Getting to the 21st Century

Voluntary Action and the Global Agenda

Books edited by David C. Korten

Bureaucracy and the Poor
Closing the Gap
(with Felipe B. Alfonso)

Community Management
Asian Experience and Perspectives

People-Centered Development
(with Rudi Klauss)

Getting to the 21st Century

Voluntary Action and the Global Agenda

David C. Korten
People-Centered Development Forum

KUMARIAN PRESS

Dedicated to

Dr. Soedjatmoko

January 10, 1922 – December 21, 1989

Whose wisdom and example taught me
the meaning of global citizenship in its fullest sense.

and to my daughters

Diane and Alicia

Whose emerging sense of their own global citizenship
inspires my hope for the future.

Printed in the United States of America
94   93   92   5   4   3

Cover design by Marilyn Penrod

Library of Congress Cataloging in Publication Data

Korten, David C.
    Getting to the 21st century : voluntary action and the global
agenda / David C. Korten.
        p. cm. -- (Kumarian Press library of management for
development)
    Includes bibliographical references and index.
    ISBN 0-931816-85-8. -- ISBN 0-931816-84-X (pbk.)
    1. Non-governmental organizations--Developing countries. 2.
Non-governmental organizations. 3. Economic assistance--
Developing countries. 4. Economic assistance, Domestic. 5. Economic
development--Environmental aspects--Developing countries. 6.
Economic development--Environmental aspects. 7. Voluntarism--
Developing countries. 8. Voluntarism. 9. Green movement--
Developing countries. 10. Green movement. 11. Peace movements--
Developing countries. 12. Peace movements. I. Title. II. Title: Getting
to the twenty-first century. III. Series.
HC60.K67   1990
338.9'009172'4--dc20   90-4211
                                                                        CIP

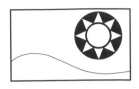

CONTENTS

Tables

Figures

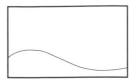

PREFACE

The development industry, created during the past four decades to respond to a global commitment to alleviating poverty, is in a state of disarray. The landscape is littered with evidence of the failures of official development efforts to reach the poor. The largest of the multilateral and bilateral assistance agencies have responded to the failure by focusing once again on accelerating economic growth. They argue that if adequate growth rates can be sustained, the poor will be swept along with the tide of rising incomes. The argument is reassuring, but reflects more a hopeful myth than a pragmatic reality.

While the poor are being carried along as on a tide, it is not that of the rising of buoyant economies. Rather they are caught in the tides of flood and drought, desertification, communal violence, unrestrained population growth, and the ebbing of employment and income generating opportunities.

Private international assistance agencies have focused their attention on the needs of the growing numbers of casualties of these unfavorable tides, by responding with relief and welfare measures that temporarily relieve the worst symptoms of development failure. Seldom do cither private or official assistance agencies address the causes of the human suffering that they profess to be combating. More often they close their eyes to the causes in the interests of "pragmatism."

Development has become a big business, preoccupied more with its own growth and imperatives than with the people it was originally created to serve. Dominated by professional financiers and technocrats, the development industry seeks to maintain an apolitical and value-free stance in dealing with what are, more than anything else, problems of power and values.

It is becoming evident that the hope for dealing with the global development crisis rests not with the development industry, but with the great social movements of contemporary society including the peace, environment, women, and human rights movements. It rests with people who are driven by a strong social commitment rather than by the budgetary imperatives of huge global bureaucracies. It rests in particular with the more forward-looking nongovernmental organizations (NGOs) of the South that find themselves immersed in the political, environmental and economic struggles of the poor with whom they work and that lack the luxury of closing their eyes to the real nature of the problem. Yet these Southern NGOs remain dependent on Northern donors whose funding policies and procedures are grounded in old myths about development and the processes by which it is achieved.

An important impetus for decisive action comes from the growing realization in both North and South that our planet is gripped in an environmental crisis, a problem that cannot be ignored. Fine tuning of a failed system is no longer adequate. The realization is beginning to dawn that we have placed so much pressure on the natural environment that continuing with business as usual is likely to have intolerable consequences for rich and poor alike. There are indications that the crisis is creating a readiness to question basic assumptions that did not exist even as recently as 1987.

At issue is the most fundamental of assumptions, i.e., that continued pursuit of economic growth as the focal development priority is an option. If, as suggested by a substantial body of evidence, the wealth consuming countries of the North are stressing the global ecology to its limits, there are three ways to address the issue: 1) press for continued conventional economic growth in both North and South and face an almost certain failure of global ecosystems; 2) leave the poor of both North and South to live in perpetual poverty; or 3) pursue drastic measures to reduce the demands that the overconsumers of both North and South place on the environment to give the poor scope to achieve a decent human existence. These are not *happy* choices. They are, however, the *only* choices.

THE BACKGROUND OF THE BOOK

In early 1989 I circulated to a few colleagues a draft paper in which I explored the implications of important trends of the decade of the 1980s for U.S. private voluntary organizations (PVOs) in the 1990s. I outlined key elements of the current global crisis and argued that citizen action is critical to their resolution. The development assistance agency that had funded me to prepare the paper asked that I remove all references to its financial sponsorship. The issues raised were too controversial. This action appeared to confirm my argument that large governmental and inter-governmental assistance agencies are largely incapable of providing the needed leadership to resolve the problems of poverty, environment and social conflict addressed in this book.

The paper, though only in draft, took on a life of its own, circulating through the photocopy press. It was passed hand-to-hand by people in the voluntary sector who found that it articulated concerns that they felt had been ignored too long and needed serious airing. Invitations started coming in, not only from important U.S. PVOs, but also from voluntary and governmental organizations in other countries, to help them plan and present workshops on issues raised by the paper. Additional perspectives and insights began to emerge as a result of these discussions. Rather than revise the paper, I decided to write this book.

Getting to the 21st Century marks a significant advance in my personal search for answers to the difficult and frustrating dilemma of why development has not worked for the poor in most Southern countries. The resulting intellectual journey is documented in my three previous Kumarian Press books: *Bureaucracy and the Poor, People-Centered Development,* and *Community Management.*

While writing *Community Management*, the most recent of the three, I was working for the United States Agency for International Development (AID). Though I worked under a contract arrangement through the National Association of Schools of Public Affairs and Administration, my office was located in AID missions, first in Manila and later in Jakarta. The nature of my position and funding gave me freedom to travel and to work on critical institutional issues with some of the most creative and forward-looking people in AID. Working as an insider, I had access to the top levels of country missions and the Washington bureaucracy.

My assignment was to determine how AID might deal effectively with one of development's central issues: creating a capacity in development agencies to work in a participatory mode with local people. I worked with AID missions throughout Asia on this topic over a period of some eight years.

I had gone to AID from the Ford Foundation, where my wife, Frances F. Korten, and I had worked with numerous colleagues to discover and articulate effective strategies for bureaucratic transformation that would allow development agencies of Southern countries to be effective in supporting a truly people-controlled and people-led local development. These strategies were based on the learning process concepts first described in "Community Organization and Rural Development: A Learning Process Approach" published in the *Public Administration Review* in September-October 1980. *Transforming a Bureaucracy*, edited by Frances F. Korten and Robert Y. Siy, Jr., and published by Kumarian Press, describes the successful application of these concepts and methods to the transformation of the Philippine National Irrigation Agency. The Ford Foundation played a crucial catalytic role in this case.

Those who had arranged my move to AID wanted to know whether their agency might play a role similar to that of the Ford Foundation in applying a learning process approach in its own programming. If we could make it work within the AID system, there was a possibility that AID might be able to support the transformation of development agencies in many Southern countries. Perhaps the methods might also be applied by other large donors. This was the dream to which I was committed during most of the eight years I was associated with AID.

It proved to be an impossible dream. Eventually it became clear to even the most optimistic participants in the exercise that it is beyond the capacity of AID and most other large international assistance agencies to provide leadership as catalysts in achieving the institutional changes required to empower the poor. It was a conclusion I was particularly reluctant to accept as it was not evident what other organizations might play the essential catalyst role.

Despite many staffers' good intentions, the international assistance agencies deal in money, not in the social processes that are the key to institutional change. Their staff members are preoccupied with bureaucratic procedures that leave too little time for working with counterparts on substantive development issues. They have too much money, programmed in blocks that are too large and inflexible to be used in the opportunistic ways required by institutional change initiatives. The large loans and grants made by these agencies almost inevitably direct attention away from the more effective use of local resources and toward reliance on external resources. These agencies are too controlled by short-term political changes to make long-term commitments to slow and difficult processes of institutional change.

No one, not even mission directors and senior officials in Washington, felt there was any prospect of making the changes within AID that most of us involved in the analysis felt were necessary. One senior AID official asked, "If we truly believe that community control and initiative is what development is about, what can we do?" It was a troubling question for many of us.

I began exploring other options with AID colleagues who had shared my commitment. Two of them, George Carner and Frank Young, who were then both working in Washington, suggested that voluntary organizations (VOs) might be the answer. In some programs in Haiti and Africa, AID had been looking to NGOs to assume substantial roles in project implementation. It had greater flexibility in working with NGOs than it did in working with governments and for-profit contractors. Furthermore, NGOs did not suffer from many of the inherent limitations that burdened AID.

Then it occurred to me that I had been thinking about the Ford Foundation as a donor organization and therefore had been looking to other donors to play the change catalyst role in which it had been so successful. It was one of those moments of intense insight when a deeply held, but erroneous assumption is cast away. Suddenly I realized that the qualities that allowed the foundation to be effective in this role were not so much inherent in the fact that it was a donor as in the fact that it was an independent, nonpolitical private agency able to field highly qualified staff backed by modest but adequate financial resources to work closely and flexibly with local colleagues on shared commitments. Perhaps other private agencies could do the same.

In 1986 I began to devote the majority of my time to work with

NGOs on interpreting the changing context of their work and assessing the implications for their roles and capacities. This was a liberating experience. I found myself working with people who were limited only by their own imagination and capacity, not by the artificial constraints of a public bureaucracy burdened by legions of auditors, lawyers and contracts officers. They were free to consider significant changes in their strategies and ways of working. They were not locked into a procedural and legislative straightjacket.

However, I also became aware of the extent to which many NGOs, even some of the largest, perceived their roles to be limited to peripheral actions intended primarily to alleviate the consequences of poverty for the people they could reach directly. They seldom had a clear strategic focus, often lacked technical capability, and seemed reluctant to cooperate with other organizations.

Yet, unlike the fundamental structural constraints that face most bilateral and multilateral assistance agencies, the constraints faced by NGOs are largely the self-imposed constraints of their own self-limiting vision. NGOs are capable of shedding these constraints, as many have demonstrated. Their participants need only the courage to embrace a more expansive vision of their roles and potential.

As my experience with NGOs grows, so too does my awareness of the central role of voluntary action in creating social and institutional change. I am also coming to realize that voluntary action is not limited to what VOs do. Voluntary action includes the work of countless individuals who work in formal organizations in government and business who have the courage and commitment to act in a voluntary capacity as global citizens in support of the public good, even when this may run counter to the bureaucratic imperatives of their organizations. The efforts of these citizen volunteers are as crucial to the transformation that global society must achieve during the 1990s as are the efforts of formal VOs.

Working with NGOs to create and embrace a new vision for themselves consistent with the challenges that currently face global society has led to a mutual realization that the need for a new vision extends beyond defining new directions for their individual organizations. More fundamental is the need to define an alternative vision of development itself to serve as a collective guiding beacon for voluntary action by countless individuals and organizations. The formulation of this vision is itself a collective, evolving process that must be grounded in grassroots experience.

This book is an effort to document and share what I am learning from working with a continually expanding circle of colleagues from the voluntary sector. It is addressed to these colleagues, and to countless like-minded citizen volunteers, in the hope that it will help us all to better understand and appreciate the nature and potential of our collective commitment.

THE PEOPLE-CENTERED DEVELOPMENT FORUM

The publication of this book marks a new transition in my life. In preparing the manuscript I have been pressed to examine more fully the implications of its central ideas for how I focus my energies. With a great deal of help and encouragement from friends and colleagues, this examination led to a decision to establish the People-Centered Development Forum (PCDForum).

One of the limiting qualities of voluntary action is that its diffuseness leaves even its participants with an unclear image of the special nature of their efforts. As growing numbers of volunteers embrace the concept of development as a people's movement in support of just, sustainable and inclusive improvements in human well-being, there is need for a forum within which experiences and interpretive insights may be exchanged to maintain a collective sense of perspective and direction. The PCDForum is intended to contribute to this essential function.

ACKNOWLEDGEMENTS

Much of the manuscript for this book was prepared while I was on the staff of the Institute for Development Research (IDR). I want to acknowledge the encouragement given to this undertaking by L. David Brown, Jane Covey, Mark Leach and Elizabeth Fabel of IDR.

I want to give special thanks to my wife and colleague, Frances F. Korten, who has shared in each step of the intellectual journey of which this book represents one landmark, and who has read and critiqued many of the drafts. David Beckman has read and critiqued several earlier drafts, each time offering incisive criticisms that have reshaped the presentation in important and useful ways. Robert Berg also provided extensive and valuable critical comments.

Special mention must also go to Nathan Gray, president of the Gateway Pacific Foundation, who has provided encouragement and material support in establishing the People-Centered Development Forum. Nathan has also helped me to see the possibilities for engaging a broad audience in a dialogue on the issues addressed here.

Terry George of the Ford Foundation and Becky Sawyer of the Institute of Philippine Culture contributed editorial inputs. Krishna Sondhi made the book's publication possible, and Roberta J. Buland did the final editing for Kumarian Press.

There are many other people who contributed to the book in a variety of ways. Some contributed valuable data and insights during the preparatory stages. Others have read and critiqued various drafts. Among these are Fazle H. Abed, Fermin and Lourdes Adriano, Salehuddin Ahmed, Norman Barth, Rolf Berglund, Elena Borghese, Nan Borton, Robin Broad, Tim Brodhead, Roland Bunch, Robert Busche, Tom Carter, John

Clark, Peter Davies, Thomas Dichter, Phyllis Dobyns, Anne Gordon Drabek, Kenneth Ellison, Julie Peck Fisher, Dolores Foley, Tom Fox, William Fuller, Terry George, John Gerhart, Nathan Gray, K-G Hagstrom, Thomas Hammarberg, Sam Harris, Douglas and Stephen Hellinger, Frank Hicks, Richard Holloway, Stanley Hosie, Graeme Irvine, Arturo Israel, Alicia Korten, Ron Leger, Beryl Levinger, Tina Liamzon, Carolyn Long, Karl-Erik Lundgren, Shane MacCarthy, Paul McCleary, Peter McNee, Larry Minear, Horacio Morales, Bryant Myers, Paul Petersen, Karen Poe, Agus Purnomo, David Richards, Achmad Rofi'ie, Sixto K. Roxas, August Rumansara, Emil Salim, Adi Sasono, Isagani Serrano, Robert Seiple, Elise Smith, Elizabeth Silverstein, Corazon Juliano-Soliman, F. Stephen, Beverly Tangri, Gene Thiemann, Paul Thompson, Norman T. Uphoff, Edgardo Valenzuela, Carl Wahren, Jane Watkins, Joseph Wheeler, Erna Witoelar, David Winder and Soetjipto Wirosardjono.

Each of these people, and many others, have given their time to share their thinking in ways that have had a particular influence on my own understanding of the development problem as presented in this book. Many have made useful critical comments on earlier drafts and papers on which this book is based. Many of the hundreds of participants in the conferences and workshops in which I have been involved over the past two years have also made important contributions to my thinking through their presentations, questions and comments. None of the people whose names are mentioned here bear responsibility for the opinions or for any errors of fact or interpretation that this book may contain. The views expressed are solely those of the author.

David C. Korten
Manila, Philippines

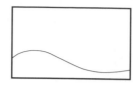

ABBREVIATIONS

ADB	Asian Development Bank
AFSC	America Friends Service Committee
AID	Agency for International Development
ANGOC	Asian NGO Coalition
BRAC	Bangladesh Rural Advancement Committee
ELCI	Environmental Liaison Center International
FPA	family planning association
GDP	gross domestic product
GONGO	governmental nongovernmental organization
IC	industrial country
IDR	Institute for Development Research
IMF	International Monetary Fund
IPPF	International Planned Parenthood Federation
JCRR	Chinese-American Joint Commission on Rural Reconstruction
LIC	low income country
LP3ES	Indonesian Institute for Social and Economic Research Education and Information
LSP	Indonesian Institute for Development Studies
NGO	nongovernmental organization
NIC	newly industrialized country
OECD	Organization for Economic Co-operation and Development
OPEC	Organization of Oil Exporting Countries
PACT	Private Agencies Collaborating Together
PCDForum	People-Centered Development Forum
PhilDHRRA	Philippine Partnership for the Development of Human Resources in Rural Areas
PO	people's organization
PSC	public services contractor
PVO	private voluntary organization
RAG	rainforest action group
RAN	Rainforest Action Network
SCC	Sudan Council of Churches
UNICEF	United Nations Children's Fund
VO	voluntary organization
WHO	World Health Organization

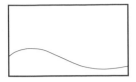

WE HAVE A PROBLEM

The decade from which we have just emerged, the 1980s, was a time of growing recognition that we live in a world in profound crisis—a world of dehumanizing poverty, collapsing ecological systems, and deeply stressed social structures. An awareness is dawning that these are not isolated problems. They represent worldwide phenomena. Each is to some extent both cause and consequence of the others. Each points to important institutional failures.

Three interlocking crises brought into bold relief during the 1980s—poverty, environmental stress, and communal violence—pose a threat to human civilization that is now more real and more important in its implications than the threat of nuclear war. Yet this new threat is different. It cannot be reduced to the problem of two world leaders facing one another, each with a finger on a nuclear button, playing a global game of chess. The principal actors in the new threat include all the people of the world—rich and poor, educated and uneducated, North and South, East and West.[1] The threat results from the collective consequences of the individual actions of every citizen of our planet. This reality, along with the breathtaking progress of East-West detente, have made traditional concepts of national security obsolete, almost overnight.[2]

The damage we are doing to ourselves and our planet is not yet so great as to be irreversible, but time is running out. The actions taken during the decade of the 1990s may well determine whether the 21st century will be a time of bold new advances for human society or a period characterized by violent struggle for survival.

We have traditionally thought of the industrial nations of the North as representing the cutting edge of development experience. We must now come to terms with the reality that the leading edge of the three-fold global crisis is found in the countries of the South. It is here that the consequences of global mismanagement are felt most acutely. Unless adequate corrective action is forthcoming, the North may find that the current Southern experience is a window into its own future—not the reverse.

VIEW FROM THE GRASSROOTS

Many of the nongovernmental organizations (NGOs) that assist the poor in the nations of the South have seen the human reality behind the dismal statistics that tell us that in all too many settings the numbers of poor are increasing, the environment is failing, and communal violence is an ever present threat. Sometimes individual NGOs have been able to shield favored groups of the poor from the forces involved. Sometimes they have even been able to help them improve their lives. Yet these NGOs see signs of the broader reality all around them. They see the despair, violence, hunger and exploitation that lead many among the poor and marginalized to embrace revolutionary movements or the security of narrow and exclusive religious dogmas and ethnic causes that encourage social cleavages and communal violence.

Table I-1: Types of NGOs

The term NGO embraces a wide variety of organizations. They include
- **Voluntary Organizations (VOs)** that pursue a social mission driven by a commitment to shared values.
- **Public Service Contractors (PSCs)** that function as market-oriented nonprofit businesses serving public purposes.
- **People's Organizations (POs)** that represent their members' interests, have member accountable leadership, and are substantially self-reliant.
- **Governmental Nongovernmental Organizations (GONGOs)** that are creations of government and serve as instruments of government policy.

For further discussion of these types of NGOs, see chapter 9. The term private voluntary organization (PVO), common in the United States, is largely synonymous with NGO.

NGO workers see directly how environmental deterioration is adding to the tragedy. They see the poor reap ever smaller harvests as the meager soils on which they depend lose their fertility. They witness the poor walking ever further for water and firewood as their wells go dry and forest cover disappears. They watch the fishermen returning at night empty-handed as the coastal waters yield fewer and smaller fish. Those who work in urban areas see the poor crowded into ghettos best described as garbage dumps and cesspools.

The poor are both contributors to and victims of the pressures that are creating these circumstances. As their numbers continue to grow, ever more people find themselves in competition with one another to squeeze an existence out of the deteriorating environmental niches that have not yet been commandeered by the wealthy for their "development" projects.

We are left with troubling questions: Is it the experience of the North or of the South that provides the most accurate window into our collective future? Or will we increasingly live in a world divided between the rich and the poor? Will the poor passively accept their fate as being of their own making? Can the North long hide from the South the extent to which its own policies and actions carry a major responsibility for sustaining, even exacerbating the crisis in the South? Can a world that has grown so small through modern communications remain a world so divided? Environmental interdependence and the ability of the poor to contribute to environmental destruction through their shear numbers, large flows of refugees from Southern to Northern countries, and the North's vulnerability to terrorist attack are only a few of the increasing number of realities that tell us that ultimately all the peoples of planet earth will share in a common future. The choices we make during the current decade may well determine what that future will be.

A NEED FOR CHANGE

The need for change becomes increasingly evident. Yet our ability to take corrective action continues to be inhibited by an interlocking set of interests that are sustained and legitimated by a development vision grounded in flawed assumptions about our natural and social reality.

Development as Growth

We have become prisoners of an obsolete vision of our global reality and the nature of human progress. This vision equates human progress with growth in the market value of economic output and subordinates both human and environmental considerations to that goal. The result has been the extravagant consumption of the world's resources by a favored few with little recognition of the social and environmental costs borne by the many. These costs have now accumulated to the point of endangering the continued well-being of everyone on planet earth.

Proponents of the growth-centered vision argue that continued growth is the only hope for the poor. There are two basic flaws in this argument. First, given existing economic and political structures, the majority of the benefits of growth accrue to those who are least in need. Second, continuation of conventional patterns of growth will likely reduce the ability of the global ecology to sustain even the levels of economic output already achieved.[3]

Development as Transformation

The critical development issue for the 1990s is not growth. It is transformation. Our collective future depends on achieving a transformation of our institutions, our technology, our values, and our behavior consistent with our ecological and social realities. This transformation must address three basic needs of our global society.

- **Justice.** Current development practice supports an extreme imbalance between over and underconsumers of the world's resources, including the natural recycling capacities of the ecosystem. This imbalance is simply unacceptable by any standard of human values. One group enjoys a sumptuous feast, while the other struggles for existence without the means to produce even a bare subsistence livelihood.

  Justice does not require equality of income, nor does it require that the productive be required to support the slothful. It does require, however, that all people have the means and the opportunity to produce a minimum decent livelihood for themselves and their families. It rejects the right of one person to self-enrichment based on the appropriation of the resources on which another person's survival depends. The transformed society must give priority in the use of the earth's natural resources to assuring all people the opportunity for a decent human existence.

- **Sustainability.** Current development practice supports increases in economic output that depend on the unsustainable depletion of the earth's natural resources and the life support capabilities of its ecosystem. Such temporary gains do not represent development so much as theft by one generation of the birthright of future generations.

  Sustainability does not require that nature be left untouched. It does require, however, that each generation recognize its obligation for stewardship of earth's natural resources and ecosystem on behalf of future generations. The transformed society must use the earth's resources in ways that will assure sustainable benefits for our children.

- **Inclusiveness.** Current development practice systematically deprives substantial segments of the population of the opportunity to make recognized contributions to the improved well-being of society. This practice breeds alienation and social conflict.

  Inclusiveness does not mean that everyone must enjoy equal status and power. It does mean that everyone who chooses to be a productive, contributing community member has a right to the opportunity to do so and to be recognized and respected for these contributions. The transformed society must assure everyone an opportunity to be a recognized and respected contributor to family, community and society.[4]

Voluntary Action

Most of the institutions on which we rely for economic and social problem-solving are themselves the creations of the growth-centered development vision and are therefore ill-suited to challenging it. While ultimately important to the transformation, at this stage they more often act as inhibitors than facilitators.

Inspired world leaders who are driven by a new vision unbounded by conventional prejudice and ideology have an essential role. Mikhail Gorbachev stands as a leading example of such a leader who has made an incalculable contribution toward creating new potentials for East-West cooperation in this transformation. However, such leaders are all too rare.

Furthermore, the leader can only create the enabling conditions. Ultimately the people must seize the opportunities available to them to recreate their institutions in ways that better serve their needs—as the people of Eastern Europe are now doing.

Our concept of and approach to development must undergo a transformation every bit as rapid and profound as the changes in political and economic institutions now sweeping Eastern Europe. Given the profound, broadly-based and highly personal nature of the needed transformation, voluntary citizen action will have an essential role. Such action includes not only the work of organizations, but also the efforts of individuals who have the courage to seek changes from within the established institutions of society.

A People-Centered Vision

A number of NGOs throughout the world are giving attention to the definition and projection of a people-centered development vision that embraces the transformation agenda. This vision looks to justice, sustainability and inclusiveness as the defining principles of authentic development. It views development as a people's movement more than as a foreign-funded government project. It looks to government to enable the people to develop themselves. It seeks a synthesis of the change objectives of the environmental, human rights, consumer protection, women's and peace movements. It seeks a new human consciousness in which the more nurturing, enabling and conserving dimensions of female consciousness gain ascendance over the more aggressive, exploitative and competitive dimensions of male consciousness that have so long dominated the social and economic life of human societies.

The vision is gaining clarity and followers through an evolutionary, experience-based process that involves countless individuals and organizations. The movement of which this vision is a product, however, remains incipient and lacks a defining self-awareness. *Getting to the 21st Century* is intended to contribute toward strengthening this identity and self-awareness.

Growing NGO Self-Awareness

Many NGOs became increasingly aware during the 1980s that the leadership needed to deal with the underlying causes of the human tragedy was not being provided by governments. Governments and international agencies themselves came to acknowledge the ability of NGOs to do what many governments have proven unable to do, i.e., to get a range of essential goods and services to the poor. Yet growing numbers of NGOs also recognized that their own efforts were too meager, and too often focused on the *consequences* of system failure rather than the underlying causes of this failure. Their financial resources were negligible and their modes of working were largely irrelevant to the real issues.

In their attempts to deal with this reality some NGOs have sought increases in government funding to expand their service delivery capabilities. Others have questioned the nature of their more conventional roles and asked whether they may need to rethink their own approaches to development actions to get at the real causes of the human suffering that motivates their action. The latter often come to the conclusion that the more distinctive contributions of NGOs to local, national and global development go well beyond their traditional, legitimate, but limited, concerns with service delivery. *Getting to the 21st Century* attempts to illuminate the larger mission of the voluntary sector as a development force.

OVERVIEW

The book is divided into four parts. Part I examines the lessons of the 1980s, describing the decade as simultaneously one of crisis, denial, and newly emergent opportunities. In the end, it became a decade of awakening, leaving us with a hope that the 1990s can achieve the transformation so essential to prepare our entry into the 21st century.

Part II points up the importance of what a society believes about itself in determining how it behaves. It introduces the argument that to overcome the current global crisis it is necessary to renew our vision of who we are and what we hope to become. More specifically, it calls for a new development vision that leads to just, sustainable and inclusive improvements in human well-being. The growth-centered development vision that has prevailed during the past four decades has failed to meet this test. Furthermore, export-led growth strategies, the current favorite of adherents to the conventional vision, lead to policies that reinforce the dualistic economic structures of the colonial era and their unjust, unsustainable and noninclusive use of national resources. The critical elements of an alternative people-centered development and a supporting equity-led sustainable growth strategy are outlined.

Part III focuses on the voluntary development sector. It examines the distinctive nature and role of this sector and the evolution of the strategies of its constituent organizations from relief and welfare, to community development, to catalyzing institutional and policy change. It suggests that in the future greater attention must be given to the facilitation of development as a people's movement that utilizes the full potentials of self-directing voluntary social energy.

Part IV outlines a development agenda for the 1990s. It focuses on the need for system transformation as a prelude to new patterns of economic growth that will be more just, sustainable and inclusive, suggesting that the global system will not sustain continued growth as conventionally defined. The priority must be to achieve the transformation that will make further growth a viable possibility without risking either social or ecological collapse. Many of the elements of the transformation agenda are outlined, with a focus on achieving a better balance between the over- and the under-consumers of environmental resources. Implications for the voluntary sector are examined.

NOTES

1. The term South is used here essentially as a synonym for Third World or developing countries. North is used as a synonym for First and Second World, industrial, or developed countries. The North/South terminology presents a greater symmetry than the First World/Third World terminology. There is less implication that one advances by becoming more like the other.

The North/South terminology gained currency in relation to Southern demands for the creation of a New International Economic Order. In that context, the term clearly denoted power blocks with conflicting interests. More recently NGOs have begun to use the North/South terminology in a less conflictive sense as a way of grouping countries that share broadly similar historical circumstances. Some argue that such terms oversimplify the differences among countries included in one block or another and place too much stress on the differences between the two blocks. These are valid criticisms. At the same time, intellectual discourse depends on the use of categories and generalizations and a book of this type would be almost impossible to write without some terminology for dealing with the broad groupings of countries that define an important part of our human reality.

2. See Jessica Tuchman Mathews, "Redefining National Security," *Foreign Affairs,* Vol. 68, No. 2, 1989, pp. 162–77; *The Developing World: Danger Point for U.S. Security,* A report commissioned by Mark O. Hatfield, Matthew F. McHugh and Mickey Leland (Washington, DC: Arms Control and Foreign Policy Caucus of the U.S. Congress, August 1, 1989); and Michael Renner, "Enhancing Global Security," in Lester R. Brown *et al., State of the World 1989* (New York: W. W. Norton & Co., 1989), pp. 132–53. The Managua Declaration issued by the Fourth Biennial Congress on the Fate and Hope of the Earth in June 1989 called for such a redefinition on a global scale, specifically an end to arms expenditures and a reallocation of resources to poverty alleviation and environmental protection as the overriding threats to human security. Reported in the *Manila Chronicle,* June 18, 1989.

3. For extensive documentation and elaboration of the argument see Ted Trainer, *Developed to Death: Rethinking Third World Development* (London: The Merlin Press,

1989); and James Robertson, *Future Wealth: A New Economics for the 21st Century* (London: Cassell Publishers Limited, 1990).

4. The principle of inclusiveness reflects a value premise that human well-being involves more than being a consumer of adequate food, clothing and shelter. To have a full sense of one's own humanity depends on having the self-respect that comes from being a productive and respected contributor to the community. Welfare programs can meet basic human needs, but they can never confer self-respect.

In its application, the principle of inclusiveness calls attention to the inherent limitation of strategies that focus on either the powerful or the powerless to the exclusion of the other. Injustice is almost the inevitable consequence of excluding the powerless. Yet to confine consciousness-raising efforts to the powerless, as some voluntary organizations have been inclined to do, misses the fundamental reality that while it is possible to substitute one power holder for another, it is probably beyond the means of human institutions to eliminate power holders all together.

Class conflict is real and we must deal with it, but even "successful" communist revolutions have not eliminated class and class conflict. As the people of Eastern Europe are now making clear, communist governments have only substituted one set of privileged power holders for another. We must find other approaches to resolving the conflict based on a combination of structures and values.

PART I

THE 1980s: AN AWAKENING

Futurists told us throughout the 1970s that underlying forces accumulating within global society would pose fundamental challenges to established values, institutions, interests, and modes of working. Some predicted disaster. Others predicted new heights of human accomplishment and prosperity. Others saw a choice point, arguing that neither disaster nor utopia were preordained. Both were possible. The outcome would depend on the collective choices of people throughout the globe. A positive outcome would depend on profound changes—some called it a transformation—in our values and institutions.

The 1980s provided evidence that we are in fact at a critical historical choice point. This was most dramatically demonstrated by the evidence of growing environmental destruction. It became undeniably clear that we were engaged in the collective act of destroying the life support capabilities of planet earth. The message the futurists had given us took on new urgency. Their models had suggested that the planet would experience a collapse of major environmental systems in the mid-21st century.[1] They were dismissed as pessimists. Now we might say that in fact they were pollyannas. The forces of collapse are already building at a far more rapid rate than they had predicted. The 1990s may provide us with our last window of opportunity to reverse these trends. With each passing day the accumulating environmental and human damage wrought by the crises make such reversal more difficult.

The threat of environmental collapse was not the only reason to characterize the 1980s as a decade of crisis. We also saw a dramatic deepening of poverty in many areas of the world and widespread communal violence—indications of failure in our social, as well as our environmental, systems. While limited data make it difficult to quantify trends with regard to the incidence of poverty and communal violence, there is substantial reason to expect future increases in both as an almost inevitable consequence of continued environmental deterioration and the resulting increase in competition for available environmental resources.

Appropriate corrective action was seriously impeded during the 1980s because of a strong tendency to respond with denial to the growing crisis of system failure. The United States led the way in denying the existence of any fundamental problem. Those who called attention to evidence that environmental and social crises were deepening were once again dismissed as doom-sayers. People and nations borrowed against their financial and environmental futures to reassure themselves that nothing fundamental had changed and that they could continue, as usual, the business of profligate consumption.

Yet the events of the decade also created new opportunities, the most dramatic of which was the breathtaking progress of East-West detente and the opening of Eastern Europe. In almost a matter of months the threat of nuclear holocaust gave way to new possibilities for East-West cooperation to address the crises of poverty, environment and communal violence that now are becoming recognized as the primary threats to global security.

The final years of the 1980s saw an important awakening, a move beyond denial to a new recognition of need and opportunity—and a growing commitment to action. It has become evident to most responsible citizens that denial is an unaffordable luxury.

Few among us as yet grasp the full implications of the changes that must be faced if we are to address the underlying causes of our collective crisis. We face the need for a basic transformation of values and institutions to bring us into alignment with an alternative vision of our collective future as inhabitants of planet earth. Our obsession with development as growth in the consumption of material goods must give way to a new vision of how we define human progress.

The following chapters provide a brief review of the decade from each of three perspectives: crisis, denial and opportunity. This review defines the scope of the challenge that currently faces human society in its effort to rethink the meaning and processes of local, national and global development.

NOTE

1. See Donella H. Meadows et al., The Limits to Growth (New York: New American Library, 1972).

CHAPTER ONE

DECADE OF CRISIS

Three interrelated global crises were burned into the human consciousness during the 1980s: poverty, environmental failure and social violence. These three crises relate directly to three major areas of development failure: justice, sustainability and inclusiveness. These failures demonstrate that the systems by which we manage our relationships with one another and with our natural environment are not working. Past approaches to development have, in too many instances, exacerbated the problem. Failure to acknowledge and correct the sources of this failure during the decade of the 1990s will most surely turn the 21st century into a global nightmare.

POVERTY

The global commitment to the development of the nonindustrial countries first emerged nearly forty years ago. The accumulated experience of these years is varied and complex. Important gains have been made. Some countries have emerged as celebrated success stories. It has been estimated that the percentage of the population of non-communist developing countries falling below the poverty line decreased from 46.8 percent in 1960 to 30.1 percent in 1980.[1]

No Time for Rejoicing
Any rejoicing at these accomplishments must be tempered, however, by a recognition that the poverty line used in the above calculation is set at $50 per capita 1960 purchasing power—the income required to support minimally adequate calorie replacement at average levels of activity. In other words, those whose rise above the poverty line we celebrate have risen only above the level of absolute deprivation.[2] So long as they devote *none* of their income to clothing, shelter or other nonfood indulgences they need not go to bed hungry each night.

Our rejoicing at this progress must also be tempered by the fact that population growth rates of approximately 2.5 percent a year in the countries of the South mean that in absolute terms there were more people living below the poverty line in 1980 than there were in 1960.

According to the World Bank the number of people throughout the world (excluding China) with inadequate diets increased from 650 million to 730 million between 1970 and 1980.[3]

The trend toward increasing numbers of people with inadequate diets accelerated in the 1980s, along with reported declines in life expectancy, per capita calorie supply, and real wages.[4] As a world economy burdened by both financial and environmental debt went into decline in the late 1970s, Southern countries experienced steep drops in per capita gross national product.[5] Just as the poor are usually the last to benefit from economic expansion, they also commonly bear the worst burdens of economic decline—a reality thoroughly confirmed by the experience of the 1980s.

It is estimated that by 1988 the number of people who lived in households too poor to obtain the food necessary to maintain energy levels sufficient for work had risen to one billion, or 20 percent of the world population.[6] The human meaning of the statistics was burned into the global conscience by the images produced during the African famines. From 1980 to 1987 the Sub-Saharan African countries experienced an annual decline of 2.9 percent in per capita income. Oil exporting and heavily indebted countries also experienced annual declines in real per capita income during this period.[7]

Food Security

Declining world food security creates ominous future prospects for the economically and politically weak—who inevitably bear the brunt of the burden of declining food security. Between 1950 and 1984, per capita food production increased by 40 percent worldwide. Since 1984, however, persistent annual declines in per capita grain output—a total drop of 14 percent—brought 1988 per capita food output back to the 1970 level. Roughly 11 percent of the decline was offset by drawing down food stocks. The remaining 3 percent represented reduced food intake.[8] In the meantime world buffer stocks have been largely depleted.

Even more alarming is the indication that the record levels of world grain production achieved in the early years of the decade were achieved at the expense of unsustainable mining of topsoils and groundwater supplies, and that the unusually high temperatures and severe droughts that contributed to the decline may reflect long-term trends.

An unbroken history of expansion in land area under cultivation came to an end in 1981. The land devoted to grain production has since declined by 7 percent.[9] The continuing rapid loss of agricultural land to urban and industrial uses combines with loss due to environmental mismanagement to make a reversal of the overall trend unlikely. Efforts continue to bring additional land under cultivation. However, most remaining uncultivated lands are marginal and ecologically unstable.

If the application of agricultural technology remains constant at today's standard, the Food and Agriculture Organization of the UN estimates that by the turn of the century sixty-four countries will be unable to meet the food needs of their population. Twenty-nine of these countries are in Africa.[10]

At best we must anticipate a slowing of growth in per capita global food production. At worst we may face declines, even as competition for available supplies grows.[11]

Economic and Environmental Refugees
To be a refugee is to experience a particularly degrading form of poverty. The refugee typically lacks not only economic resources, but has been deprived even of national identity. One's very right to exist is called into question.

Political refugees have long been a reality of human society. The number of refugees created as a consequence of wars, insurrections and despotic regimes stood relatively constant at around 13 million throughout the 1980s.

There was, however, a sharp increase in economic and environmental refugees. The phenomena of economic refugees became particularly visible to the United States during the decade with the relentless influx of refugees from Mexico, Central America and the Caribbean.

Less well-documented is the global increase in environmental refugees who have been displaced because the areas where they once lived have become unfit for human habitation because of desertification, soil erosion, chemical or nuclear contamination, persistent flooding, or other such conditions. The number of such refugees is estimated by the World Watch Institute to be at least 10 million.[12]

ENVIRONMENT

Prior to the 1980s the aesthetic problems and discomfort caused by polluted air and water were the most visible indications of the environmental crisis. The relative ease with which progress was made toward solutions of these problems in selected localities contributed to a reduction of concern.

More than Aesthetics
The 1980s brought home the reality of more fundamental environmental threats, evidence that human society might be well along toward making large portions of its world uninhabitable. No longer was the environmental crisis a future possibility. Rather, it had become a current reality.

People everywhere experienced record high temperatures and severe droughts. Scientific opinion eventually confirmed our worst fears. There was good reason to believe that the predicted global warming trend produced by excess combustion of fossil fuels was a current reality. Prospects of rising sea levels resulting from melting polar ice caps seemed increasingly plausible.

Lowered water tables, loss of top soil, destruction of coastal fisheries, chemical contamination of drinking water supplies and residential lands, depletion of the protective ozone layer, water logging and salination of prime agricultural lands, pollution of beaches, record floods, and the build-up of radioactive wastes all impinged directly on ever more lives and reached proportions that could not be ignored.[13]

Increasing Population Pressure
The problem is exacerbated by increasing population pressures. In 1987 the world population passed the 5 billion mark. At current birth rates it will double again in 40 years. In the latter half of the 1980s, population was growing at the rate of 82 million persons per year. By the latter half of the 1990s it is expected to grow by 91 million annually.[14] A projected 876 million people will be added to the world population during the next decade, enough to completely populate a new India plus a new Ethiopia at their current sizes. This growth will be concentrated in the poorest and most environmentally degraded countries, the very countries that have the least prospect of being able to accommodate it.[15]

Given that environmental systems are already stretched to the breaking point and a major portion of the global population is already living in abject poverty, a further doubling of the population seems unlikely. In the absence of voluntary control, population growth will almost certainly be brought into check through a combination of ecological collapse, starvation and communal violence. Those who oppose voluntary family planning on moral grounds eventually will have to confront the ultimate moral consequences of the barriers they have thrown up against efforts to avoid this human tragedy.[16]

SOCIAL INTEGRATION

The crisis of social integration is revealed in the pervasive communal violence and drug dependence that characterized the 1980s. Both reflect a fundamental alienation that is played out in anti-social and self-destructive behaviors.

Communal Violence
By communal violence I refer to violence that occurs among people who share the same national boundaries and identity. According to Sivard there were twenty-five active "wars" in 1988. All but three were communal wars in the sense that they primarily involved citizens of a single country killing one another. All, except for South Africa, were in Southern countries. In total these wars had killed about three million people—80 percent of them civilians.[17]

The forces of communal violence dominate our perception of world events, with no evident sign of abatement. Sometimes the violence is along well-defined religious or ethnic lines as in Ireland and Israel. In other instances the violence is more random and its motives ill-defined as in the pervasive violence of America's urban slums or the incidents on the Los Angeles freeways of one motorist shooting another. The extreme manifestation of a breakdown of the state and civil order is found in the horror of Beirut, a once beautiful and prosperous city that has become a permanent battlefield on which rival ethnic and religious factions press their claims through unrestrained armed violence. The potential for increasingly dire consequences in ethnically diverse countries such as India is evident and a cause for increasing concern among responsible citizens there. Events in Eastern Europe have created cause for concern that what might follow the retreat of communism may not be liberal democracy so much as a rebirth of factionalism and conflict based on age old ethnic, religious and cultural rivalries.[18]

There is strong evidence that the nature of organized violence is changing. The conventional war that pits the army of one nation against that of another, both adhering to international conventions regarding the conduct of warfare and the treatment of prisoners and civilian populations, is rapidly becoming a quaint historical curiosity.

In contemporary warfare the fighting is increasingly between religious, ethnic and political factions that share a common national border and nationality—or even among units of the same national army, as in the December 1989 coup attempt in the Philippines. Governments are now more likely to engage their armies against their own citizens than against a foreign power. The line between warfare and communal violence becomes blurred. The line between combatant and civilian is similarly blurred, and the rules of "civilized" warfare are freely ignored.[19]

While the increasingly diffuse and pervasive nature of contemporary violence makes trends difficult to quantify, the groups that work most closely with the victims of this violence report that the 1980s have seen a worldwide escalation in levels of violence. This was reflected in the number of conflicts, their duration and the resulting toll in human suffering.[20]

According to the Independent Commission on International Humanitarian Issues, "We live in a time of violence.... Ethical barriers have broken down, fundamental moral values are questioned and man is engulfed by waves of fear and insecurity."[21] The search for moral guidance, security and identity in an age of insecurity and personal alienation has encouraged the growth of religious fundamentalism and ethnic separatism, with their related sense of self-righteousness and intolerance of social diversity. This alienation has fueled the forces of local level religious and ethnic violence, forces that now seem to run deeper than the political competition between East and West.

Increasing Drug Use and Trafficking

Americans spend $150 billion annually for illegal drugs, five times the amount spent for oil imports. Related crime, law enforcement, prison and treatment costs add up to an additional $100 billion a year. Drug use causes 5,000 deaths in the United States annually and accounts for a quarter of U.S. AIDS cases. In major U.S. cities the majority of people arrested for crimes are drug abusers.[22]

But the worst consequences of the appetite of Americans and other citizens of the North for drugs are being felt in the producing countries. The financial opportunities created by the Northern drug market have led to the domination of major producing countries by drug cartels that buy politicians and destroy the ability of governments to maintain the rule of law.

Colombia's Medellin-based cocaine cartel earns an estimated $3–$6 billion a year, compared to the government's annual budget of $4.6 billion. Numerous officials who have attempted to stop the drug traffickers have been killed by the cartel—including two supreme court justices, a minister of justice, an attorney general and the commander of a special anti-narcotics police. Judges have been forced either to accept bribes or be assassinated. It is an offer few can refuse. The environment also suffers. The clearing of forests to grow drugs is clogging Colombia's rivers with silt and damaging its shellfish industry.[23]

In Peru, drug traffickers have created an informal alliance with Peru's rebel movements to join in attacks against military forces and government representatives in drug-growing regions. Thus programs aimed at increasing legal economic activities are excluded and the regions become even more dependent on the drug trade.[24]

In Panama, General Noriega, indicted in the United States for his role in drug trafficking, ran the government of Panama much as any drug boss might run his personal syndicate. The people of Panama suffered the consequences.

A fairly recent phenomenon has been a rapid increase in the numbers of addicts in drug-producing countries. Colombia now has an estimated 500,000 drug users. Pakistan, also a major drug producing country, has become a net importer of opium to supply its 600,000 heroin addicts.[25]

There has been tendency to view the crises of the 1980s as somehow unrelated. This is a serious error. We are reaching the natural limits of an era of rapid population growth and unrestrained resource consumption by the fortunate few. The patterns of growth in both population and consumption have accentuated injustice and undermined the legitimacy of the social institutions that have supported that injustice. The resulting sense of alienation and loss of hope fuels the problems of drugs and violence. Only by acknowledging the failures and the interlinked nature of their causes can we hope to deal with them.

NOTES

1. Irma Adelman, "A Poverty-Focused Approach to Development Policy," in John P. Lewis and Valeriana Kallab (eds.), *Development Strategies Reconsidered* (New Brunswick: Transaction Books, 1986), p. 53.

2. Adelman, "A Poverty-Focused Approach," p. 49.

3. *World Development Report 1988* (Washington, D.C.: World Bank, 1988), p. 4.

4. *Ibid.*

5. Giovanni Andrea Cornia, "Economic Decline and Human Welfare in the First Half of the 1980s," in Giovanni Andrea Cornia, Richard Jolly, and Frances Stewart (eds.), *Adjustment with a Human Face: Protecting the Vulnerable and Promoting Growth* (Oxford: Clarendon Press, 1987), p. 20.

6. Estimate of the Brown University World Hunger Program reported in "Hunger Profile for the 1990s," *Bostid Development,* Vol. 9, Summer 1989, p. 5.

7. World Bank, 1988, p. 37. For further analysis of the data on increasing poverty during the 1980s see Cornia, "Economic Decline and Human Welfare," pp. 11–47.

8. Lester R. Brown, Christopher Flavin, and Sandra Postel, "A World at Risk," in Brown, *et al., State of the World 1989* (New York: W. W. Norton, 1989), p. 12. During these years world grain stocks fell to one of their lowest levels in decades. In July 1989 the U.S. Department of Agriculture estimated that world grain harvests for the year would be 13 million tons *below* the projected consumption of 1,684 tons, further reducing stocks. Lester R. Brown, "Feeding Six Billion," *World Watch,* Vol. 2, No. 5, Sept.–Oct. 1989, p. 32. According to "The Hunger Report: Update 1980" issued by the Alan Shawn Feinstein World Hunger Program at Brown University, if equally distributed, the total food supply available in 1986 would have been adequate to provide a basic, principally vegetarian diet, to 6 billion people or 120 percent of the world population. To provide a full but healthy diet with about 25 percent of calories from animal products that same food supply was adequate to feed only 3 billion people, or 60 percent of the then current world population.

9. Lester R. Brown, "Reexamining the World Food Prospect," in Brown, *et al., State of the World 1989,* p. 46.

10. United Nations Food and Agriculture Organization, *Land, Food and People* (Rome: Food and Agriculture Organization, 1984), as reported by Michael Dover and Lee M. Talbot, *To Feed the Earth: Agro-Ecology for Sustainable Agriculture* (Washington, D.C.: World Resources Institute, 1987), p. 1.

11. From Lester R. Brown, "The Changing Food Prospects: The Nineties and Beyond," *Worldwatch Paper 85* (Washington, D.C.: Worldwatch Institute, October 1988).

12. Jodi L. Jacobson, "Environmental Refugees: A Yardstick of Habitability," *Worldwatch Paper 86* (Washington, D.C.: The Worldwatch Institute, November 1988), p. 6.

13. Flooding in South Asia reached crisis proportions, largely due to the loss of forest cover in the Himalayas. In India the area subject to annual flooding expanded from 47 million acres in 1960 to 124 million acres in 1984, an area larger than California. In

September 1988, two-thirds of Bangladesh was under water for several days, adding further to the misery of one of the world's poorest people. Brown, "Feeding Six Billion," p. 33.

14. Lester R. Brown and Christopher Flavin, "The Earth's Vital Signs," in Brown, *et al., The State of the World 1988* (New York: W. W. Norton, 1988), p. 8. The anticipated growth during the 1990s is 13.5 times the combined population [65 million] of the four Asian "tiger economies"—Hong Kong, Singapore, Taiwan, and South Korea—that are being touted by development economists as the models for emulation by poor countries.

15. Lester R. Brown, "Analyzing the Demographic Trap," in Lester R. Brown, *et al., State of the World 1987* (New York: W. W. Norton and Company, 1987), pp. 32–36.

16. For an analysis of the relationship between population growth and social conflict see Brown, "Analyzing the Demographic Trap," pp. 32–36.

17. Ruth Leger Sivard, "World Military and Social Expenditures 1987–1988," (World Priorities, Washington, D.C.) as cited by Tom Houston, "The Greatest Need in the World Today," *Together,* July–September 1988, pp. 3.

18. S. Rajaratnam, former Foreign Minister of Singapore, expressed the view in the *International Herald Tribune* in an article titled, "The Ethnic Fires Won't Die Out," January 12, 1990, p. 4 that:
> This sort of ethnic counterrevolution will dominate domestic and international politics in Europe, Asia and elsewhere in coming decades...the paradox of the closing years of the 20th century is that while economic and technological forces are unifying the world, ethnic hatreds are threatening to split it apart.

19. Larry Minear, *Helping People in an Age of Conflict: Toward a New Professionalism in U.S. Voluntary Humanitarian Assistance* (New York: American Council for Voluntary International Action, 1988).

20. This conclusion was reported by Alexandre Hay, President of the International Committee of the Red Cross (ICRC) in a speech titled "An Appeal for Humanity," delivered at ICRC headquarters in Geneva, Switzerland on January 10, 1985. It was confirmed by a working group of international experts in *Modern Wars: The Humanitarian Challenge,* report of the Independent Commission on International Humanitarian Issues (London: Zed Books, Ltd., 1986). The conclusions and citations are from Minear, *Age of Conflict*, pp. 7–8.

21. Quoted in Minear, *Age of Conflict,* p. 9.

22. *The Developing World: Danger Point for U.S. Security,* A report commissioned by Mark O. Hatfield, Matthew F. McHugh and Mickey Leland (Washington, D.C.: Arms Control and Foreign Policy Caucus of the U.S. Congress, August 1, 1989), p. 68.

23. *Ibid.,* pp. 66–67.

24. *Ibid.*

25. *Ibid.,* p. 66–68.

CHAPTER TWO

DECADE OF DENIAL

The predominant response to the growing evidence of systems failure throughout much of the 1980s was to deny that anything fundamental was wrong. The limited solutions undertaken more often focused on symptoms rather than on causes, or called for more faithful application of past remedies. Rather than confront the fundamental nature of the problems being encountered, solutions were sought in self-serving and politically palatable actions that often as not exacerbated the real problem. The basic inclination was pervasive, as demonstrated by the following examples.

ALLEVIATING POVERTY BY HELPING THE RICH

Conventional growth-centered development strategies came back into vogue with their assumption that helping the rich to become richer would result in new wealth gradually trickling down to benefit the poor as well. These strategies represented a thinly veiled rejection of the needs of the poor in favor of getting on with the much easier task of enriching the rich. Brazil, with its shameful environmental record and some of the worst poverty to be found in Latin America, was touted as a development miracle in recognition of the additions its more fortunate citizens had made to their incomes. The cynics argued, with considerable justification, that in fact the primary purpose of the structural adjustment and export-led growth policies espoused by the major bilateral and multilateral funding agencies for the South during the decade was to increase prospects that the international banks could recover their bad loans.

Treating Symptoms

Disasters, particularly the famines in Africa, captured headlines. While some talked of the need for long-term solutions, the main focus was on providing relief supplies to relieve immediate suffering, as though the conditions involved were the result of true natural disasters that were unpredictable and basically temporary in nature. The dumping of imported grains on Southern markets in the name of economic assistance, in many instances, depressed local food prices and thereby local farm production and incomes.

UNICEF and others called for the expansion of social services, focusing attention on targeted, technical, quick fix, politically popular, "magic bullet" attacks on leading symptoms of poverty, such as infant and maternal mortality. The emphasis on immediate food assistance, and quick-fix technical services effectively drew attention away from the conditions of social injustice that create and sustain poverty and condemn children of the poor to a life with little future.[1]

Few voices called attention to the extent to which the disasters and their consequences were indeed "unnatural." In many instances they were exacerbated by the self-serving actions of governments and international agencies and were thereby basically avoidable—if we were willing to address causes rather than only symptoms.[2]

Financial Borrowing

Defying evidence for the need of fundamental economic and political reforms, many nations went on a binge of borrowing to artificially sustain economic growth—akin to a final spending spree before the day of reckoning. This provided at least the temporary illusion that the consequences of a deepening economic crisis could be avoided without the inconvenience of unpleasant reforms and hard work. The number one example was the United States, which managed in less than a decade to transform itself from being the world's leading creditor nation to being its leading debtor. Meanwhile, as real U.S. power and influence declined, a small number of more frugal nations, such as Japan, West Germany, Taiwan and South Korea established dominant positions in the world economy.

In an effort to recycle the surplus revenues of oil producing countries, Southern nations were urged, in the name of development, to engage in unrestrained borrowing. Ironically, in this process many oil producing countries themselves became net borrowers. Southern borrowing so far exceeded the repayment capacity of some countries that there was concern that defaults might bring down the global financial system. The exposés that accompanied the fall of corrupt dictatorial regimes in the Philippines and Haiti told the story of how a great deal of the borrowed money was actually used.

The biggest borrowers were generally the relatively wealthier countries and the benefits of their borrowing generally accrued to their wealthier citizens. Later, as the international financial system bordered on collapse, much of the burden of the resulting crisis was transferred to the poor. Most developing countries suffered financial and economic crisis. While tens of millions of poor people sank deeper into poverty, structural adjustment policies attempted to overcome the crisis by shifting scarce resources into production of goods for sale to foreign consumers.

Environmental Borrowing

Environmental borrowing also allowed the world's rich to continue living beyond their means for a brief additional period, while in fact exacerbating the problem and limiting future options. Financial debtor nations were encouraged to focus on export-led growth, putting available resources to work for the benefit of foreign consumers while indigenous subsistence producers were crowded onto a declining segment of the resource base. Logging, cattle, and shrimp production were major money earners and highly favored by international financial institutions, often with disastrous social and environmental consequences.[3]

Responding to high grain prices, the United States made a singular contribution to achievement of record levels of global grain production in the first half of the decade—by plowing highly erodible land, with consequent soil loss, and lowering ground water tables through pump irrigation.[4] The United States was not alone in mining its soil and water resources. Countries throughout the South mined their soils, ground water, forests, coastal fisheries, energy deposits, and the international financial system, so that political and economic elites could support profligate consumption, accumulate funds in foreign assets and bank accounts, and finance large military establishments to keep the frustrations of the poor in check—all in the name of development and national security.

Financial borrowing involves only paper transactions between people. One group mortgages the future of its children to the children of another group. Financial borrowing can, and often does, have serious negative social and environmental consequences. However, these are agreements between people and nations. They can be renegotiated to reduce the detrimental consequences. Environmental borrowing is different. It involves a Faustian bargain between humanity and nature that leaves no possibility of appealing for debt relief or rescheduling, nor of default. Both the borrower and all of the borrower's children inevitably pay through loss of the ability of their planet to sustain them.

PROVIDING PALLIATIVES AS A SUBSTITUTE FOR ENVIRONMENTAL ACTION

Palliatives were offered as substitutes for serious environmental action. This was particularly evident in areas such as population control and the disposal of chemical and radioactive contaminants.

Population Control

Continued rapid population growth adds each day to the difficulty of resolving the global crises of poverty, environment and social conflict. Yet population control slipped down the list of development priorities as the United States abdicated its leadership position. A small, but vocal, minority of religious fundamentalists extended their battle against abortion into an attack on all serious family planning assistance efforts, implicitly denying the importance of population growth as a social and moral issue.

Again, palliatives were promoted as substitutes for more difficult, but essential action. Leading examples were the child survival programs that grew into prominence during the decade. Their advocates reassured the politicians with the inventive and politically popular claim that increased investment to improve the health of mothers during their reproductive years and to reduce infant mortality would resolve the population problem through a voluntary reduction in birth rates. Too often they conveniently ignored a well-documented fact: that inadequate birth spacing is one of the most important contributors to infant and maternal mortality. These advocates also failed to specify just how they expected couples without access to adequate contraceptive services to voluntarily limit their fertility.[5]

Waste Disposal
Another example of unconscionable reliance on palliatives was found in the area of waste management. Efforts to deal with the problem of chemical and radioactive contaminants were too often limited to burying them in "temporary" storage or scattering them over the landscape. Imaginative opportunists put them on boats in search of ports in Southern countries where a combination of limited environmental awareness, authoritarian control and corruption made dumping possible—for just a little while longer.

INCREASING MILITARY EXPENDITURES TO REDUCE VIOLENCE

In recent years, Southern countries have spent approximately $200 billion per year for military purposes, *four times the amount that they were receiving annually in economic aid.* Furthermore, these expenditures have been growing at a rate four times greater than their non-military spending.[6] Since 1960, the industrial countries have doubled their inflation adjusted military expenditures. Southern countries increased their military expenditures more than sixfold in this period.[7] Global military expenditures of $940 billion in 1985 exceeded the income of the poorest half of humanity.[8]

Total international trade in arms between 1967 and 1986 was valued at $635 billion in 1984 dollars, and was a significant contributor to Southern debt.[9] In a single year, 1984, global arms imports totaled $35 billion compared to $33 billion spent on grain imports.[10]

While the Western nations were reaching into their pockets to finance shipments of food to sustain starving people of Ethiopia, the

Ethiopian government was spending 42 percent of its budget to maintain the largest army in Sub-Sahara Africa.[11] It was shipping grain to the Soviet Union to pay for imported arms used for the sole purpose of killing its own citizens in order to maintain itself in power.

All too often the military expenditures of Southern governments are aimed more at protecting corrupt ruling elites from the wrath of their own citizens than at defending national borders. In many countries, the military has a major role in the illegal logging and destructive fishing operations that are destroying Southern forests and coastal ecologies.[12]

Half a million of the world's scientists are employed in weapons research. These scientists spend more money increasing the destructive power of weapons than the total spent to develop new energy technologies, improve human health, raise agricultural productivity, and control pollution.[13]

Far too little attention has been given to the multiple direct links between military expenditures and increasing human suffering and environmental degradation in Southern countries.

In many respects we lived an illusion during the 1980s, taking every available measure to avoid the hard realities of the mounting global crises and their underlying causes. Rather than act on underlying causes we preferred to deny their existence, at least where this might force us to question fundamental assumptions and challenge existing interests. Fortunately, the final two years of the decade brought hope of an increasing readiness to move beyond denial and to accept the harsh truth of our collective reality—at least in dealing with the issues of the environment and run-away military expenditures. Willingness to come to terms with poverty and irresponsible fiscal policies remains less evident.

NOTES

1. For an excellent critique of the prevailing approaches to health and child survival services see David Werner,"Empowerment and Health," The Hesperian Foundation, P.O. Box 1692, Palo Alto, California 94302, U.S.A., January 1988.

2. These include environmentally unsound policies and projects promoted by international donor agencies; and superpower backed regional conflicts, such as in Ethiopia and the Sudan, in which the rulers of contesting governments pursue "victory" with a total disregard for the well-being of their own citizens. There are a few lone voices calling attention to the human origins of these disasters. See, for example, Marck Malloch Brown (ed.), *Famine: A Man-Made Disaster*, A Report for the Independent Commission on International Humanitarian Issues (London: Pan Books, 1984).

3. See, for example, Sheldon Annis, "Costa Rica's Dual Debt: A Story About a Little Country that Did Things Right." Study prepared for the World Resources Institute by the Overseas Development Council, May 1987.

4. According to estimates of the Worldwatch Institute: "If the U.S. grain output produced with unsustainable use of soil and water is subtracted from the world total, the surpluses of the eighties disappear." Lester R. Brown, "The Changing World Food Prospects: The Nineties and Beyond," *Worldwatch Paper 85* (Washington, D.C.: Worldwatch Institute, October 1988), p. 7.

5. UNICEF, which was one of the leading offenders, now appears to be moving toward a more balanced position with greater attention to the necessity for serious attention to birth spacing.

6. *The Developing World: Danger Point for U.S. Security,* A report commissioned by Mark O. Hatfield, Matthew F. McHugh, and Mickey Leland (Washington, D.C.: Arms Control and Foreign Policy Caucus of the U.S. Congress, August 1, 1989), pp. 53 and 58.

7. Michael Renner, "Enhancing Global Security," in Lester R. Brown *et al., State of the World 1989* (New York: W. W. Norton & Company, 1989), p. 133.

8. Lester R. Brown, "Redefining National Security," in Lester R. Brown *et al., State of the World 1986,* (New York: W.W. Norton & Company, 1986), pp. 196.

9. Renner, "Enhancing Global Security," pp. 134–35.

10. Brown, "Redefining National Security," pp. 197–98.

11. *Ibid.,* p. 199.

12. In the Philippines, for example, the military is reported to be the primary source of the dynamite used in dynamite fishing, a major contributor to the destruction of the Philippines' coastal ecology.

13. Brown, "Redefining National Security," p. 199.

CHAPTER THREE

DECADE OF OPPORTUNITY

Along with crisis and denial, the 1980s also brought truly profound new developments that give us hope for the future. Not only was there an awakening to the crises we face, particularly the environmental crisis; there were also startling breakthroughs toward the creation of new potentials for dealing with the threefold global crisis.

The breathtaking speed with which events were unfolding by the close of the decade confirms that the beneficial transformation of imbedded institutions can occur more quickly than a rational person would have any reason to believe possible—if there is sufficient human commitment. The momentum has been established. It remains to be sustained and directed toward realizing the potentials now before us. This chapter reviews a few of the important new opportunities that the 1980s produced.

DEMILITARIZATION AND EAST-WEST COOPERATION

The global balance of power shifted dramatically during the 1980s. Those countries that chose to focus their energies on building economic power—specifically Japan and members of the European Economic Community—have gained enormously in global stature and power. Those countries—the United States and the Soviet Union—that have chosen to project their interests predominantly through military power have experienced a corresponding decline. The United States and the Soviet Union have been absorbed in an obsolete game with no winners, leaving Japan and the European Economic Community to walk off with the global power prize. The United States may have the B-1 bomber, but Japan owns nine of the world's ten largest banks.[1]

Perhaps because the Soviet Union had the weaker economy of the two former global superpowers, it was the first to grasp the implications of the shifting balance between economic and military power.[2] It thus took the lead in abruptly ending the cold war and redirecting priorities from arms to economic reconstruction.[3] Almost overnight, confrontation gave way to East-West cooperation in dismantling one of the world's last major colonial empires—Eastern Europe—and in reconstructing economies that had been devastated by years of communist rule.[4]

These developments create a realistic hope that the 1990s may see the end of the cold war and dramatic reductions in arms expenditures. There is also the possibility of a new era of East-West cooperation in dealing with the threefold global crisis.

ENVIRONMENTAL ACTION

The latter part of the decade produced evidence that a fundamental shift had occurred in world public opinion on environmental issues, including the emergence of a new-found environmental awareness within the Soviet Union. In 1986, a U.S. administration that had set the standard for denial of environmental issues introduced a Conservation Reserve Program that by 1987 had already helped reduce soil losses by 460 million tons a year.[5]

The World Bank, in part due to pressures from nongovernmental organizations (NGOs), began to give more than lip service to environmental issues. The United States Agency for International Development announced new environmental initiatives. Increasing numbers of NGOs throughout the world came to recognize and act on the fact that environmental deterioration was further increasing the burden faced by the already desperately poor.

The real breakthrough came in 1988. Environmental issues suddenly advanced to center stage on the global agenda, spurred in part by the publication in 1987 of *Our Common Future,* the report of the World Commission on Environment and Development[6] and by growing evidence of environmental failure. It was as if a threshold had been breached. Suddenly an awareness of the growing environmental disaster flooded into the collective human consciousness.[7] The environment became a major issue in the 1988 U.S. presidential campaign—with each leading candidate vying to prove himself the more aggressive environmental advocate. In recognition of the extent to which environmental issues had dominated the news during 1988, in its first issue of 1989, *Time* magazine named The Endangered Earth "Planet of the Year" and warned of impending environmental catastrophe.

There remains a wide gap between awareness and action. However, increased consciousness creates possibilities for actions in the 1990s that seemed all too remote even in 1987.

PEOPLE POWER

The triumph of people power over armed tyrants was one of the extraordinary developments of the 1980s. In setting after setting people said no to tyranny and won, usually with little or no violence.

Democratization

The decade saw an upsurge in people's movements and voluntary development initiatives, including a new and broadly-based commitment to democratization.[8] The ferment was particularly evident in Latin America and the Eastern bloc countries, which began to move toward market economies and democratic governance. The Philippines and Haiti captured the global imagination in 1986 with the overthrow of corrupt family dictatorships. Democratic pressures grew in South Korea and Taiwan.

At the same time the 1980s provided a sobering demonstration that the institutions, values and self-discipline required to sustain an open democratic society take time to build. The path from oppression to freedom is seldom smooth. This was demonstrated by the subsequent setback to the liberalization process in China, as well as the difficulties experienced following the restoration of democracy in the Philippines and Haiti.

It is still too early to claim a final victory for freedom and democracy. However, events have demonstrated beyond reasonable doubt that these are indeed universal human values without an East or West, North or South. So too have events shown that tyrants depend on the acceptance of their tyranny by the tyrannized. When the people refuse to acquiesce, the power of the tyrant evaporates. Ultimately power flows not from the barrel of the gun, but from the will of the people. People power is the supreme power.

Citizen Diplomacy

A citizen's peace movement strengthened and played an important role in building people-to-people linkages across the divide that separated the superpowers, reducing mutual suspicion and creating pressures on governments to reassess outdated positions.[9] In growing numbers private citizens concluded that peace and the relations between peoples are too important to be left to governments whose leaders are often far removed from the values and aspirations of their citizens. As a consequence, local governments in various parts of the world responded to citizen pressures to develop their own foreign policies and established sister-city relationships to foster direct citizen-to-citizen diplomacy.

Women

Among the most important people power advances of the decade was the progress made toward releasing women power as a development force. The contributions of women to development have become increasingly recognized, resulting in progress in many countries toward relieving restrictions on female participation in political and economic activities. There is growing confirmation that women bring a fresh and much needed ethical perspective to bear in solving society's problems.

Women may prove to be the force that will reshape Japan's archaic political system and open the way for using more of the country's enormous wealth to increase the standard of living of the Japanese people. In the Philippines, Cory Aquino, the housewife in the yellow dress, restored democracy to the Philippines, bringing to that position a moral commitment that makes her a beacon of light in the midst of the traditional male crony politicians who have tried to unseat her by using the traditional methods of Philippine politics—guns, goons and gold.

Much yet remains to be done. However, the forces unleashed by the feminist movement have become too powerful to be reversed and the gains will surely continue.

Development Role of Civil Society

The 1980s saw a growing rejection of the myth that government is the sole legitimate agent for development decision making and the management of development resources. It is now widely accepted that civil society has an essential, if not central, role in both. Where corresponding changes in policy have resulted, new possibilities have been opened for mobilizing a far greater range of human talent, institutional capacity and social energy in the service of development than governments could ever hope to achieve.

Much of the effort to expand the role of civil society has focused on freeing up markets so that economic competition can work its magic. One of the more important advances in this area has been a new awareness of the importance of the informal sector in providing livelihood opportunities for the poor. Stimulated in part by the success of the Grameen Bank in Bangladesh and the Institute for Liberty and Democracy in Peru, it is now widely recognized that when systemic procedural and financial constraints to self-help are removed, the poor are excellent credit risks and highly effective in creating their own employment. As a consequence, the more progressive donors, governments and NGOs have begun to move beyond limited "livelihood projects" to look more broadly at the need for financially viable systems of rural credit and the elimination of barriers that prevent small producers from gaining access to the facilities and legal protection offered by participation in the "modern" sector.[10]

Many donors and governments also came to appreciate the important and distinctive development roles of NGOs during the 1980s. NGOs, in turn, began to take themselves more seriously, making commitments to strengthen their capacities to provide leadership on important policy issues. These advances prepare the way for a substantially new development dynamic in the South in which the people take the lead and government enables the people to develop themselves.

Again the victory is far from complete. There are many vested interests that benefit from governmental regulation and monopolization of development resources. The first step has been taken, however, toward breaking that monopoly.

INFORMATION INTENSIVE TECHNOLOGIES

The decade saw a wide range of advances in information-based technologies. The computer matured from a massive and prohibitively expensive number cruncher accessible only to big government and big business to a powerful decentralized personal communication and global networking tool. The bio-technology revolution progressed from science fiction to proven application, with the potential to fundamentally reshape industries such as agriculture and health. Advances in materials science resulted in substituting readily available materials, such as silicon, for depletable resources, like copper. Together these advances caused a continuing reduction in the amount of physical resources required to perform any given function.

The technologies that create the most important opportunities for our future are information-based. They use knowledge as a resource, commonly substituting information for materials in performing useful work. Information, among all the resources on which improvements in human well-being depend, is unique. It is nondepletable and is infinitely divisible. It is nearly costless to replicate and the original owner can give it away without losing the use of it. Though the uses of information-based technology can be environmentally devastating, such as in applied nuclear technology, information is itself a nonpolluting resource and its use as a substitute for physical material can greatly ease the burden we place on our environment. The use of bio-technologies to increase plant yields per hectare while reducing requirements for fertilizer, insecticides and irrigation is only one example.[11]

In the end, the 1980s came to a tumultuous conclusion as a decade of awakening and opportunity. It left us with a realistic hope that the 1990s might truly be a decade of transformation. If so, then the coming decade may prepare the way for new heights of human accomplishment in the 21st century. Yet the awakening remains only partial and is only the first step toward change. The real work has just begun. We must be clear on more than the tragedy we hope to avoid. We must commit ourselves to a new vision of society and of the path we take in search of human progress. This is the topic to which we turn our attention in Part II.

NOTES

1. Citibank is the only U.S. bank to rank among the top ten. Japan's banks now account for 40 percent of all international bank assets, up from 20 percent in 1983. Japan's thirteen largest banks have a combined stock market value of $470 billion. The combined value of the fifty largest U.S. banks is $110 billion. David C. Hale, "Global Finance and the Retreat to Managed Trade," *Harvard Business Review,* Vol. 90, No. 1, January–February 1990, pp. 150–51.

2. The world still refers to the United States and the Soviet Union as the two world superpowers. That is partly historical and partly a reflection of the reluctance of either Japan or Western Europe to flex the muscle inherent in their economic power—a more useful power than the possession of weapons that no sane person would ever use. Furthermore, Western Europe has not yet fully consolidated its economic power, which it plans to do in 1992.

3. I recently read a book published in 1986 on the nuclear threat and the need to build citizen level communication links between the United States and the Soviet Union as a means of increasing communication and reducing the nuclear threat. The fact that the issues discussed, if not the plea for citizen diplomacy, had in such a short period come to seem so dated was for me a powerful statement as to the depth and speed of the changes we are presently confronting.

4. It may be argued that China, with its continued domination of Tibet and Mongolia, still remains a major colonial empire.

5. Lester R. Brown, "The Changing World Food Prospects: The Nineties and Beyond," *Worldwatch Paper 85* (Washington, DC: Worldwatch Institute, October 1988), p. 49.

6. Commonly known as the Brundtland Report, it was published by the Oxford University Press in Oxford, England.

7. Robert Ornstein and Paul Ehrlich, *New World, New Mind: Moving Toward Conscious Evolution* (New York: Doubleday, 1989) argue that culturally and biologically the human species has been conditioned to ignore small changes in its environment. Selective perception allows us to filter out incremental change in order to be more conscious of the more abrupt changes that traditionally have signaled potential threats to our security—such as the appearance of a large tiger in the cave entrance. This previously functional characteristic has resulted in a systematic filtering out of information regarding persistent, but incremental changes in our environment. Now it seems that the changes are coming with sufficient speed and magnitude that they have finally begun to register on the human consciousness as the threat they truly are.

8. According to Freedom House, political rights increased in fifty-six developing countries between 1973 and 1987, against a decline of political rights in thirty-three. As reported in Alan Woods, *Development and the National Interest: U.S. Economic Assistance into the 21st Century, A Report* (Washington, DC: U.S. Agency for International Development, 1989), p. 45.

9. Don Carlson and Craig Comstock (eds.), *Citizen Summitry: Keeping the Peace When it Matters too Much to be Left to Politicians* (New York: St. Martin's Press, 1986).

10. A leading exponent of this concept is Hernando de Soto of the Institute of Liberty and Democracy in Lima, Peru. His ideas are presented in *The Other Path* (New York: Harper & Row Publishers, 1989).

11. Information technologies are no panacea. Obviously people cannot live by information alone. Furthermore, while the objectives of society are generally best served by making information freely available, those who control information often have a substantial economic interest in monopolizing control over its use.

In understanding the issues involved in policy making regarding information as a resource and the assignment of rights to its use the distinction that some economists make between *use* value and *market* value is important. Use value refers to the value of the benefit that a person will derive from actually using a resource to meet some need. Thus use value is determined independently of considerations of the items market value, i.e., the price it might command if sold in open bidding. Thus for an individual the use value of life sustaining amounts of water and air are very high, even though in most settings their market value is nil. By contrast, for most people the actual use value of a diamond is very low. There are few people who cannot survive without one. Its market value, however, may be very high.

Most resources are indivisible. A person cannot sell or share them without giving up their use and the option of selling them to another party on the market. Information is different. Generally it is infinitely divisible. It can be shared without compromising the ability of the person who shares it to continue using the information. The market value of the information will surely decline as it is shared because people will not pay for that which is freely accessible. However, the total use value increases because much larger numbers of people are able to avail of its benefits without depriving anyone else of actual use benefits. For this reason the public interest will in most instances be maximized to the extent that useful information is freely shared—so long as reasonable incentives are maintained to encourage the creative processes involved in generating new information.

PART II

TOWARD A JUST, SUSTAINABLE AND INCLUSIVE SOCIETY

During the 1980s, the dominant reality for the people of the South, after forty years of development commitment, was widespread poverty, a deteriorating environment, and pervasive fear of arbitrary violence. A great deal more than an unfortunate downturn in the international economic cycle was involved in creating these conditions and it is unlikely that they can be alleviated merely by fine tuning economic policies, as some would have us believe. The causes are deeply imbedded in our institutions, which in turn are the creations of our collective vision of the nature of our world and of what constitutes human progress. To resolve the global crises we must achieve basic changes in the ways in which we think and act. To paraphrase Kenneth Boulding, we need to stop thinking and acting like cowboys on the open plain and begin to think and act like astronauts who recognize that their lives depend on maintaining the supplies and life-support systems of their spaceship.

The chapters of Part II focus specifically on the need to redefine our vision of development progress—to move beyond the growth-centered vision that places the emphasis on economic output toward a people-centered vision that gives primacy to people, ecology and society.

For many decades nations and individuals who pursued the growth-centered vision were highly successful, even though many of its implicit assumptions have always been invalid. There were enough natural resources relative to demand that one could just as well act as if they were limitless without being seriously inconvenienced. If one resource became unduly scarce another was substituted. To the extent that there were perceived to be limits to the ability of the environment to absorb discarded wastes they seemed to be of little relevance. Jobs and human well-being were at stake. One could not place the environment before people—and profits. Those whose economic interests were at stake regularly expressed their pious concern for the less fortunate: How, they asked, could the poor hope to arise from their misery if economic expansion were curtailed for the sake of preserving a few rare bird species?

The success of those who pursued the growth-centered vision was so great that its promised bounty became a dream of the vast majority of the world's population, their hope for a better life. Though many of us are still reluctant to acknowledge it, the 1980s provided a growing body of evidence that it is a false promise born of a vision based on a badly distorted view of the nature of the world in which we live.

The world's physical and ecological resource base is not adequate to provide affluence, at least as currently defined, for all people. Furthermore, given existing institutional structures, the benefits of additional increments of production accrue first to the already well-to-do, and only marginally, if at all, to those who are most in need.

The endless expansion of economic output can no longer be viewed as a panacea for what ails human society. Growth is an answer only to the extent that it is preceded by a fundamental transformation of structures and values to ensure that it will be a just, sustainable and inclusive growth—a profoundly different kind of growth than the growth we have known.

The following chapters examine how the shared beliefs of society shape behavior and human progress. Chapter 4 suggests that in contrast to the claim that "seeing is believing," in fact what we believe often determines what we see. Thus beliefs about reality may sometimes play a more dominant role than reality itself in shaping the development of human societies.

Chapter 5 examines the critical elements of the growth-centered development vision, their underlying assumptions, and their value implications. Chapter 6 looks at the post-colonial experience broadly shared by many Southern nations, and points out how application of the policy orientations of the growth-centered vision contribute to sustaining basic patterns of economic and social relationships more reminiscent of the colonial era than of the relationships appropriate to modernizing societies.

Chapter 7 outlines the critical elements, assumptions and values of an alternative people-centered development vision. Chapter 8 takes a step toward operationalizing this alternative vision in a sequenced equity-led sustainable growth strategy.

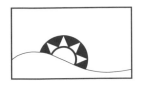

CHAPTER FOUR

BELIEVING IS SEEING

Some years ago, Thomas Kuhn, one of the most influential modern writers on the nature of scientific thought, introduced the concept of the paradigm.[1] A paradigm is a set of basic ideas, thoughts or beliefs about the nature of reality. These beliefs serve as a lens through which we filter day-to-day perceptions of our world. While the old proverb tells us that seeing is believing, it might be more accurate to say that believing is seeing. Because of its influence on what we see the lens of our belief system is a powerful determinant of how we act.

IDEAS CHANGE HISTORY

It is the relationship among belief, perception and action that gives ideas revolutionary power. Throughout history certain ideas have come into currency that have had the power to lift a veil from the eyes of those who embraced them. The flood of new insights that results brings a great sense of elation and power. A truly powerful new lens can stimulate the release of massive social energies toward a reordering of human institutions and behavior on a grand scale.

 The most widely cited example of an idea that had the power to reshape a world view, and ultimately the lives, of millions of people was Nicolaus Copernicus' discovery that the earth rotates around the sun. This discovery, along with the contributions of Galileo, Descartes and Newton ushered in the new age of science. Before their time it was well-known, and readily observable to all reasonable and educated people, that the sun and the heavens rotated around the earth. Such people saw the earth as the center of the universe and the focus of attention of the gods and spirits who ruled it. As they could find no consistent order to the movement of the stars they concluded that the universe was ruled by gods and demons who gave it a life of its own beyond ordinary logic and calculation. Thus, knowledge of the workings of our world was considered to be the province of priests and sorcerers who had the ability to make connections with the moving spirits and to access their magical powers.[2]

The simple idea that the earth in fact rotates around the sun represented a fundamental change in perspective. With that change came the realization that there was indeed order to the movements of heavenly bodies and these could become known and predicted through observation and calculation. This discovery introduced a new age of positivistic science built on the perception of a mechanical universe. The reality of the universe had in no way changed. How people perceived it, however, changed dramatically. That change in perception or vision contributed to fundamental changes in social institutions and opened possibilities for undreamed of technological advances. It also separated the world of action from the world of values.

Karl Marx introduced the idea of class conflict into our view of society. His was a lens with substantial analytical power, opening profound new insights into the human condition. For millions of people it became not simply a tool, but a theology. It led to the creation of the Marxist states that ultimately came to control the lives of a substantial portion of the world's population, sustaining for much of this century one of the most profound of historical contradictions, the imposition of tyranny in the name of humanitarianism and justice.

Right or wrong, ideas have power. Even lenses with the power to reveal important truths can do great harm if the wearer becomes so dependent on them as to become unable to see any other reality.

The women's movement represents still another example of the power of an idea, the idea that the subordination of women is political and social—not biological—in its origins. This idea has released new forces in society that are reshaping the family, the work force, political institutions and economies.

The central models and values of economics regarding the appropriate ways to organize societies for productive activity and measure their performance represent another example of the power of a set of ideas with the ability to shape history. The vision of development that economic science fostered and legitimated proved enormously liberating, leading to a large-scale mobilization of resources that lifted a substantial minority of the world's population to previously unimaginable levels of physical luxury.

The growth-centered vision further nurtured the ideal that through the application of a set of logical prescriptions, the prosperity of one and all could be assured—a lofty and worthy goal. Indeed the vision in large measure drew its legitimacy from its promise to deliver this outcome. Unfortunately, this same vision now holds us captive to ways of thinking and acting that are increasingly inappropriate and self-destructive to the point of threatening to destroy our environment, push ever increasing numbers of people into exactly the condition of poverty it promised to alleviate, and tear asunder the social fabric of human society.

FROM COWBOYS TO ASTRONAUTS

The central problem of the growth-centered development vision was graphically described by Kenneth Boulding in 1968 in his classic distinction between a cowboy and a spaceship economy.[3] The cowboy lives on the open frontier. He takes what he wants from nature wherever he finds it. His frontier is vast and its resources seemingly inexhaustible. He drops along the trail whatever trash or belongings no longer serve his need to be swept away by the forces of nature. The vision of cowboy economics is that of a world best described as a limitless open plain that supplies resources and waste disposal services without end.

The cowboy economy is geared to extracting the most conveniently available resources from its environment and converting them into whatever products satisfy its wants. Any item that is no longer immediately useful is simply discarded to be disposed of by nature. Performance is measured in terms of the market value of the throughput of resources. The faster resources are mined, processed, and discarded, the more prosperous the people are considered to be.

Spaceship economics is grounded in a fundamentally different vision, that of a spaceship hurtling through space with a human crew and a precious, limited supply of resources. Except for the radiant energy of the sun, the continued existence of the crew and the functioning of their life support systems depend on the conservation of the ship's resource stock. This reality dictates the basic principles of the spaceship economy.

Following the logic of Boulding's analogy, increases in the wellbeing of the spaceship's occupants necessarily depend on their becoming more efficient and effective in the sustainable use and recycling of existing resources to meet first their needs, and then—to the extent surpluses are available—their wants. For any resource to be discarded, and therefore lost forever to the inhabitants of the spaceship, is an indicator of serious system failure. The goal is to extend the life of products, rather than to increase the rate at which they are discarded; and to substitute information-based technology for materials in the design of life-enhancing systems and products.

Life on a spaceship can be sustained only through the cooperation of all of the spaceship's inhabitants. Each must feel a stake in maintaining the system and be willing to accept its allocation of available resources as just. We may conclude from this that no increase in economic output in the spaceship can be counted as an advance unless it is based on sustainable processes *and* translates into justly distributed benefits for the spaceship's inhabitants.

The spaceship analogy is a powerful tool for conceptualizing the current dilemma of human society. Temporary gains in economic output based on environmental borrowing in fact leave us poorer. They represent *de-development* by any reasonable definition and should be handled accordingly in our economic accounting. Actions that impoverish one group to multiply the riches of another must also count as a reduction in the well-being of the whole. They too must be classified as *de-development*. They reveal the injustice of the system and undermine the social consensus essential to sustain it. The consumption of resources for uses that ultimately diminish rather than increase human well-being, such as investments in military hardware, must also count as *de-development.*

Nature is now drawing our attention to the fact that the vision by which we are living is as contrary to our reality as was the pre-Copernican vision that the earth revolved around the sun. We have all along been living on a spaceship, not on a limitless plain. There are now too many of us, our aspirations are too great and our technology too powerful to continue to live by the old myth. We must now learn to see and think in ways more consistent with our true reality. We must learn to link human systems and technologies to environmental systems in ways that enhance the overall productivity of the combined ecological system to humanity's long-term benefit.

The challenge of making a transition to the application of spaceship economics in the management of earth's resources must be embraced equally by both agricultural and industrial societies, by both the "developed" and the "underdeveloped." Unless we all, both North and South, come to embrace a vision more consistent with our collective reality, we will suffer dearly in the years ahead.

HISTORICAL PRECEDENT

We may find comfort in the fact that this is not the first time in human history that societies have gone through profound transformations in basic perceptions, values and institutions.[4] We have already mentioned the profound changes in institutions and values that came with the new age of science. Other important transitions have been successfully negotiated when societies moved from hunter/gatherer to pastoral to agricultural to industrial economies. Each of these transitions brought its own trauma. Each brought as well, new opportunities that led to major advances in human civilization.

We must be aware, however, that the present transition differs from earlier historical transitions in several important ways:

- Changes are now coming at a much more rapid rate.
- All of human society is engaged simultaneously.
- Currently available knowledge and technology give us far greater conscious awareness of the alternatives and increased opportunities for choice.
- Failure to make correct choices will limit the possibilities open to human society for many generations to come.

■ A successful transition requires that we take more significant steps than at any other point in human history toward the elimination of poverty and warfare from the human experience.

The choices to be made are too important to be left to politicians, technocrats and bureaucrats. The people's voice must be heard in defining the vision that drives these choices, as the people will bear their consequences.

NOTES

1. See Thomas S. Kuhn, *The Structure of Scientific Revolutions* (Chicago: University of Chicago Press, 1970).

2. For a more complete discussion see Kuhn, *Revolution;* and Willis Harman, *Global Mind Change: Promise of the Last Years of the Twentieth Century* (Indianapolis: Knowledge Systems, Inc., 1988), pp. 3–10.

3. Kenneth E. Boulding, "The Economics of the Coming Spaceship Earth," in Henry Jarrett (ed.), *Environmental Quality in a Growing Economy* (Baltimore: The Johns Hopkins University Press, 1968), pp. 3–14. Also in David C. Korten and Rudi Klauss (eds.), *People-Centered Development: Contributions toward Theory and Planning Frameworks* (West Hartford: Kumarian Press, 1984), pp. 63–73.

4. See Harman, *Global Mind Change;* Robert E. Neil, "What Makes History Happen?" in Korten and Klauss (eds.), *People-Centered Development*, pp. 33–46; Fritjof Capra, *The Turning Point: Science, Society and the Rising Culture* (New York: Simon and Schuster, 1982); and Alvin Toffler, *The Third Wave* (New York: William Morrow and Company, Inc., 1980).

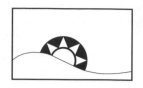

CHAPTER FIVE

COWBOY ECONOMICS:
THE GROWTH-CENTERED VISION

Development thought and action in most countries of both North and South has been dominated for decades by a growth-centered development vision.[1] This vision has spanned the ideological division between East and West, being as dominant in socialist as it is in capitalist societies. It is a vision informed by the world view of Boulding's cowboy economics described in the previous chapter.

The events of the 1980s have revealed many limitations of this world view to the point that it is becoming difficult to find true champions of many of its underlying premises. However, on balance, the economic policies of most countries and international institutions continue to follow prescriptions grounded in its logic.

To highlight the choices we face and thereby to give clarity to the alternatives, I have chosen to review the basic prescriptions, premises and values of the growth-centered vision in their more purist form. Some readers may find the representation that follows to be something of a caricature. If so, I hope they will find it a caricature that enhances their understanding of critical issues.

In its pure form, the conventional vision defines development almost entirely in terms of growth in the economic value of the output of the society's productive systems, without regard to the impact on resource stocks and environment, or even actual contributions to human well-being. National progress and well-being are reduced to a single indicator, the growth or decline of total economic output as valued by the market, i.e., as determined by what those with money are willing to pay to satisfy their *wants*. No weight is given in such calculations to the *needs* of the poor who have no money to participate in the market.

Outputs that do not pass through a formal market are often discounted or ignored in the calculation of the value of total output. Thus the worth of what a farmer produces for the consumption of his family is either excluded or assessed only at wholesale value.[2] Similarly discounted are the food production and processing, water supplying, household maintenance and child-care activities of the housewife; and the value of the work of the informal urban sector, such as the street vendors, scavengers and repairpersons—who comprise a growing percentage of the urban population. For those who wear the conventional lens, these outputs do not exist or are substantially undervalued. Attention is focused instead on the budgets of government and the sales and investments of major enterprises, especially those corporations with sales that flow into international markets and contribute to foreign exchange earnings.

CENTRAL ROLE OF CAPITAL INVESTMENT

Wearers of the conventional development lens commonly presume that growth in output is achieved primarily through the productive investment of domestic savings and foreign grants, loans and investments.[3] Since it is assumed that the rich are more likely than the poor to save and invest additions to their income, there is an implicit preference for increasing the incomes of the rich. Unlike the rich, it is expected that the poor will only spend their money for food, clothing, social obligations and other unproductive consumption items.

There has also been a related and longstanding assumption among many proponents of the growth-centered vision that authoritarian regimes are more effective than democracies in mobilizing domestic savings and channeling them to the most productive investment areas. Such regimes are considered to be less subject to populist pressures to increase labor benefits, public services and other consumption expenditures that divert resources away from "productive" purposes.[4]

There is also an expectation that most growth-promoting investments in Southern countries—such as for infrastructure, industry and input intensive agriculture—require the import of capital goods, technology and technical assistance. This creates a demand for foreign exchange, and a special interest in policies that will increase exports, substitute local production for imports, or attract foreign investment capital, assistance grants and loans—all in order to improve the exchange position.[5]

When most international assistance agencies were created, it was assumed that their primary function would be to transfer investment capital in the form of loans and grants from developed to underdeveloped countries. These agencies were created specifically to manage such transfers. They were labeled "development" institutions and the activities they funded were by definition "development." The perspectives of the growth-centered development vision became institutionalized in what became very powerful international organizations.

POLICY ORIENTATION

The development efforts of the past forty years have seen many pass-ing fads with respect to favored policies. Should the focus of invest-ment be on industry or agriculture, export promotion or import substi-tution? Should the preference be for state or private enterprise, for planned or free markets? What priority should be given to basic services for the poor? In general, however, these debates have taken place within the boundaries of the growth-centered development vision.[6]

The frequent debates may obscure the extent of agreement among proponents of the conventional vision on more fundamental points. However, though their perspectives are now in transition, they have over the decades been inclined to favor:

- Increasing economic specialization to concentrate productive re-sources on those products and services in which the country has a comparative advantage in the international marketplace.
- Making investments that support the rapid extraction of resources for export to increase foreign exchange earnings.[7]
- Mobilizing foreign equity or loan financing for large-scale capital investments.
- Minimizing restrictions on private investors, both foreign and domestic.
- Fully utilizing available foreign loans to stimulate the domestic economy.
- Concentrating capital in large units to achieve the economies-of-scale needed to compete in foreign markets.
- Encouraging the flow of labor out of agriculture and into the cities to ensure an adequate labor supply for industrialization.
- Keeping labor costs low to provide an attractive climate for foreign investment and to maintain international competitiveness.
- Postponing political development (democratization) so that govern-ment can undertake the measures required to meet the needs of economic growth before being subjected to populist demands that may divert resources from productive uses.[8]

ACTING AS IF. . .

The actions that have followed from the pursuit of the growth-centered vision imply a number of underlying assumptions. Specifically the vision encourages acting as if:

- The earth's physical resources are for all practical purposes inex-haustible. (The explicit argument is sometimes made that science will come up with suitable substitutes for any resource that be-comes exhausted or prohibitively expensive to recover.)[9]
- The environment has a virtually infinite ability to absorb waste.

- Poverty is simply the result of inadequate growth, which in turn results from inadequate capital investment.
- The international markets in which a country is competing are freely competitive without subsidies or restraints that give competitors from some countries an advantage over others.
- Foreign borrowing is used for productive capital investments that will generate foreign exchange for repayment.
- Those workers who are displaced from agriculture or other rural resource-based occupations, such as fishing, by productivity enhancing capital investments will be readily absorbed in industrial employment in urban centers.
- Market forces will automatically distribute development benefits.

Because of the strong belief in automatic market responses, structural issues relating to the *distribution* of economic benefits tend to be neglected. Concerns with people's participation enter into consideration only in relation to participation as labor and consumers, i.e., in enhancing the performance of the economy.

VALUE ORIENTATIONS

In addition to encouraging action based on these dangerously risky assumptions, the conventional vision involves implicit value preferences that tend to be anti-people and anti-environment. Specifically:

- It is strongly biased toward the *wants* of affluent consumers—especially foreigners, to the neglect of the *needs* of domestic consumers—especially the poor.
- It undervalues natural resources and discourages resource conservation.
- It values equally any increase in economic activity, irrespective of whether it is sustainable or contributes to improved human well-being.
- It assumes that the laborer exists to serve the economy, rather than the reverse.
- It legitimates the concentration of ownership of productive assets in corporate structures that separate the control of these assets from the communities that depend on them.

These value orientations are generally only implicit. Even among those who are outspoken proponents of the vision, there are few who explicitly advocate or defend them. Often the value premises of the vision are simply unexamined.[10]

The outcomes of the growth-centered vision and its underlying policy prescriptions are likely to be substantially influenced by existing structural conditions. Where pre-existing structures serve to distribute rather than to concentrate economic and political power, there is a reasonable prospect that participation in the benefits of economic growth may be broadly shared. Where this condition is not met, the result is likely to be an increasing concentration of economic and political power, with limited opportunity for the poor to gain a voice either in the marketplace or in the political process.[11] There are also tendencies toward institutionalizing the practice of absentee ownership on a global scale. This contributes to a lack of commitment to people and place, and undermines the sense of community and resource stewardship essential to sustainability.

THE BASIC NEEDS STRATEGIES

The basic needs strategies that gained prominence during the 1970s, and are still advocated by organizations such as UNICEF, are a variant of, usually an add-on to, a classical growth-centered development strategy. Generally, they concentrate on service delivery as a means of simultaneously reallocating the benefits of economic growth and preparing people for participation in the economic system.[12]

Building Social Capital
Advocates of a basic needs strategy generally accept that, particularly in its early stages, the benefits of growth may be inadequately allocated by the market. The common explanation is that the limited social capital of most members of the population, particularly their levels of education and health, reduce their productive potential and thereby their ability to participate in the market as laborers and consumers.

The underlying assumption that the market does indeed work is retained. The implicit argument is that the problem for the poor is that they do not come to the market with adequate education, skills and physical strength to attract employment on favorable terms. To help the poor make up their deficiency, advocates of the basic needs strategy call on governments to transfer wealth from those who have benefitted from growth to finance compensatory services for the poor. In part this compensates for their inability to meet their own needs. In part it is intended to prepare them to gain a place in the labor force. The wealth transfer may be international through assistance agencies, or domestic through use of the government's taxing authority.

Participation
There tends to be considerable discussion of people's participation in the implementation of basic needs strategies. The focus, however, is usually on how to get people to participate as co-producers in implementing service delivery projects initiated and controlled by government. This form of participation is more accurately described as mobilization than as empowerment.

Outcomes
Actions in support of basic needs strategies generally result in aug-

menting social service budgets, staff and facilities. However, the results for the poor are often difficult to distinguish from relief and welfare programs aimed purely at relieving some of the worst consequences of poverty. The results are seldom sustainable, nor do they necessarily enhance economic participation. Too often poverty involves fundamental structural barriers that limit access to productive assets, markets and fair wages. These barriers are seldom addressed by basic needs strategies, which consequently tend to leave the poor in a perpetual state of dependence.

Though proponents of the growth-centered vision found themselves on the defensive during much of the 1970s, the vision remained largely intact and regained ascendance in the 1980s. It found its purest expression in the structural adjustment policies of the multilateral banks—the findings of the 1960s and 1970s regarding social consequences of pure growth strategies apparently forgotten. Once again, if the poor were suffering it was presumed to be because there was not enough growth to be shared. It is a convenient premise for those with the political and economic power to capture growth's benefits.

A concerted attack was made during the 1980s by the development community on the structures that restrain growth, while remaining largely silent on the structures that restrain justice. Predictably the poor suffered. The primary concern for social welfare came from the advocates of basic needs strategies, arguing for greater investment in human services to give adjustment a "human face." The terminology was apt. The basic services for which they pleaded were best characterized as a facade, putting a more palatable face on actions that are based on flawed analysis and theory, rather than coming forward in support of more basic, but politically controversial reforms.

Neither pure growth, nor growth with basic needs, strategies have contributed much to dealing with the root causes of poverty. Yet they largely dominated the foreign assistance and development policy agenda during the 1980s. We will see in the following chapter how, as a partial result of this dominance, foreign assistance has probably contributed more to strengthening the dualistic enclave structures of colonial economies than to advancing structural reforms toward justice, sustainability and inclusiveness.

NOTES

1. Current examples of documents that advocate a largely unexamined growth-centered vision are the recent report by Alan Woods, the former administrator of the United States Agency for International Development, *Development and the National Interest: U.S. Economic Assistance into the 21st Century* (Washington, DC: Agency for International Development, 1989); and the World Bank's world development reports for 1988 and 1989. Unfortunately, even the much-heralded report of the World Commission on Environment and Development [the Brundtland Commission] is an example. It is one of the more comprehensive and authoritative statements available

on the limits of our finite planet. Yet it acknowledges no contradiction between the reality it documents so faithfully and its own optimistic call for a revival of growth as the cure for poverty. The World Commission on Environment and Development, *Our Common Future* (Oxford: Oxford University Press, 1977), pp. 49–52.

2. If the family had purchased the same food in the market to meet its needs it would be valued at the full retail price.

3. The growth-centered vision has long treated domestic savings and foreign borrowing as though they were equivalent sources of the capital required to drive economic growth. This is a fundamental fallacy that has contributed materially to the current global financial crisis. Savings and debt are not and never have been the same thing. Savings are accumulated through disciplined reduction of consumption. Furthermore, savings do not create an obligation to another person. On the contrary, they strengthen independence. Borrowing creates only a requirement for future discipline. It creates dependence on the lender.

Since savings are created through discipline their use is likely to be disciplined. The one who borrows more often rejoices in his good fortune in having received money for which he did no work and made no sacrifice and spends it accordingly. It is even more so with countries because the persons who make the decision to borrow and who benefit from the borrowing are seldom the same ones as those who will bear the burden of repayment. The temptations created for politicians are nearly irresistible.

4. Atul Kohli, "Democracy and Development," in John P. Lewis and Valeriana Kallab (eds.), *Development Strategies Reconsidered* (New Brunswick: Transaction Books, 1986), p. 156, observes that the assumption that nondemocratic governments would be more successful in limiting consumption and boosting national savings was built into the early growth models of the Harrod-Domar type and cites Jagdish Bhagwati, *The Economics of Underdeveloped Countries* (New York: McGraw-Hill, 1966), p. 204, as a proponent of this view. Milton J. Esman and Norman T. Uphoff, *Local Organizations: Intermediaries in Rural Development* (Ithaca: Cornell University Press, 1984), pp. 48–49, provide a brief review of the literature arguing this point. Samuel P. Huntington, *Political Order in Changing Societies* (New Haven: Yale University Press, 1968), was one of the leading proponents of the view that popular mobilization should be restrained in the early stages of economic growth.

There have been exceptions, especially by those advocates of the growth-centered vision whose ideological commitment is not to growth per se, but specifically to capitalist growth. Thus, while the conventional vision was central to the official ideology of the Reagan administration, Reagan theorists also embraced democracy as a major part of the pluralism necessary to foster capitalism.

While no international assistance agency would admit to a preference for working with authoritarian governments, it is usually easier to negotiate large project agreements with authoritarian governments because the approval process is not subject to public scrutiny and debate. Furthermore, most international assistance agencies have taken explicit measures to avoid the public debate characteristic of decision making in democratic societies by treating the documentation on prospective projects as privileged information available only to agency and recipient government personnel. Steps are being taken within the World Bank to change this practice, but this long overdue change is coming slowly.

5. Though the politicians, whose primary concern is to maintain control over state power, may occasionally wear the lens of the growth-centered vision, they wear it only as an auxiliary lens when it serves their purpose, as it often does. However, they

seldom allow it to obscure their vision of the true goal—political power. It is more often the development technocrat who wears the conventional growth-centered development lens exclusively. These technocrats populate universities, planning bodies, finance ministries, and many other institutions of business and government.

6. It might be argued that the brief period during the 1970s when there was serious discussion of basic needs and the participation of the poor was an exception.

7. The economic gain from resource exploitation is calculated as the difference between costs of extraction and sale price. Current economic accounting practices make no allowance for depreciation of resource reserves.

8. AID has recently moved to an explicit policy position in support of pluralism and democratization based on the contrary argument that pluralism is essential to the effective function of the capitalist economy.

9. While historically it has been more or less the case that science has found substitutes for critically scarce resources, the proposition has not been seriously tested on a significant scale. We cannot know for sure that this assumption will prove to be either true or false in the future for any given critical resource. If true, it means we could sacrifice important gains by seriously attempting to preserve environmental resources it may turn out we don't need anyway. On the other hand, the consequences if we should assume the assumption is true and it proves to be false could well be intolerable for global society. For a discussion of this calculus see David Pearce, Anil Markandya, and Edward B. Barbier, *Blueprint for a Green Economy* (London: Earthscan Publications, Ltd., 1989), pp. 10–11; and Robert Costanza, "What is Ecological Economics?" *Ecological Economics,* Vol. 1, No. 1, 1989, pp. 1–7.

10. The high priests of the vision generally discourage such examination of underlying values with the claim that these models are based on objective value-free science. While they may be value-free in the sense that they avoid addressing value issues, their application has highly value-laden consequences.

11. In the 1960s there was thorough documentation of the fact that when growth occurs in countries with highly inequitable social, political and economic structures the benefits of that growth go primarily to the already rich and powerful. The poor become both comparatively and absolutely poorer. See, for example, Irma Adelman and Cynthia Taft Morris, *Economic Growth and Social Equity in Developing Countries* (Stanford: Stanford University Press, 1973). As my Indonesian colleague, Adi Sasono, puts it: "The rich get richer and the poor get children." These findings gained considerable prominence in the late 1960s and early 1970s. They gave rise to the concern with basic needs or growth with equity strategies that sought to correct the imbalances primarily by channeling funds to social services to help the poor make up for deficiencies in need satisfaction.

12. One orientation toward basic human needs stresses building the capacity of the poor to obtain gainful employment to meet their own basic needs. The other considers basic human needs to be a fundamental human right and calls on government to supply services to insure they are met directly. For further discussion see Robert L. Ayres, *Banking on the Poor* (Cambridge, MA: MIT Press, 1983), pp. 76–91.

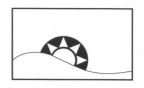

CHAPTER SIX

REVIVING THE COLONIAL ECONOMY

The drive for economic power was an important motivating force behind colonialism. Colonies provided assured access to cheap raw materials and captive markets for the industries of their colonial masters. Control over colonies was established and maintained through military intervention, religious conversion and the collusion of local elites who ensured the passive obedience of the masses in return for a share in the profits.

Prior to colonization, most traditional agricultural societies were largely self-contained production systems devoted primarily to subsistence agriculture supplemented by some artisan production. Productivity and consumption were relatively stagnant and there was little trade beyond the local community.[1] When foreign colonizers arrived, they imposed externally oriented economic enclaves on portions of this closed agrarian world to produce minerals, cash crops or other primary products for export and sale in foreign markets.[2]

The rural component of the colonial enclave economy produced cheap commodities for export and was generally the primary interest. The urban component provided the banking, port and transportation services required to support the extractive rural enclaves and to ship their output to foreign buyers. Earnings from export sales were used to purchase industrial consumer goods for the people employed in the enclaves and any investment goods required by enclave enterprises. The traditional subsistence agricultural sector remained relatively undisturbed. Its role was only to supply workers for estates and supporting facilities as required and to produce the food surplus to feed them.[3]

During the 1980s, international assistance funding and policy guidance sought to orient the productive capacity of Southern countries to the needs of foreign consumers, while opening their markets to foreign producers. Those ruling elites who collaborated stood to gain handsomely, through strengthening their control over both the economic enclaves that commanded national resources and the new flows of credit that were promised in return for their cooperation.

It was like a case of *deja vu*, of colonialism revisited. The exports were now a combination of primary and industrial products produced by cheap labor. However, the basic pattern of economic dualism geared to the needs of foreign interests remained much the same. Perhaps the major difference was that now debt took the place of military occupation or religious conversion as the instrument of control. Though presumably unintentional, credit dependence turned the nations of the South into the equivalent of the peasant debt-slave who is at the perpetual mercy of the moneylender, forever unable to get ahead of the game to establish economic independence.[4]

ECONOMIC ENCLAVES

One might anticipate that the first and most fundamental priority of post-colonial development would have been to dismantle the structures of the dual economy. As argued by Ranis:

...the primary task of early post-independence transition growth is to break down the compartmentalization of the domestic economy by achieving a much closer integration between a more dynamic domestic agriculture sector and both the agricultural and services components of the enclave economy.[5]

This advice from Ranis is supported by the research of Adelman and Morris, which demonstrates that dualistic development

is accompanied by an absolute as well as a relative decline in the average income of the very poor. Indeed, an initial spurt of dualistic growth may cause such a decline for as much as 60 percent of the population.[6]

Under dualistic or bimodal economic structures, economic growth is concentrated in agricultural and industrial enclaves that are linked primarily to foreign suppliers and markets, with few backward and forward linkages to the domestic economy.[7] These enclaves have little rationale for their location other than the opportunity to exploit the host country's cheap labor and resources at the least cost—ultimately to the detriment of the majority of its citizens. More and more of the natural resource base is pulled into the enclave portion of the dual economy as the economic power of the enclave increases.

The productive returns from the resources that have been shifted from the traditional to the enclave economy are then added to the wealth of the already prosperous individuals who control the enclave and its resources. Heavily represented among these individuals will be the family and cronies of those who control state power and their loyal supporters from within the military.

In most post-colonial countries the lines between the enclave and traditional economies have become blurred, and a substantial number of people who have found places for themselves at the margins of the enclave economy have received apparent benefits. This has tended to obscure the extent to which the basic structures of dualism have remained intact, leaving a substantial portion of the population to scratch out its subsistence in the traditional sector from a continuously declining resource base.[8]

The survival of the dualistic economic structures in the post-colonial era is easily explained by the interests of a dominant ruling elite and the predispositions of international assistance agencies committed to the growth-centered development vision. A modern sector, able to command an increasing share of national resources in the name of development, serves the interests of foreign consumers, as well as local elite and foreign business interests. The people, who struggle to obtain their subsistence from whatever resource bases have not been commandeered for "development" by the modern sector, lack an effective political voice and thus can command little attention to their plight. Political power is concentrated in the hands of those who have the most to gain from preservation of the dualistic economic structures.

THE DOMINANT STATE

Following the emergence from colonialism of the new nations of the South, a number of circumstances converged to create, legitimate and sustain an authoritarian dominance of the state over civil society, the suppression of pluralism, and the use of state power to serve the interests of exploitative elite elements.[9] There were often convincing arguments in favor of the actions that supported these outcomes.

The leaders of new nations found themselves ruling deeply fragmented societies comprised of competing ethnic, religious and linguistic groups that lacked experience with the responsibilities of democratic citizenship. Although these leaders possessed few resources, they faced demands to bring the instant prosperity that freedom movements had promised. Yet the economies of the newly liberated countries were geared more to the needs of the metropolitan societies of their former colonial masters than to the needs of domestic populations. Local cultures often harbored traditional notions of authoritarian leadership that the lifestyles and administrative practices of colonial rulers did little to dispel. The traditional elites, through which colonial powers commonly governed, also had their own interests in maintaining privileged positions.

These conditions created strong pressures for firm direction from the state. There was no shortage of aspirants eager to provide that direction. The disorder that many post-colonial nations experienced often created broad popular support for the authoritarian ruler who promised to bring order and produce improvements in living standards. For example, disorder bordering on chaos during the Sukarno years in Indonesia ushered in the Suharto regime in 1965 and legitimated the latter's use of the military and a strong centralized bureaucracy to impose order. Similarly, by the time Ferdinand Marcos declared martial law in the Philippines in 1972 a breakdown in civil order, characterized by private armies in the provinces and random shootouts between gun carrying playboys and thugs in the streets and bars of Manila, had created a climate of acceptance for anything that would restore order to society.

International development assistance played an important role in establishing the dominance of state power. When the nations of the North came forward with their own commitments to support the efforts of Southern governments to achieve economic growth, their support took many forms. Whatever its form, however, the assistance was most always channelled through central governments—strengthening their control of national resources and weakening their accountability to their own citizens. Even assistance targeted to the poor, usually taking the form of welfare handouts administered by governments, reinforced and legitimated existing power relationships.

The development technocrats who emerged as advisors to the newly formed states also played a role. The planning models in which they were trained assumed the presence of a strong central decision-making unit that could allocate available capital to its most productive uses. The rationality of the decision process could not be maintained if decision making were subjected to the ebb and flow of open democratic competition among interest groups. Thus many technocrats advised delaying political development as a luxury that resource poor, newly independent nations could not afford.

In many Southern nations such forces led to state dominance over civil society in setting national goals and arbitrating conflicting resource allocation priorities. The stronger this dominance became, the more the small group that controlled state power achieved nearly exclusive control over all avenues for significant political and economic advancement in the society.

PATRONAGE AND CORRUPTION

In countries with more pluralistic institutional settings, the distribution of economic and political power provides many avenues for personal advancement and many arenas for economic and political competition. When the state becomes supreme, there is ultimately only one real prize, the control of state power. All other competitions become inconsequential in comparison. Indeed, those who control state power in this context set the rules for and ultimately control the outcome of all other competitions. The benefits to those who acquire this power, and to their families and cronies, become enormous.[10] The costs of losing it become unthinkable.

It is quite natural for those who control power to use it first to ensure their own positions, creating vast networks of patronage to this end.[11] The greater the injustice that this creates, the more important the military becomes as a means of sustaining social order among the excluded masses. So the wise ruler gives the military special treatment in the allocation of patronage resources.

The major patronage resources of the Southern state are of several types. Among the more important are: 1) natural resource wealth, including oil, minerals, forests and large tracts of land for agricultural estates; 2) import/export licenses and quotas that give their holders near monopoly power over goods and commodities that cross the nation's borders; 3) grants of industrial monopolies, sometimes in the form of control over state enterprises; and 4) foreign assistance funds and foreign commercial credit. The dynamics of the patronage process are a substantial contributor to the stripping of environmental resources, the consolidation of lands into agricultural estates, the use of the power to regulate trade to create marketing monopolies, the creation of protected inefficient industries, and the accumulation of excessive foreign debt.

Traditional obligations to family mean that members of the ruler's extended family are often major beneficiaries of the patronage system. The line between corruption, exercising one's family responsibilities, and astute politics nearly disappears within the typical setting of many post-colonial nations.

The patronage system tends to concentrate economic and political power in the hands of elite elements who are mainly interested in collecting rents and tribute. It is rare that those so favored prove to be driven by the entrepreneurial challenge to increase productive efficiency and thereby generate true value-added in a competitive market. Their interests are well served by the preservation of dualistic economic structures.

ROLE OF INTERNATIONAL DEVELOPMENT ASSISTANCE

Prior to the 1980s there was substantial ambiguity in the thrust of international assistance policies with regard to their stance on dualistic economic structures. While the dominant resource flows fairly consistently served to strengthen economic and social dualism, there were instances in which a portion of these flows were used in ways intended to achieve greater economic integration. These have included support for land reform, mass education, small farm agricultural development, cooperatives development, and small and medium enterprises. Seldom, however, are these efforts comprehensive, sustained, or part of an overall development strategy aimed at transforming dualistic structures. As will be discussed later, this helps to explain why there are so few true development assistance success stories beyond those of Taiwan and South Korea.

It was only during the 1980s that international development assistance became clearly and unambiguously focused on supporting policies that strongly reinforced the dualistic tendencies of assisted economies. This clarity of focus was given a strong assist by the perception in 1983-84 that the entire international financial system had become endangered by Southern debt. The threat was exacerbated by the slackening of economic growth in most developing countries, often with little prospect of resuming. The indebted countries found their interest costs, and thereby their debt service payments, skyrocketing, at a time when the foreign markets for their products were shrinking or growing more slowly.[12]

Development assistance became focused on helping developing countries recover financial stability and economic growth through policy lending in support of structural adjustment. The policies advocated were strongly biased toward the promotion of export-led growth, directing international assistance to the support of domestic enclave economies and their links to the international economy.[13]

Indebted countries were offered the promise of new lending in return for acceptance of a package of structural adjustment policy reforms that advocates claimed would remove barriers to economic efficiency and promote export-led growth. Specifically, structural adjustment packages were supposed to:[14]

- **Increase exports** to cover debt repayment and imports, and to restore credit-worthiness. Specific actions included removing export tariffs and quotas, setting realistic exchange rates to make exports more competitive and imports more expensive, and concentrating investment capital on export-oriented industries.
- **Reduce deficits in public budgets** by curtailing public spending for salaries and subsidies, including subsidies for public enterprises and social services.
- **Reduce distortions in the allocation of economic resources** and unproductive rent-seeking behaviors[15] by relying on the market rather than government to set prices and allocate resources. Recommended actions included reducing or eliminating price controls (including minimum wages), investment regulations, and licensing requirements.
- **Open the domestic economy to international competition** by reducing or eliminating import duties and quotas.

THE DISTORTIONS OF STRUCTURAL ADJUSTMENT

The failures of structural adjustment policies in relation to the poor reflect the general failure of the growth-centered development vision. The architects of structural adjustment have concerned themselves only with those structures that promote growth. They have partially or totally neglected those that determine whether growth will be just, sustainable, or inclusive. It would seem to be a case of partial blindness induced by the lens of their chosen vision.

Selective Perception?

Proponents of structural adjustment invariably cite the experience of the four Asian "tiger" economies—Singapore, Hong Kong, Taiwan and South Korea, plus Japan, to validate their promotion of the export-led growth strategies that structural adjustment is supposed to support. With the exception of Japan, these are the most prominent of the newly industrialized countries (NICs) that countries throughout the South are being advised to emulate. Their economic performance is indeed impressive. The relevance of their experience and the lessons it suggests for other Southern countries bears critical examination.

As small city-states, one of which remains a colony, the experience of Singapore and Hong Kong is hardly relevant to most Southern countries, except perhaps as models for large, sophisticated export processing zones. The experience of Japan, South Korea and Taiwan, on the other hand, yields important lessons that go well beyond the policies advocated by proponents of export-led growth.

In their purest expression, the policies called for by proponents of export-led growth center on two actions: 1) open national borders and eliminate government interference in the free international flow of trade and capital; and 2) adopt an "outward looking" economy heavily oriented to production for export markets.[16] When proponents of this strategy examine the Asian success stories, they seem to see only those aspects of the NIC experience that support their favored prescriptions. As we noted in chapter 4, "believing is seeing."

The growth-centered lens seems to screen out from the wearer's vision the fact that the three relevant Asian countries built their economic growth on a foundation of radical land reform, significant investments in education, strong voluntary population programs, the development of dense networks of local organizations in their rural areas, and policies aimed at increasing rural incomes and developing domestic markets. As discussed further in chapter 8, equity-oriented structural reforms generally preceded and provided the foundation for the push to rapid growth. In this respect the strategies of Japan, South Korea and Taiwan might be more accurately characterized as *equity*-led than as *export*-led. Furthermore, even today, contrary to the advice being given to their prospective competitors, each continues to maintain protected domestic markets that give its own agriculture and industry an advantage over foreign competitors.[17]

Another country that, until very recently, has been cited as an example of the miracles produced by export-led growth strategies is Brazil. In Brazil there was indeed a strong push for export-oriented growth—without prior efforts to create an equity base. Impressive increases in levels of economic activity were achieved. However, it takes a true devotee of the growth-centered vision to classify Brazil as a development miracle. Brazil achieved its "miracle" through "economic liberalization" policies carried out by an authoritarian regime that strongly favored the interests of business, including foreign investors, over those of its own people. Labor unions were suppressed and expenditures on social services were limited.[18]

In addition to rapid growth, the outcomes of the Brazil miracle include some of the worst poverty and income disparities to be found anywhere in the world; wasteful borrowing to finance economically unsound and useless showcase development projects;[19] a debilitating debt burden that at one time threatened to destabilize the global financial system; and short-sighted, uneconomic environmental policies that threaten the global ecology. In 1988 Brazil experienced an inflation rate of 934 percent.[20] This is the kind of economic "miracle" the world—and the people of Brazil—could well do without.

Certainly there is need for significant reforms in the South, especially to reduce corruption and increase reliance on competitive market forces. There is no difficulty in finding examples of misguided government policies and gross mismanagement of economies.[21] There are good reasons for reducing public subsidies. These are seldom targeted to the poor, and yet they generate budget deficits that are funded through inflationary monetary policies of which the poor bear the major burden. There may even be an argument for cutting back on expenditures for government administered social services—on the grounds that for reasons of corruption and mismanagement they seldom reach the poor.

However, reforms directed purely to stimulating economic growth within an existing dualistic structure will almost inevitably lead to worsening income inequality.[22] Even where a portion of available development resources is specifically targeted to the poor, unless consequential attention is given to correcting inequalities in asset distribution, that assistance is likely only to draw attention away from reforms that are essential for authentic development progress.

To pursue an export orientation before an institutional foundation supportive of an equitable broadly-based growth is in place, is surely to put last things first.[23] It represents a denial more than a replication of the Asian success stories.

Importance of Domestic Market Development
If there is no development of the domestic market, new large-scale industrial projects must necessarily be export-oriented. Without building up a broadly-based local industrial infrastructure, as was established in Japan, South Korea and Taiwan, these projects are also likely to be substantially dependent on imported technology, capital equipment and inputs. Experience demonstrates that the actual value added domestically by the countries that seek the path of enclave, export-oriented industrialization is a small percentage of total export earnings. The result is further strain on foreign exchange resources to keep these industries supplied with inputs.[24] Overall, such dynamics create a strong tendency toward steady increases in income inequities and foreign exchange imbalances.[25]

Furthermore, without real command over the technologies being applied by their export industries, countries following this path remain technologically dependent. What they are selling is mainly cheap labor, tax breaks, and trade preferences—a weak foundation for an industrial economy. The growth that is achieved is of uncertain sustainability—dependent on the willingness of laborers to continue living in poverty, the depletion of natural resources, and the fickle economic and political dynamics of international markets and trade restrictions.

Still another fallacy of the NIC strategy is an implicit assumption that there are sufficient international markets to absorb the industrial products that the aspiring NICs will produce. In reality, the drive to NIC status is resulting in increasingly vicious competition among the aspirants: on the one hand, to offer the cheapest, most docile labor force and the most attractive financial incentives to lure transnational investment away from other countries; and, on the other hand, to gain access to the available export markets. This has contributed directly to labor suppression and exploitation as necessary competitive measures that must be taken by countries that wish to outbid their neighbors.[26]

Hypocrisy
In addition to selective perception, there is more than a little self-serving hypocrisy in the policy recommendations that the Northern industrial countries are pressing on Southern governments through the multilateral financial institutions they dominate.[27] John Clark has done a comparative analysis of the performance of industrial countries (ICs) and low income countries (LICs) on a number of key policy prescriptions recommended under structural adjustment. Except where otherwise noted, the following analysis is from Clark based on 1980 World Bank data.[28]

- **LICs must reduce wasteful, market distorting subsidies.** ICs spend about 18 percent of their gross domestic product (GDP) on subsidies, while LICs spend 6 percent.
- **LICs must reduce public expenditures, including those on bloated public bureaucracies.** Central government expenditures represent 29 percent of GDP in ICs and 22 percent in LICs (1987 data).[29] Furthermore, ICs spend 4 percent of GDP on public sector wages compared to 2.5 percent for LICs.
- **LICs must direct a higher proportion of their budgets to capital spending in contrast to recurrent expenditure.** LICs devote 16 percent of their budgets to capital spending in contrast to 6 percent for ICs. Unfortunately, much of LIC capital spending is swallowed up by loan principal repayments.
- **LICs must accept cuts in social services in order to encourage greater investment and saving.** LIC governments spend 8 percent of their budget on the social sectors, compared with 56 percent for the ICs. LICs have a higher proportion of GDP directed to investments and savings than do ICs.

■ **LICs must reduce their budgetary and current international payments accounts deficits.** Compared with those of the United States, LIC budget and current account deficits pale into insignificance. The United States, which has led the way in setting the agenda for reform in the South, set a new global standard during the 1980s for borrowing, selling off its own resources to foreigners, and engaging in budgetary gimmickry to sustain wasteful spending far beyond its means. The total current account deficit (before official transfers) for all LIC countries in 1987, with their nearly three billion people, was some $17.6 billion. The current account deficit of the United States, with some 240 million people, was $142 billion for the same year.[30]

One must wonder why those who are so outspoken about wasteful subsidies and expenditures on social services by Southern governments have so long been silent on the military spending of these same countries, including large expenditures of foreign exchange for military hardware purchases that add substantially to debt burdens to no productive end.[31] Similarly, if the multilateral banks truly believe in the importance of the Asian experience, why aren't they pressing as strongly for asset reform, mass education, increasing rural incomes, population programs and the development of strong rural organizations as they are for export promotion and the removal of trade barriers? What is the driving force behind the structural adjustment policy prescriptions? Why, during the 1980s, did the international assistance agencies turn their attention to the reform of policies and practices that previously they had implicitly condoned and in some instances even financed?[32] If their concern were to improve conditions for the world's poor, they surely would have emphasized a different set of structural prescriptions.

PUTTING INTERNATIONAL BANKS FIRST

The primary function of the International Monetary Fund (IMF) is to ensure the integrity and function of the international trade and financial system.[33] Thus it should come as no surprise that the IMF has rather consistently given priority to debt repayment over other objectives in its negotiations with debtor countries. Sometimes this is interpreted, probably correctly, as giving higher priority to helping the international commercial banks recover bad loans than to protecting the interests of the people of the South.[34] That is the IMF's job.

As experience was gained with structural adjustment and its biases become evident, the World Bank moved somewhat more easily to a developmental approach that gave more attention than did the IMF to growth and to compensatory programs for the poor. By the end of the decade the World Bank was offering assistance to indebted countries in negotiating favorable settlements with commercial creditors.

Though the World Bank would appear to be relatively more concerned than the IMF with the interests of the borrowing countries, the
reality remains that, on balance, structural adjustment packages call on
assisted countries to orient their economies to the needs of foreign
consumers and investors. The approach of the multilateral banks to
dealing with the needs of the poor has yet to move seriously beyond
efforts to provide compensatory services. Indeed, the fact that poverty
is hardly mentioned in the 1988 and 1989 editions of the *World Development Report,* the major publication through which the Bank commu-
nicates its current views on economic and development policy to the
world, suggests that the World Bank still does not see the issue of
poverty as particularly central to economic and monetary policy.[35]

Borrowing countries are normally assured that by generating the
foreign exchange to repay international debts, they can restore their
credit ratings and obtain new loans to finance economic growth. Indeed the multilaterals have commonly held out the promise of new
loans as an incentive for accepting politically unpopular adjustment
prescriptions. It is a curious package of advice and incentives that the
multilaterals have offered. New borrowing means new debt. Debts
must eventually be repaid, as the banks stressed throughout much of
the 1980s.

Is new borrowing really a solution to the problem? Or does it
merely postpone the day of reckoning? What of international borrowing in general? Is it the key to development progress as the lending
institutions would seem to have us believe?

If foreign borrowing is used for productive investments that generate new foreign exchange earnings in excess of debt servicing payments, then it is a sound policy. Too often, however, foreign borrowing
in the name of development is used for purposes that are not productive and that represent decidedly unsound use of debt such as for
"showcase" projects, or simply as an artificial economic stimulus and a
means of financing current accounts deficits.[36] Unfortunately, the incentives for both the borrowers and the lenders in the international
system to limit the use of credit to financially sound projects are few.
The individuals who make the decisions as borrowers and lenders all
have a great deal to gain from maintaining a large flow of new loan
capital, while being nearly certain that the burden of repayment (for
the borrower) and collection of "bad" loans (for the lender) will fall on
others, not on themselves.

Where borrowing is used primarily to stimulate the economy and
to cover chronic current account deficits, the economy and the government become dependent on continuous increases in the net annual
inflow of foreign resources to achieve growth targets. Every year debt
service payments increase, and the amount borrowed must also increase to maintain a net inflow of resources. The country becomes
"addicted" to loans. As with the heroin addict, each dose must be a bit
larger than the last to get the same high. When the ceiling on borrow-

ing is reached, net flows turn negative, creating a drain on the economy and painful withdrawal symptoms.

Multilateral banks have been severely criticized for the impact of their structural adjustment policies on reducing services for the poor.[37] More surprising is the lack of condemnation for their role in encouraging and facilitating the accumulation of the debt in the first place and their continuing role in maintaining borrowing countries in a condition of debt dependence.[38] Acceptance of the conventional growth-centered vision and its emphasis on capital transfers is so pervasive that it has taken a remarkably long time for people to seriously question the irony of offering more debt as the answer to too much debt. Fortunately, such questions are finally being raised.

In assessing the adequacy of our existing assistance agencies, it must be borne in mind that the major multilateral assistance agencies are banks. They have two products to offer: advice and loans. For low income countries they also have highly concessional loans, which are subjected to even less vigorous economic criteria than are more conventional loans, because they contain a large element of "free" money.[39] They are still loans, however, which means that they add to the total debt burden of a country.[40]

The two products of the multilateral banks—advice and loans—come together in their increasingly popular policy based lending. World Bank staff members like to think that the primary contribution of the Bank to development is intellectual. Much of the Bank's advice, however, is tied to lending and there are few within it who believe that there would be much interest in the advice if it were not directly tied to large loan packages.[41]

Multilateral banks have a strong interest in promoting borrowing as the key to development progress. They cannot contest that premise without challenging their own existence. Yet that premise must be contested, along with the premise that export-led growth is the road to national prosperity for Southern countries.

Conventional development assistance must bear a substantial share of the blame for the increases in poverty, environmental destruction, and communal violence experienced by Southern countries. This assistance has failed to achieve the reforms that would reduce or eliminate the economic and political dualism that makes a substantial contribution to creating and sustaining these conditions. To the contrary, it has all too often served to legitimate and sustain, or even strengthen, these dualistic tendencies.

The current commitment of most assistance agencies to imposing structural adjustment policies supportive of export-led growth exacerbates the problem of underdevelopment. Not only is the strategy bad social policy, it is also bad economic policy. The fervor with which these policies are being promoted forces us to ask to what extent the underlying motives of the governments of the Northern industrial nations have changed consequentially since the days of colonialism. Past experience also raises questions regarding the extent to which we can expect either the multilateral or the bilateral assistance agencies to provide effective leadership toward solutions. They are a central part of the problem and have a substantial stake in the status quo. For this reason, development during the 1990s must be driven by a new vision and rely on new sources of leadership.

NOTES

1. Based on Gustav Ranis, "The Dual Economy Framework: Its Relevance to Asian Development," *Asian Development Review,* Vol. 2, No. 1, 1984, p. 40.

2. *Ibid.*

3. *Ibid.*

4. It has become a bonanza for the North. Not only are indebted Southern nations being required to orient their economies to produce for the needs of the North, but at the same time the bill for past borrowing has come due with a vengeance. In 1982 the net international transfer of financial resources from North to South was $29 billion in favor of the South. Then the flows shifted as the bills came due and new loans dried up. By 1987 the net flow was $34 billion from Southern nations to the North. Since 1987, both the IMF and the World Bank have become net financial drains on the South, with loan servicing collections exceeding total disbursements. Richard E. Feinberg and Catherine Gwin, "Reforming the Fund: Overview," in Catherine Gwin and Richard E. Feinberg (eds.), *The International Monetary Fund in a Multipolar World: Pulling Together,* Overseas Development Council Policy Perspectives, Series No. 13 (New Brunswick: Transaction Books, 1989), p. 15. Essentially what this means is that Southern countries are not only pressed to sell their goods to the North at whatever prices are offered, they have to return the money they received from them as loan repayments.

5. Ranis, "Dual Economy," p. 40.

6. Irma Adelman and Cynthia Taft Morris, *Economic Growth and Social Equity in Developing Countries* (Stanford: Stanford University Press, 1973), p. 189. In 1986 Adelman reported more recent data showing that "between 1960 and 1980, income inequality in the entire group of non-communist developing countries increased substantially." Irma Adelman, "A Poverty-Focused Approach to Development Policy, in John P. Lewis and Valeriana Kallab (eds.), *Development Strategies Reconsidered* (Washington, DC: The Overseas Development Council, 1986), p. 52. This was even before the economic debacle of the 1980s that exacerbated these tendencies.

7. See Bruce F. Johnston and Peter Kilby, *Agriculture and Structural Transformation: Economic Strategies in Late-Developing Countries* (New York: Oxford University Press, 1975).

8. For documentation of this process in the Philippines see George Carner, "Survival, Interdependence, and Competition among the Philippine Rural Poor," in David C. Korten and Rudi Klauss (eds.), *People-Centered Development: Contributions Toward Theory and Planning Frameworks* (West Hartford: Kumarian Press), 1984, pp. 133–43.

For documentation from Africa see Tessa Marcus, *Commercial Agriculture in South Africa: Modernizing Super-Exploitation* (London: Zed Books, Ltd., 1989); and Maureen Mackintosh, *Gender, Class and Rural Transition: Agribusiness and the Food Crisis in Senegal* (London: Zed Books, Ltd., 1989).

9. For an excellent analysis of this history and the forces behind the emergence of authoritarianism in Southern countries see Ambassador Soedjatmoko, *The Primacy of Freedom in Development,* edited by Anne Elizabeth Murase (Lanham: University Press of America, 1985). The following discussion draws freely on Soedjatmoko's analysis.

10. These realities seldom reach public attention. Even the international press is cautious for the simple reason that those who write the truth about odiously corrupt national leaders find their publications and their reporters banned. It is a high price. Sometimes they provide passing glimpses that give some hint of the iceberg below the surface, as do the periodic country analyses that appear in *The Economist.* In most reporting, however, the whole truth is seldom spoken, in deference to the sensitivity of the sovereign rulers of friendly nations. Occasionally, events unfold to lift the veil on the reality. Such was the case in February 1986 when within a period of less than three weeks President Jean Claude Duvalier fled Haiti and President Ferdinand Marcos fled the Philippines, both in disgrace, both aboard U.S. military planes. Stories of their greed, corruption, and brutality poured forth in the international press. Before that we had obtained a glimpse into the reality of President Anastasio Samosa of Nicaragua whose troops bombed his cities in a last desperate move to retain his absolute hold on the politics and economy of Nicaragua, even after every responsible element of the society not on his immediate payroll had aligned against him. Then came General Manuel Antonio Noriega of Panama, a common thug who ruled the country and its military much as a mafia chief, and became so deeply involved in the drug trade that even the CIA had to abandon him. If only we could dismiss these as the exceptions. They are not. The true exceptions are the small handful of national leaders whose personal integrity and commitment to democratic process remain above question.

11. It is important to note that in many traditional societies it was widely accepted that an official office was like a grant of property from a grateful monarch to be used for one's personal enrichment so long as the interests of the monarch were served. In Amharic, the national language of Ethiopia, the word for "to rule," *nagasa* translates literally "to collect tribute." David C. Korten, *Planned Change in a Traditional Society: Psychological Problems of Modernization in Ethiopia* (New York: Praeger, 1972), p. 72. The Ethiopians also have a proverb that says: "He who does not enrich himself while in office is a fool." Such perspectives are by no means unique to Ethiopia. They were also part of the feudal tradition in Europe.

No leader rules alone. Even where the ruler has a strong commitment to honesty and democratic processes, he or she is faced with the reality of the culture of the elites upon whose assent continued rule depends. This is the dilemma of Corazon Aquino in the Philippines. There are few, other than the crooks and opportunists who would like to displace her before the end of her elected term, who would question her own ethics, including her total integrity and commitment to the democratic process. However, she cannot totally deny her own family, some members of which do not share her values. She has had to fill thousands of key positions with appointees, in some instances appeasing powerful political interests on whose support she depends. Among these interests is that of the military. Among its members are elements that are little more than goons for hire by local mafia chiefs beyond the control of the central government. Niall O'Brien, *Revolution from the Heart* (New York: Oxford University Press, 1987) provides account after chilling personal account of what this means for the rural poor in the Philippines. Yet to purge these elements is to risk still another military coup attempt. These are realities of governance in Southern countries.

12. The combination of the global economic recession and record interest rates that precipitated the crisis had resulted in large part from the fiscal irresponsibility and economic mismanagement of Northern countries, in particular the United States.

13. For a comprehensive review of the specific policy guidance provided to the Philippines by the IMF and the World Bank and its consequences in the early 1980s, see Robin Broad, *Unequal Alliance, 1979–1986: The World Bank, the International Monetary Fund, and the Philippines* (Manila: Ateneo de Manila University Press, 1988).

14. This summary is based on *World Development Report 1987* (Washington, DC: The World Bank, 1987), primarily chapter 2 "From Recovery and Adjustment to Long-Term Growth," pp. 14–35. It also benefits from Colin I. Bradford, Jr., "East Asian 'Models': Myths and Lessons," in Lewis and Kallab (eds.), *Development Strategies Reconsidered,* pp. 115–28.

15. Rent seeking refers to efforts to capture any surplus value that has not been created through productive investment or effort. According to the World Bank, "Rent seeking embraces lobbying activities designed to capture the rents—that is, scarcity premiums—that are attached to licenses and quotas." See Box 4.7 "Rent Seeking and Directly Unproductive Profit Seeking," *World Development Report 1987* (Washington, DC: The World Bank, 1987), p. 76. Use of the term rent seeking behavior is commonly a euphemism for corruption. Licenses and quotas almost invariably carry an economic benefit to those fortunate enough to obtain them that is far in excess of the fees that are legally charged for them. Therefore those with the power to grant these benefits commonly charge an additional "rent," i.e., demand a bribe.

16. For an uncompromising and incorrectly titled defense of the classical argument by one of its leading proponents see Jagdish N. Bhagwati, "Rethinking Trade Strategy," in Lewis and Kallab (eds.), *Development Strategies Reconsidered,* pp. 91–104. For what might be considered almost a caricature of the purist position on export-led growth strategies see the special issue of *The Economist,* September 23, 1989 on the theme "A Survey of the Third World: Poor Man's Burden." Many of the ills of prevailing economic policies are accurately identified. The problem is in the prescription offered and the fact that it is grounded only in a narrow band of economic theory to the disregard of institutional reality. For a development economist's critique of the pure neoclassical interpretation of the Asian tiger's experience see Colin I. Bradford, Jr., "East Asian 'Models': Myths and Lessons."

17. Many trade barriers remain in Japan, South Korea, and Taiwan even though these countries are now major economic powers in their own right. According to *Business Week,* August 7, 1989, p. 2, "A growing cadre at the highest levels of the U.S. government, business and academe is discarding the hope that the Japanese will ever subscribe to free-market rules." See the summary description of the cover story for that issue. South Korea is reputedly the most restrictive of the three. In October 1989, a visit by the U.S. Special Trade Representative to Seoul to press for a wider opening of the country's closed agricultural and industrial markets sparked strong criticism from Koreans and an attack by radical students on the residence of the U.S. ambassador. Peter Maass, "Seoul Radicals Invade Home of U.S. Envoy to Protest Trade Pressure," *International Herald Tribune,* October 14–15, 1989, p. 2.

18. See Alfred Stepan (ed.), *Authoritarian Brazil* (New Haven: Yale University Press,

1973); and Sylvia Ann Hewlett, *The Cruel Dilemmas of Development: Twentieth-Century Brazil* (New York: Basic Books, 1980) as cited by Atul Kohli, "Democracy and Development," in Lewis and Kallab (eds.), *Development Strategies Reconsidered,* pp. 158–518.

19. A list of economically, socially, and environmentally unsound projects that account for the majority of Brazil's foreign debt is documented by Bertrand Schneider, *The Barefoot Revolution: A Report to the Club of Rome* (London: Intermediate Technology Publications, 1988), p. 29.

20. Jeffrey Sachs, "Making the Brady Plan Work," *Foreign Affairs,* Summer 1989, p. 91.

21. Numerous examples are cited in "A Survey of the Third World," *The Economist,* September 23, 1989, which correctly notes that "Bad government has long been the biggest obstacle to economic development in the third world." (p. 3) Simply eliminating government from the picture to give private enterprise a free hand is hardly a solution, however, given that much of the South's agriculture and industry is owned by the same folks who have been responsible for the bad government.

22. This was one of the arguments raised by Gustav Ranis against donor plans for substantially augmenting foreign assistance to the Philippines under the Philippine Assistance Program/Multilateral Assistance Initiative. "The Philippines, the Brady Plan and the PAP: Prognosis and Alternatives," Yale University, May 1989, unpublished.

23. Though it is certainly not in the sense of Robert Chambers' admonition to put the last (the poor) first. *Rural Development: Putting the Last First* (London: Longman, 1983).

24. Robin Broad and John Cavanagh, "No More NICs," *Foreign Policy,* Number 72, Fall 1988, pp. 87–89.

25. For further discussion of these dynamics see Jeffrey B. Nugent and Pan A. Yotopoulos, "Orthodox Development Economics versus the Dynamics of Concentration and Marginalization," in Korten and Klauss, *People-Centered Development,* pp. 107–20.

26. Broad and Cavanagh, "No More NICs," p. 85.

27. The World Bank does believe that structural adjustment is needed by some Northern countries as well. Its *World Development Report 1986* criticized the agricultural policies of Northern countries and their protective trade policies. However, the Bank has no leverage over the Northern countries.

28. John Clark, "World Bank and Poverty Alleviation—An NGO View." Paper prepared for the 1988 Meeting of the World Bank-NGO Committee, Oxfam, Oxford, U.K., p. 3. Data are from *World Development Report 1988* (Washington, DC: World Bank, 1988), pp. 109–10. (Personal communication with the author.) Copies are available from the Development Policies Unit, Oxfam, 174 Banbury Road, Oxford OX27DZ, England. Clark is a policy adviser to Oxfam United Kingdom and an NGO member of the World Bank-NGO Committee.

29. World Bank, *World Development Report 1989* (Washington, DC: World Bank, 1989), pp. 184–85.

30. Based on World Bank, *World Development Report 1989*, pp. 164-65 and 198-99.

This represented a deficit of $5.87 per person for the LICs and $591.67 per person for the United States. For the LICs the deficit was 2 percent of per capita income. For the United States it was 3.2 percent. These figures for foreign debt do not include the sale of U.S. businesses, farms and real estate to foreigners that generated further funds to support profligate and unsustainable spending.

31. Barber B. Conable, President of the World Bank, did raise the question of military expenditures in a recent speech and it has been suggested that the World Bank may become more outspoken on this issue. UNICEF officials are also beginning to speak out on this issue. It is long overdue.

32. Though I focus much of my criticism in this chapter on the multilateral banks as the leading exponents of structural adjustment and export-led growth strategies, these banks are the agents of individual governments that ultimately bear the responsibility. The policies of these governments are also played out through their bilateral assistance agencies. In the Philippines the primary thrust of USAID's commitment is to support the development of export processing zones and "growth-centers" (essentially export processing zones without the fence), an extreme expression of the distortions that undermine meaningful development progress in the Philippines and elsewhere in the South.

33. This is, of course, an essential and legitimate function. However, the line is not always clear between protecting the ability of the system to continue functioning and protecting the profits of the international banks, even in the face of irresponsible lending policies.

34. Sachs, "Making the Brady Plan Work," p. 87–104, maintains that until 1988 the focus of U.S. policy, which strongly influences IMF and World Bank policy, was to help the banks recover their loans. The Baker Plan, introduced in 1985, sought to restructure existing debts and to increase access to new borrowing so that borrowing countries would be able to repay old debt while at the same time increasing their net inflow of new funds to restore economic growth. The concept might be characterized as a giant international financial pyramiding scheme similar to a well-known form of financial fraud practiced by some financial con men. In fact, from 1982–1988, the banks received most of the interest due them, though new lending declined and net financial flows were negative for many countries. In 1989, the deteriorating situation in debtor countries finally pressed the U.S. to recognize that foreign policy concerns had to receive higher priority in addressing the debt issue. The Brady Plan was introduced in 1989, emphasizing debt reduction schemes that essentially encouraged the lending banks to acknowledge the loses many of them had already written off against their income taxes as bad debts. (Personal communication with Robin Broad.)

35. Clark, "World Bank and Poverty Alleviation," observed that though there are many World Bank reports and speeches on poverty, the 1988 edition of its *World Development Report*, barely makes reference to poverty in 185 pages of text dealing with current priorities in economic and development management [except for a half page box presenting evidence that poverty is on the increase] until the last page, which reminds the reader that, "Reducing poverty remains the ultimate challenge of development policy." The final three brief paragraphs suggest how this may be done, summarizing its conclusions with the statement, "Fiscal prudence sets the groundwork for growth—the precondition for defeating poverty in the long run."
    I decided to look through the Bank's *World Development Report 1989* to see to what extent Clark's observations had influenced its preparation. In the 132-pages of text that constitute the body of the report I found the word "poverty" used four times—

all in one brief section calling attention to how the poor are destroying the environment (pages 14–15). I could not find a single use of the word elsewhere in the 132 page body of the report, though I also found four uses of the word "poor." One was in a reference to how Ghana had "kept structural adjustment on track while helping the poor." The second was a reference to "a bank's poor health." There is a reference to "poor management" and a reference to "poor risk selection." It might make a good game to amuse the kids. "Who can find the words 'poverty' or 'poor' in the World Bank's *World Development Report 1989*?" I surely missed one or two. In fairness, there is a chapter in the *Report* devoted to "Issues in informal finance" that deals with the informal economy at some length, though with astonishing success in avoiding any reference to poverty or poor people in discussing the segment of the economy that is their primary refuge.

It is wholly inexcusable that the major annual policy study of the organization considered to be the intellectual leader in setting the global development agenda could so neglect the single most central issue legitimating public funding of international development assistance. However, progress is being made. Poverty is to be the central theme of the *World Development Report 1990*. This will be a welcome edition of this important document. However, until poverty becomes a central concern of Bank thinking about the world economy, public finance and financial systems—the themes of the 1988 and 1989 reports—rather than a special issue for separate attention divorced from concerns about economic and financial policy, it cannot be assumed that poverty is truly central to the Bank's concerns and the foundation of its policy guidance.

36. Sixto K. Roxas provides an analysis of this mode of thinking in relation to development planning in the Philippines in "Industrialization through Agricultural Development," a speech before the Philippine Agricultural Economics and Development Association, August 25, 1989. Susan George, "The Debt Crisis: Obstacle to Development or Path to Democracy?" Briefing Paper No. 14 of the Australian Development Studies Network, October 1989, argues that much of the debt of Southern countries can be accounted for by borrowing to pay for petroleum and other forms of current consumption, purchase weapons, capital flight back to Northern banks, 'Pharaonic' projects, and interest payments on variable interest loans.

37. One of the World Bank's own simulation studies concludes, "If contractionary adjustment packages can survive three years of sharply deteriorating social indicators, income distribution will probably improve—but people below the poverty line will probably suffer irreparable damage in health, nutrition, and education." Summary conclusion on the cover of François Bourguignon, William H. Branson, and Jaime de Emlo, "Adjustment and Income Distribution: A Counterfactual Analysis," WPS 215, Working Paper, Country Economics Department, The World Bank, Washington, DC, May 1989. For a comprehensive review of the consequences of structural adjustment for the poor see Giovanni Andrea Cornia, Richard Jolly, and Frances Stewart, *Adjustment with a Human Face: Protecting the Vulnerable and Promoting Growth* (Oxford: Clarendon Press, 1987).

38. There are a few exceptions. A recent column by Paul Craig Roberts in *Business Week* charged the World Bank with creating a new debt crisis on top of the existing one by "churning out ever larger loans to its least credit-worthy borrowers." Those who stand to benefit according to Roberts are "the development bureaucracy, the U.S. banks with loans to Latin American and other underdeveloped countries, the U.S. companies that sell to the developing countries, and the congressmen in whose districts these banks and companies are located." As reported in *World Development Forum*, Vol. 7, No. 2, January 31, 1989.

39. See Nick Eberstadt, "The Perversion of Foreign Aid," *Commentary,* Vol. 79, No. 6, June 1985, p. 23.

40. There are exceptions, such as when a new loan is used to buy back previous loans at a discount or to restructure high interest debt into low interest debt. There are inherent limits to this type of lending.

41. The Asian Development Bank has a small grant fund for funding project preparation costs. The World Bank has a few hundred thousand dollars in grant funds for NGO projects. However, for all practical purposes the multilateral banks are limited to solving problems with loans.

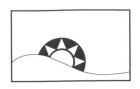

CHAPTER SEVEN

THE PEOPLE-CENTERED VISION: AN ECONOMICS FOR SPACESHIP EARTH

Growth-centered development puts economic growth ahead of people and the ecology on which their well-being depends. We need an alternative vision in which the well-being of people and the living systems of the planet that is their home come first. This vision must serve as our guide to the transformation of our values and institutions—the central development priority of the 1990s.

Momentum is growing behind a people's dialogue toward the collective discovery and articulation of a people-centered development vision. This vision is evolving inductively through a global social learning process, gradually gaining in clarity and definition. Although there are countless contributors to this process from both North and South, there seems to be a broad consensus on basic values and principles. Many of these are outlined in "The Manila Declaration on People's Participation and Sustainable Development" reproduced in Appendix A of this volume.[1]

WHAT IS PEOPLE-CENTERED DEVELOPMENT?

If development is more than simple undifferentiated growth in economic output, then what else is it? The following definition is a synthesis of numerous dialogues involving countless colleagues from around the world.

Development is a process by which the members of a society increase their personal and institutional[2] capacities to mobilize and manage resources to produce sustainable and justly distributed improvements in their quality of life consistent with their own aspirations.

For most people this definition seems obvious, hardly worth belaboring—until they realize that it bears almost nothing in common with prevailing definitions that equate development either with industrialization, or more broadly with increases in economic output. The above definition emphasizes the *process* of development and its essential focus on personal and institutional capacity. It embodies the principles of justice, sustainability and inclusiveness. It acknowledges that only the people themselves can define what they consider to be improvements in the quality of their lives.

The people-centered development vision is grounded in a world view that perceives earth to be a life-sustaining spaceship with a finite store of physical resources.[3] Its only external and virtually inexhaustible resource is sunlight. Thus the quality of life of its inhabitants depends on maintaining a proper balance between its solar energized regenerative systems, its resource stocks and the demands that its inhabitants place on these systems and resources.

The assumptions and value orientation of the people-centered development vision set its policy preferences clearly apart from those of the prevailing growth-centered development vision. Each will be examined in turn.

ASSUMPTIONS OF FACT

The people-centered development vision embodies a number of empirically verifiable assumptions about our physical, political and economic reality.

- The earth's physical resources are finite.
- The productive and recycling capacity of ecological systems can be enhanced through human intervention, but this enhancement cannot exceed certain natural limits.
- Governments by nature give priority to the interests of those who control power.
- Political and economic power are closely linked in that possession of either increases the holder's ability to exercise the other.[4]
- Markets are important allocation mechanisms, but all markets are imperfect and by their nature give priority to the *wants* of the rich over the *needs* of the poor.
- Just, sustainable and inclusive communities are the essential foundation of a just, sustainable and inclusive global system.
- Diversified local economies that give priority in the allocation of available resources to meeting the basic needs of community members increase the security of individual communities and the resilience and stability of the larger national and global economies.
- When the people control the local environmental resources on which their own and their children's lives depend, they are more likely than absentee owners to exercise responsible stewardship.

Values Orientation
The people-centered vision is also grounded in several explicit values.
- The first priority in the use of earth's resources should be to allow all people an opportunity to produce a basic livelihood for themselves and their families.

- Current generations have no right to engage in levels of nonessential consumption that deprive future generations of the possibility of sustaining decent human living standards.
- Every individual has the right to be a productive contributing member of family, community and society.
- Control of productive assets should be broadly distributed within society.
- Sovereignty resides in the people. The authority of the state is granted by the people and therefore may be withdrawn by them.
- Local economies should be diversified and reasonably self-reliant in producing for basic needs.
- People have a right to a voice in making the decisions that influence their lives and decision making should be as close to the level of individual, family and community as possible.
- Local decisions should reflect a global perspective and an acceptance of the rights and responsibilities of global citizenship.

POLICY PREFERENCES

Both the factual assumptions and value preferences of the people-centered development vision advocates play a major role in shaping their policy preferences. These preferences commonly differ markedly from those of the growth-centered development advocates. For example, advocates of the people-centered vision will commonly:
- Seek economic diversification at all levels of the economy, beginning with the rural household, to reduce dependence and vulnerability to the market shocks that result from excessive specialization.
- Give priority in allocating local resources to the production of goods and services to meet the basic needs of the local population. The goal is to create a national and ultimately an international economy comprised of interlinking self-reliant local economic units that have a degree of insulation from the shocks of national and international systems and a stake in conserving their local environmental resources.
- Allocate a portion of surplus local productive capacity (beyond what is required to meet local basic needs) to produce goods and services for export to national or international markets. Exports should feature products with a high value-added relative to their content of physical resources. The goal here is to achieve optimal gains for the local community from "external" trade while conserving physical resources to the future benefit of the community.
- Strengthen broadly-based local ownership and control of resources by pursuing policies that: 1) allow communities substantial jurisdiction over their own primary resources; and 2) give individual producers control or ownership of their means of production. This would involve measures such as land reform, aquarian reform[5] and

policies favorable to locally-owned small farms and enterprises, member-controlled cooperatives, and employee-owned corporations.[6]

■ Encourage the development of a dense mosaic of independent, politically conscious voluntary and people's organizations that strengthen the direct participation of citizens in both local and national decision-making processes, and provide essential training grounds in democratic citizenship.

■ Develop strong locally accountable, financed and democratically elected autonomous local governments that give residents a strong voice in local affairs.

■ Establish transparency in public decision making and strengthen communication links between people and government.

■ Provide economic incentives that favor recovery and recycling over extraction and exploitation.

■ Focus on the returns to household and community in choosing among investment options.

■ Favor industrial investments that: 1) strengthen diversified small and intermediate scale production; 2) use environmentally sound, resource-conserving, labor-using technologies; 3) add value to local resources and products; 4) serve and enhance competitive efficiency within domestic markets; and 5) strengthen backward and forward linkages within the economy.

■ Favor intensive, smallholder agriculture based on the use of high productivity bio-intensive technologies.[7]

■ Give preference to advanced information-intensive technologies over those that are materials-intensive and resource-depleting.[8]

■ Give priority to the mobilization of local resources, savings and social energy. Avoid dependency creating debt financing, particularly foreign debt, except for clearly productive purposes that will generate the resources for repayment.

■ Give high priority to investments in education that build the capacity of people to take charge of their own lives, communities and resources and to participate in local, national and global decision processes.

■ Encourage an acceptance of shared responsibility for the well-being of all community members and a reverence for the connection between people and nature.

The people-centered vision favors human well-being and environment sustainability over additions to economic output, domestic over foreign markets, local financing and ownership over foreign borrowing and investment, and economic self-reliance over dependence on the international trading system. It welcomes participation in the global community, but from a position of independent strength—not external dependence.

TRANSFORMATION AS THE AGENDA

Guided in their development by the growth-centered vision, the institutions of our society are geared to producing growth for the benefit of the few without regard to social or environmental consequences. This is the heart of the failure of these institutions to ensure justice, sustainability and inclusiveness. Continued focus on growth as the solution to the crisis of our small planet in the absence of a transformation of our vision and our institutions will only serve to deepen the crises of poverty, environmental failure and social disintegration.

Growth is important, but it must be a new kind appropriate to our condition. For this reason we must address ourselves to transformation as the development priority of the 1990s.

NOTES

1. A collection of early contributions from many writers toward the articulation of such a vision is presented in David C. Korten and Rudi Klauss (eds.), *People-Centered Development: Contributions Toward Theory and Planning Frameworks* (West Hartford: Kumarian Press, 1984). Nongovernmental organizations (NGOs) have had an important part in the articulation of this vision, as reflected in the Manila Declaration and a conference report on *NGO Strategic Management in Asia: Focus on Bangladesh, Indonesia, and the Philippines* (Manila: Asian NGO Coalition, 1988). Further discussion of the NGO role in this process is presented in the introduction to Part III of this volume.

Important new contributions to a growing body of economic thought directed to defining an underlying theory and policy frameworks for people-centered development include James Robertson, *Future Wealth: A New Economics for the 21st Century* (London: Cassell Publishers Limited, 1990); and Herman E. Daly and John B. Cobb, Jr., *For the Common Good: Redirecting the Economy Toward Community, the Environment, and a Sustainable Future* (Boston: Beacon Press, 1989). More classic contributions include Mark A. Lutz and Kenneth Lux, *The Challenge of Humanistic Economics* (Menlo Park: The Benjamin/Cummin Publishing Company, 1979); and Hazel Henderson, *Creating Alternative Futures: The End of Economics* (New York: Perigee Books, 1978). The reader is urged to consult these sources for a deeper and more thorough treatment of the arguments and their empirical foundations than can be provided here.

There are also recent stirrings within some of the official aid agencies toward the search for a new vision. UNICEF has had a critical role in directing the attention of the development community to human needs, though its thinking is generally oriented to welfare programs based on improving human services rather than to challenging the basic growth model. There are early indications that this may be changing. Meetings on the international development assistance agenda for the 1990s being planned by the Development Assistance Committee of the OECD dealing with concerns such as participation, environment, and gender issues will provide opportunities for innovative thinking. There is even evidence that important new currents of alternative development thought may be emerging within the World Bank. See *Sub-Saharan Africa: From Crisis to Sustainable Growth, A Long-Term Perspective Study* (Washington, DC: The World Bank, 1989).

2. The term *institutions* in this definition refers to the enduring systems of structures, rules, customs and values that shape the behaviors and relationships of people within a society.

3. See the discussion of Kenneth Boulding's concept of "spaceship economics" in chapter 4 of this volume: "Believing is Seeing."

4. Adi Sasono refers to it as the Gold Rule: "He who has the gold rules." Under authoritarian rule the reverse is also true: "He who rules gets the gold." It is a ruthless and painful symmetry.

5. Aquarian reform refers to measures intended to give local small fishermen control over their aquatic resources to protect them against encroachment by trawler operators and others who mine the local aquatic resources for the short-term gain of a few powerful investors.

6. There has been a long experience of government-controlled cooperatives. There have been similar abuses of employee stock ownership plans in corporations that are structured in such a way as to insulate management from stockholder control and potential take-overs without giving employee owners any real voice in decision making. These are not the type of cooperative or employee-owned firm we have in mind here.

7. For a useful review see Michael Dover and Lee M. Talbot, *To Feed the Earth: Agro-Ecology for Sustainable Development* (Washington, DC: World Resources Institute, 1987).

8. Information is the one resource that is nonpolluting and increases its value with use. Many of the more important advances in technology, particularly in bio-technology and materials science, allow us to use knowledge or information to reduce the amount of physical material and energy required to perform the same amount of work. The growth-centered vision has focused attention on efforts to substitute capital for labor in an effort to increase returns to capital. The challenge of the current age is to substitute information for materials and energy in an effort to increase returns from each unit of physical materials or energy use. For a fascinating examination of the impact on the restructuring of the American economy resulting from the substitution of information for materials see James Cook, "The Molting of America," *Forbes,* November 22, 1982, pp. 161–67.

CHAPTER EIGHT

EQUITY-LED SUSTAINABLE GROWTH: FROM VISION TO STRATEGY

While there is growing consensus on the broad outlines of a people-centered development vision, much remains to be done toward translating it into an operational strategy for national development. Though many of the NGOs that have provided leadership in the vision's definition are deeply engaged in village level development action, few among them have been involved at the policy levels where national development strategies are defined.[1]

It is important that NGO leaders educate themselves about the policy choices involved and give greater attention to the translation of broad value commitments into national strategies appropriate to the specifics of their national context. Important progress may be expected in this regard over the next few years as more NGOs and their coalition bodies realize the need to engage as advocates of well-defined national strategies that embody the principles and values of the people-centered development vision.[2]

The general outlines of such a strategy are proposed in this chapter. It has been labelled an *equity-led sustainable growth* strategy.[3] This label describes the strategy's essential nature and helps to position it within the context of current development debates.

The equity-led sustainable growth strategy inverts the popular concept of a growth with equity or growth with redistribution strategy. The latter generally calls for pushing growth first, sidestepping needed structural reforms and then correcting benefit distribution problems by strengthening social services to make up deficiencies in basic needs through the redistribution of surpluses. The former calls for starting with equity by breaking down the structures of dualism, and thus making equity the foundation of a broadly-based integrated or uni-modal growth.

The starting point for defining a basic framework for the *growth* dimension of an equity-led sustainable growth strategy is, ironically, the experience of Taiwan, South Korea and Japan—the same success stories put forward by advocates of export-led growth to bolster their case. Of course the way those of us who wear the lens of a people-centered development vision interpret the lessons of this experience is quite different from the interpretation of those who wear the growth-centered lens.[4]

The experiences of these three countries provide only a partial model for a people-centered development strategy. They do not serve as models of environmentally sustainable development. Nor are they models of democratic political process. Quite the contrary. Consequently they are useful to us here only in providing a useful framework for making growth more broadly-based, integrated, equitable and economically sound. Beyond this there is need for substantial modification to arrive at a strategic framework that also embodies the sustainability and democratization dimensions of people-centered development. It must be noted that there are no immediately evident national-scale demonstrations of an equity-led sustainable growth strategy. These remain to be invented.

THE ASIAN TIGERS REVISITED

The Asian "tiger" economies—Singapore, Hong Kong, Taiwan, South Korea and Japan—are all distinguished by superior export performance and high rates of economic growth.[5] However, exports represent only the tip of the economic iceberg for these countries. The *institutions* of these economies that support this tip, and how they were developed, are seldom mentioned by the proponents of export-led growth. Yet this institutional foundation is basic to the strength of these economies. It is this foundation that has allowed people to share broadly in economic success and provided these countries with the resilience to adapt to changing economic conditions.[6] One might well argue that the export performance of these countries is more a consequence of their economic success, than its cause. Before pursuing this theme further, however, it is necessary to examine the basic relevance of the East Asian economic success stories for other Southern countries.

The Three Most Relevant East Asian Successes
Hong Kong and Singapore are unique among the countries of the world. Both are sea-port city-states with no consequential rural sectors. They were established solely to serve as colonial trading centers and military posts. Furthermore, both are small, not only as countries, but even by the standard of world cities. Hong Kong, with a population of 6 million people is twenty-eighth among world cities. Singapore, at less than 3 million is tiny. India alone has seven cities with larger populations. The world has seventy.[7] As noted in chapter 6, Hong Kong and Singapore make interesting models for the development of strategically located seaport cities as sophisticated export processing zones, but the relevance of their experience as development models for other Southern countries is decidedly limited.

Taiwan, South Korea and Japan are of broader relevance. Taiwan

(20 million people) and South Korea (44 million) fall within the mid-range of Southern countries and have important rural sectors. Japan (123 million) is larger than all four tigers combined. It also followed a strategy in achieving its dominant position in the world economy that in key respects resembles the strategies of Taiwan and South Korea.

There are, of course, important differences among the specific development experiences of these three countries. Their successes were also a product of a combination of their own strategies and particular historical circumstances that no longer prevail. It is not my intent to examine the details here, but rather only to review the broad outlines of their experience that are particularly useful in defining an economic strategy consistent with the values and perspectives of a people-centered development vision.

Institutional Foundations
For all of the five countries named above, their success as industrial exporters was built on strong integrated domestic economies with institutional foundations that helped to achieve broadly-based participation in the growth process. All five had made major investments in achieving high levels of adult literacy and education.[8]

The three countries with consequential rural sectors—Japan, South Korea and Taiwan—each instituted comprehensive and radical land reform, resulting in agricultural sectors that consisted predominantly or exclusively of small farms. These three countries were also distinguished for their strong local administrations and member managed, multitiered local organizations, including cooperatives, irrigation societies, farmer associations, and women's and youth organizations.[9]

While none of these societies had consistently democratic national administrations, the available evidence, according to Uphoff, suggests that their rural organizations were substantially member-controlled and served as effective vehicles for the articulation and upward communication of popular concerns. These rural organizations were also effective in facilitating downward communication from the government to the people. The combination of education, land reform, and local organization played an important role in controlling the formation or moderating the influence of local power monopolies that elsewhere have seriously distorted and limited the development of local economies. They also made it difficult for the center to establish a complete power monopoly over the periphery.[10]

Increasing Rural Productivity
An equity-oriented institutional base prepared the way in these countries for measures aimed at increasing the productivity of the two most important rural assets, land and people. This consisted of increasing crop diversification and improving agricultural technologies. The institutional base contributed to a reasonably just distribution of the gains from the resulting increases in value-added per hectare of agri-

cultural land among members of the rural population.

This institutional base also made it both possible and natural for Taiwan, Korea and Japan to follow what Bruce Johnston has characterized as an *unimodal* agricultural strategy. The unimodal strategy focuses on increasing the productivity and incomes of the small family farm with an emphasis on labor-using, capital-saving technologies.[11] It involves a broadly-based integrative approach to rural development that avoids the creation of economic enclaves.

Other late developing countries have commonly followed *bimodal* agricultural strategies that perpetuate the dualistic structures of the colonial economy, as described in chapter 6. Under the bimodal strategy agriculture sector resources are concentrated on commercial farms and plantations that feature the use of labor-saving, capital-using technologies. This enclave agricultural sector remains relatively isolated from the parallel rural economy of small subsistence farms. The economic gains of the bimodal strategy are concentrated in the hands of a small number of wealthy land owners and investors whose preferences are likely to be for imported products. Consequently, this strategy makes little contribution to the development of the internal market.

One of the important benefits of the unimodal strategy is that it expands the internal market for industrial goods and services. In Taiwan, South Korea and Japan these markets became the initial base for the demand-driven development of small rural industries to serve the needs of the rural population, including provision of agricultural inputs and processing. Countless small- and medium-size industrial firms emerged in the rural areas, subject to the competitive discipline of local markets. This emphasis on rural industries was strongest in Taiwan where in 1961, only 16 percent of factory jobs were located in Taipei, the capital city.[12]

Growth of Urban Industry

Substantial increases in rural productivity, incomes and industry *led* the expansion of the urban industrial sector in Taiwan and South Korea.[13] Once the rural economy had established a foundation for the expansion of urban industry, the rural areas gradually released workers to the cities. Increases in agricultural productivity insured the food supply of these workers. The rural market, including the input needs of its industries, insured a demand for their products.

As the urban industrial base grew, increasing attention was given to export markets, building on the foundation provided by domestic markets to cushion domestic industries against the volatility of the international marketplace. Export-oriented industries emerged within complex systems of domestic supplier relationships that included countless small and intermediate-size firms. The combination of domestic markets and supplier relationships created highly integrated, diversified and resilient national economies that commanded the technologies on which they depended and were able to capture domestically a substantial portion of the value added of their exports.

The Role of Government

Government played an important role in setting the policies that shaped development of the economies of these countries. The strength of government involvement varied among the Asian tigers. Hong Kong was probably the closest to the pure free market approach favored by current conventional wisdom. However, Korea's interventionist government departed substantially from prevailing free market orthodoxy.[14]

In Japan, Taiwan and South Korea government's hand was particularly strong in land reform and education. It was also important in setting policies and programs that significantly reduced population growth. This helped to ensure that the benefits of gains from asset distribution and productivity growth were not simply absorbed by expanding populations.

Furthermore, government played an important role in setting priorities for the growth of particular economic sectors and provided combinations of incentives and protection to orient market forces toward these priorities, including, eventually, export-promotion.[15] The governments of Japan, South Korea and Taiwan also took a variety of measures to provide their own agriculture and industries with substantial protection from foreign competition.

Given the substantial hand of government, it must be noted here that those who favor authoritarian rule in setting the direction of national development generally find more support for their cause in the historical experience of Japan, Taiwan and Korea than do the champions of democracy. The issues are complex. Each had a government that held corruption within reasonable bounds and was subject to strong external pressures of a special historical nature in support of fundamental institutional reforms, particularly land reform.[16] Similar reforms in other countries are likely to require a larger degree of broadly-based popular political support.

The Lessons of Asian Success Stories

History is complex and not easily summarized under simplistic labels. Even by the most accommodating standards, however, the export-led growth label does not convey an accurate image of the development strategies of Japan, South Korea and Taiwan. Their strategies were oriented to growth, but that growth is more accurately described as equity-led than export-led. Countries interested in replicating the Asian success stories should give early priority to creating the enabling conditions for broadly-based participation in a dynamic economic growth process.

AN EQUITY-LED SUSTAINABLE GROWTH STRATEGY

The equity-led *sustainable* growth strategy outlined below builds from the basic pattern of economic transformation found in the historical experience in the Asian countries, adds attention to environmental sustainability, and addresses the need to mobilize democratic forces in support of the asset control reforms that provide the foundation of the strategy.

Six Stages

The suggested elements of an equity-led sustainable growth strategy have been divided below into six sequential stages. While reality never follows such tidy conceptualization, this characterization of sequential stages is intended to help clarify issues and priorities relating to the phased sequencing of policy action.[17]

Stage I: Preparation for Change

- Make a substantial commitment to basic education in an effort to achieve near universal literacy and numeracy. This education should build relevant livelihood skills and develop the consciousness and skills of active citizenship and environmental stewardship.
- Establish strong guarantees of freedom of speech and association. Minimize restrictions on NGO formation and funding. Encourage the development of a strong NGO sector, particularly the formation of a dense mosaic of community level people's organizations.
- Modernize and professionalize the judiciary to strengthen the rule of law.[18]
- Streamline and professionalize the military, reducing its size and increasing its discipline and commitment to constitutional law and civilian rule.[19]
- Reduce restrictions inhibiting the release of the economic, political and social power of women.
- Increase the authority and functions of local governments, including their control over local tax revenues, and increase their accountability to local electorates.
- Carry out public education campaigns intended to educate the general public to the need for and power of the equity-led growth model, so that all societal elements may see why the strategy is essential to long-term viability and how it opens new opportunities for themselves.
- Strengthen programs to curtail population growth and to expand preventive health services nationwide.
- Move to Stage II as a base of political support and human resource capacity is established.

The essential task of Stage I is to create a political and institutional context that will allow for the successful implementation of the asset reform measures to be introduced in Stage II.

Stage II: Asset Reform and Rural Infrastructure

- Implement a radical redistribution of productive assets, particularly land, making use of NGOs, people's organizations and local governments to assume a leading role in implementation.[20]
- Promote cooperatives and corporate employees ownership schemes.
- Invest in basic infrastructure to open up remote rural areas and reduce communications costs.[21]
- Strengthen rural phone systems and other communications links to reduce rural isolation.[22]
- Establish or expand local mediation mechanisms to facilitate the peaceful resolution of individual and group conflicts and reduce burdens on the court system.
- Phase in Stage III as asset reform is implemented so that the new asset holders have immediate support in increasing the productivity of those assets.

Asset reform is the heart of the overall strategy. Steps to open up the rural areas, which are also central to Stage II, might well be considered important preparation for asset reform, however, including these in Stage I would increase the danger that urban elites will co-opt even more of the available assets before asset reform is implemented.

Stage III: Agricultural Intensification and Diversification

- Increase the value-added of small farm units through intensification and diversification, adding high value crops to generate cash income alongside those grown for family consumption.
- Emphasize nonpolluting bio-intensive/regenerative technologies that minimize requirements for purchased inputs.[23]
- Expand credit services to smallhold farmers and small businesses.
- Improve local agricultural processing and marketing facilities, with an emphasis on independent, farmer-controlled cooperatives.
- Take steps to strengthen the internal competitiveness of domestic markets by eliminating marketing cartels and insure that publicly licensed common carriers accept shipments from all qualified shippers without price or other discrimination.[24]
- Limit the importation of food products that can be produced locally at a reasonable cost, with special care to protect local farmers from imported food products favored by foreign subsidies.
- Review and adjust pricing policies to eliminate biases against small rural producers—such as artificial price ceilings on agricultural and aguacultural products, overvalued exchange rates and the heavy taxation of farm produce.
- Phase in Stage IV as agricultural value-added increases and the rural market for appropriate industrial products grows.

Here the primary concern is to increase rural productivity and incomes, and thereby to strengthen the local market for basic products that are within the capacity of small rural industries to produce.

Stage IV: Rural Industrialization

- Provide incentives and assistance for the establishment of small- and medium-scale rural industries to serve the needs of the rural people for services, capital goods, agricultural inputs and agricultural processing.
- Implement policies that minimize burdensome licensing and regulatory barriers to the entry of small- and medium-size firms.[25]
- Eliminate subsidies or other preferential treatment for large-scale industries, such as controls and subsidies that give large, capital intensive industries an unfair advantage over small- and medium-size firms and entrench inefficient industrial monopolies.
- Encourage productive efficiency by insuring that domestic markets remain competitive, while providing protection to local small- and medium-scale producers from competition from better established, subsidized and highly capitalized foreign competitors.
- Phase in Stage V as required to meet domestic demands that exceed the capacities of small- and medium-size rural industries.

It is during this stage that the rural economy moves from a primary reliance on agriculture to a more mature and integrated rural economy that is able to capture a major portion of the value-added potential of agricultural production.

Stage V: Urban Industrialization

- Gradually shift priorities to expansion of urban industries that have strong backward and forward linkages to the rural agricultural and industrial sectors. Unless the country is very small, the growth of these industries should be governed primarily by the growing needs of local markets and consumers.[26]
- Undertake Stage VI once urban industries have satisfied domestic demand and achieved adequate efficiency to compete in foreign markets.

During this stage the country consolidates its technical base and strengthens its competitive efficiency, moving to the production of more sophisticated products using advanced technologies that by this stage the domestic economy should be able to command.

Stage VI: Export Promotion

- Encourage the use of residual production capacity to serve foreign markets with products that have a high value-added relative to their content of physical and environmental resources.

The goal here is to earn necessary foreign exchange to participate in international markets while exporting as little of the country's physical resources as possible.

This presentation is intended only to provide a framework for encouraging thinking and debate about priority setting in positioning resources to support an equity-led strategy. It is not intended as a blueprint. Every country enters the 1990s with its own history and circumstances against which it must define the specifics of an appropriate strategy. Furthermore, more detailed analysis and debate may reveal a need to revise the framework in some of its details for both political and technical reasons.

The Essential Logic of an Equity-led Strategy

Any effort to refine the framework presented here should recognize that the essential logic of an equity-led sustainable growth strategy is found in its choice of priorities for the sequencing of development interventions. It is specifically the emphasis on institutional transformation as the point of departure that most clearly distinguishes the equity-led strategy of the people-centered development vision from a conventional growth strategy.

An essential task of the equity-led growth strategist is to analyze the extent to which existing circumstances do or do not provide the foundation for movement to a more advanced stage. For example, does the country have a functioning legal system? If not, is there reason to believe that it is a necessary precondition for successful introduction of the asset reform measures of Stage II? If so, then work on legal reform or the establishment of an alternative system of dispute resolution may be an essential first priority before directing attention to land reform.[27]

Reform of Asset Control

In line with arguments regarding sequencing, the asset redistribution of Stage II represents the true heart of the equity-led sustainable growth strategy. All prior elements of the strategy prepare for asset reform and all subsequent elements build on it. There are several reasons why asset redistribution is central, particularly in agrarian societies. The most obvious is to give people access to productive resources. This is aimed at a threefold benefit. The first is the intensive management and application of these resources to optimize their productive potential. The second is to increase the likelihood that the benefits from the drive to growth will be widely shared. The third is to establish a link between the long-term environmental viability of the resource and the family that depends on it for its livelihood.

Land reform is particularly a key, especially in countries with high ratios of population to productive land, in providing the basis for agricultural intensification. Large farms have an advantage over small farms in boosting labor productivity through the heavy use of capital investment, mechanization and chemical inputs. Small farms, however, have the advantage in terms of labor absorption and output per hectare. This is the more appropriate priority in land- and capital-scarce, labor-surplus economies.[28] The small farm unit is also particularly well suited to the intensive inputs of management and labor on which the application of advanced environmentally sound bio-intensive technologies depend.[29]

An equally important purpose of asset reform is to help break the power monopolies of the traditional land-owning, rent-collecting classes that keep the majority of the population in bondage and suppress the release of social energy critical to a vitalization of the rural economy. It is necessary to reorient these classes toward more progressive entrepreneurial activities, particularly the development of rural industries.

In some more extreme instances, local power brokers operate much as legally protected crime syndicates, enforcing their will through the use of thugs, bribery and even private armies.[30] They may appropriate local assets, control local trade, and pursue activities such as illegal logging and drug operations that are major contributors to environmental damage.[31] Breaking the power of these barons is essential if the rule of law is to be established and rural markets are to be opened to vitalizing competition—both of which are essential to a dynamic rural economy. This is why fundamental reforms are required in the judiciary and the military during Stage I in preparation for the asset distribution of Stage II.

At the same time, as important as asset reform may be in some countries, it is quite possible that for a given country it is not at issue. There are countries in which control over productive assets is already broadly distributed. Under such happy circumstances the strategy may be revised as appropriate to local conditions.

Role of International Assistance

Strong political and financial support from the international community, including through bilateral and multilateral assistance agencies, is likely to be especially important during the first two stages of the equity-led sustainable growth strategy. An important role for Northern voluntary organizations (VOs) will be to create political support for appropriate diplomatic action by Northern governments and the setting of relevant policy conditions by international assistance agencies.

Only grant funded international financial assistance is appropriate to stages I and II. Debt financing for the types of activities involved in the early stages is inherently inappropriate. Creating debt service burdens before economic expansion is well along will likely jeopardize both transformation and economic expansion, biasing attention prematurely toward export promotion to support debt repayment. This would be essentially a subversion of the strategy and a return to the colonial enclave economy.

During all stages of strategy implementation, international assistance should give special attention to assisting in the development and application of nonpolluting, resource conserving, information-based technologies. This should include attention in every activity to treating waste products as a resource for recovery and reuse.[32] Rather than transferring environmentally obsolete technologies from the North to the South, the South should insist on taking the lead in the development and application of environmentally appropriate technologies throughout all stages of development.

BUILDING POLITICAL WILL

The political barriers to an equity-led sustainable growth strategy are self-evident.[33] Conventional strategies that concentrate only on growth serve the interests of those who already hold power and who are thus positioned to capture the benefits of that growth. An equity-led strategy calls for concentrating first on reforming the structures that give the power holders their ability to capture these benefits. Obviously this is not an idea around which power holders can be expected to rally with enthusiasm.

For this reason the most important underlying task of Stage I is to build the political will to proceed with the reform of asset control in Stage II. Specifically, Stage I seeks simultaneously to:

- *Strengthen the forces supporting reform* by introducing educational and organizational initiatives aimed at increasing the political participation of those who stand to benefit by the more fundamental reforms; and,
- *Reduce the barriers to reform* by: 1) creating an appreciation among power holding elites of the economic opportunities that would open for them under an equity-led sustainable growth strategy and of the increasing violence, environmental deterioration and economic stagnation they may expect for themselves and their children if they successfully oppose such a strategy; 2) increasing the impartiality of the courts and police in enforcing the law; 3) professionalizing the military as disciplined defenders of the constitution; and 4) strengthening press freedom to increase accountability and the transparency of decision making.

AN INCLUSIVE PEOPLE'S MOVEMENT

The upsurge in commitment to political democratization that swept the world in the 1980s greatly strengthens the forces in support of Stage I reforms. People power is the key, though its expression must involve more than short-lived mass demonstrations. The expressions of people power as a force for reform must be sustained and channeled through a combination of mass organizations, individual voluntary initiatives and VOs. The resulting social energy must be directed toward transformation of the institutions and values that drive unjust, unsustainable and exclusive growth. In short, development must become a people's movement.

Unlike Marxist social movements, however, the people's development movement cannot be of class against class. It must at once raise class-consciousness among both the powerful and the powerless and yet be inclusive of all classes—joined in a commitment to resolution of the crises that ultimately threaten all whose lives and well-being depend on the security and integrity of spaceship earth. A nonviolent world is an essential goal of the movement and its means must be consistent with that goal. The movement must seek the transformation of existing institutions through their regeneration, not their destruction or further immobilization. Finally, the power must reside with the people, not with some self-appointed vanguard that rules in their name. It must build from and support the people's self-help development efforts.[34]

The ability of the movement to link domestic and international political forces is likely to be crucial to its success. Creating the conditions for Stages I and II should be a priority concern of both national and international VOs, especially in their organizing, advocacy and public education activities. There is a natural division of roles here. It is most appropriate for national VOs to take the lead in direct organizing, education and advocacy within their own countries, with support from the international VOs in lobbying Northern governments and international assistance agencies.

Though many of the governments and international agencies that have dominated the setting of national and international agendas are captives of narrower interests and a development vision that serves those interests, there are many people within them who share the commitment of VOs to a people-centered vision. These people are important participants in the people's development movement. However, they are severely constrained by the political and bureaucratic imperatives of the institutions in which they work. There are many opportunities for VOs to form alliances with these individuals to strengthen their hand in bringing change within the agencies in which they work.[35]

In many instances effective results at national levels, particularly in countries with authoritarian regimes, require broad collaboration at the international level among voluntary organizations and networks spanning dozens of Northern and Southern countries. Such alliances are being formed and strengthened. They have the potential to build a broad climate of public support that focuses political pressure on otherwise nonaccountable governments in ways that may not be possible through purely domestic initiatives.

VOs, particularly those with broadly-based constituencies, have increasing opportunities to reshape the agendas of governments and public international assistance agencies, in part through their participation in national and international policy fora, as will be discussed further in chapter 13. It is essential that a substantial number of VOs pursue these opportunities.

The 1990s will tell the story of whether the growth-centered development vision maintains its hold on human society or whether it gives way to a new and more timely vision. This decade is crucial, for if we have not established a new vision in the global consciousness by the dawning of the new century, humankind's window of opportunity will almost certainly have passed and we will be left to suffer the consequences of our failure.

NOTES

1. Many NGOs have programs that extend much beyond single villages. Some are in fact very extensive in scope and may have well-defined program plans and budgets. This, however, is a different matter than having a development strategy aimed at economic transformation based on a well-defined development theory. Among the few NGOs that seem in my opinion to have true development strategies of consequential scale are the Foundation for Community Organization and Management Technology headed by Sixto K. Roxas in the Philippines and the Institute for Liberty and Democracy in Lima, Peru headed by Hernando de Soto. Of these, the de Soto initiative, aimed at legitimizing and strengthening the urban informal sector through policies that give it the benefits of legal protection and access to the resources of the formal sector, has a longer history and is the better known internationally.

The Sixto Roxas initiative is one of the only NGO rural development initiatives I have seen that is built on a true theory of rural economic transformation. It defines an economic district of some 22,000 households to be assisted in developing themselves into a geographically defined economic unit. These households are organized into clusters that link into and ultimately provide the governance structure for an incorporated management unit that services the households as economic units. The management unit is evaluated on the basis of its contribution to increasing household incomes and bringing all households above a defined poverty line. Emphasis is placed on increasing agricultural value-added per hectare and on the development of vertically integrated processing and marketing facilities to increase the locally retained value-added from agricultural production. Sophisticated management information systems highlight unutilized land resources so that their productive development may be targeted by the community. Further information may be obtained from the Foundation for Community Organization & Management Technology, Inc., Ground Floor, Centrum Building, 104 Perea Street, Legaspi Village, Makati, Metro Manila, Philippines.

2. These events are occurring so rapidly that they are nearly impossible to track except on a personal basis in the countries in which one has an involvement in the relevant networks. For example, in 1989 in Indonesia LP3ES and LBH began convening a monthly working group of leading Indonesian intellectuals and NGO leaders to examine issues relating to a sustainable development strategy for Indonesia. A separate, but parallel initiative was being undertaken by another Indonesian NGO, YPMD, to join national and provincial governments with the NGO community in an effort to define a people-centered development strategy for Irian Jaya province.

In the Philippines, the Philippine Rural Reconstruction Movement (PRRM) has established a policy analysis unit that is studying people-centered strategy options for the Philippines. PhilDHRRA, another Philippine NGO, is asking assistance from a group of local economists to help educate Philippine NGO leaders on key development policy issues and to work with the NGO community to define a framework for assessing current policy proposals for consistency with an equity-led sustainable growth strategy. A tour of the United States in November 1989 by ten Philippine NGO leaders under the auspices of the Gateway Pacific Foundation resulted in publication of a shared development vision that outlines a strategy for national development, and the formation of the Green Forum, a coalition that by March 1990 had a membership of more than 500 Philippine NGOs, people's organizations, and religious groups committed to the articulation and realization of an alternative development vision. This group is rapidly moving to the forefront of efforts to create both a political force and an intellectual center for an alternative equity-led development strategy. It is supported in the U.S. by the Philippine Development Forum, which was created as a parallel initiative.

In India the Lokayan Movement, which has its own journal, the *Lokayan Bulletin,* brings together activities from nonparty political organizations and movements and other concerned citizens in support of a people's development movement. It has an explicit goal of bringing the thinking, values, aspirations and experiences of the marginalized sections of society into the mainstream of educational, economic and political thinking.

3. I am indebted to Frances F. Korten for suggesting the term "equity-led growth." Adelman, who has been a long-time proponent of this concept and whose ideas have substantially influenced the formulation of the strategy outlined here calls it "redistribution before growth." Irma Adelman, "A Poverty Focused Approach to Development," in John P. Lewis and Valeriana Kallab (eds.), *Development Strategies Reconsidered* (Washington, D.C.: The Overseas Development Council, 1986), pp. 49–65.

A classic study produced by the World Bank and the Institute of Development Studies at the University of Sussex in the 1970s was titled "Redistribution with Growth." Hollis Chenery, Montek S. Ahluwalia, C.L.G. Bell, John H. Duloy, and Richard Jolly, *Redistribution with Growth* (London: Oxford University Press, 1974). It outlined a variety of alternative approaches to dealing with the problem of poverty, including transferring existing assets to poverty groups. However, it rejected this alternative as politically infeasible and advocated instead the concentration of investment (foreign assistance resources) on building the capacity of the poor to be productive. Essentially the argument was that the wealthy would be less resistant to the idea of concentrating new increments of productive capital on the poor than to the idea of redistributing existing productive assets. It was a politically pragmatic choice that assumed away the fundamental issues of power relationships. In the end what the study advocated was more a variation on the more conventional growth-centered strategy than an alternative to it. For further discussion see Robert L. Ayers, *Banking on the Poor* (Cambridge, MA: The MIT Press, 1983), pp. 75–91.

4. I suspect readers whose sympathies are with other development models might, with some justification, argue that I am also a victim of the "believing is seeing" syndrome. I can make no claim to being immune to this weakness. There remains a need for considerable further review of these experiences from a variety of perspectives by people with access to a richer data base than I have at hand in an effort to see and understand the entire picture of the experience of these countries and to interpret its broader implications. No matter what lens one wears in the study of the experience of these countries, there remains the fundamental reality that global circumstances have changed dramatically since these countries achieved their success. Any lessons drawn from their experience must be adapted accordingly.

5. For references see chapter 6.

6. I am indebted to Sixto K. Roxas for stimulating many of the insights into the Asian tigers experience as outlined in this chapter through discussions and his numerous papers, including Sixto K. Roxas, "Strengthening the Capability of the Philippine Food Industry to Address the Crucial Issues of Food Supply, Demand, Technology and

Marketing in the Context of Regional and Global Competition," Notes for the Food Congress of the Philippine Chamber of Food Manufacturers on Innovative Approaches to Food Sector Development (undated, circa 1989, unpublished); Sixto K. Roxas, "Recovery, Reconstruction and Reform in the Philippines," presentation before the Japanese JCCI Mission, 15 March 1988; and Sixto K. Roxas, "Industrialization through Agricultural Development," a speech before the Philippine Agricultural Economics and Development Association, August 25, 1989.

7. Based on 1985 population statistics from the table, "Population of World's Largest Cities" in *The World Almanac and Book of Facts 1989* (New York: St. Martin's Press, 1989), pp. 738–39.

8. Masao Fujioka, "Alleviating Poverty Through Development: The Asian Experience," *Development*, 2/3, 1988, p. 27; and Irma Adelman, "Development Economics—A Reassessment of Goals," *Development Economics*, Vol. 65, No. 2, May 1975, pp. 302–09.

9. For a detailed analysis of these structures and their relationship to the national development strategies of Taiwan, South Korea and Japan, see Norman T. Uphoff (ed.), *Rural Development and Local Organization in Asia: East Asia*, Vol. 2 (Delhi: MacMillan India, Ltd., 1982). A comprehensive treatment of the rural development strategies of these countries, with a focus on their organizational dimension, is also provided by Edgar Owens and Robert Shaw, *Development Reconsidered: Bridging the Gap Between Government and People* (Lexington: D. C. Heath and Co., 1972).

10. For an assessment see Norman T. Uphoff, "Introduction to East Asian Cases," in Uphoff (ed.), *Rural Development*, pp. 1–11.

11. Bruce F. Johnston, "Agriculture and Economic Development: The Relevance of the Japanese Experience," *Food Research Institute Studies*, Vol. 6, No. 3 (1966), pp. 251–312; Bruce F. Johnston and Peter Kilby, *Agriculture and Structural Transformation: Economic Strategies in Late-Developing Countries* (New York: Oxford University Press, 1975); and Bruce F. Johnston and William C. Clark, *Redesigning Rural Development: A Strategic Perspective* (Baltimore: The Johns Hopkins University Press, 1982).

12. During that point in history, countries with dualistic development strategies typically had from 50 to 60 percent of their industrial employment located in their major urban center. This ran to a high of 83 percent in the Ivory Coast (Senegal). Owens and Shaw, *Development Reconsidered*, p. 117.

13. The *zaibatsu* were already a force before and during Japan's agrarian revolution.

14. Bradford, "East Asian Models," p. 119.

15. *Ibid.*, pp. 115–28.

16. In Japan land reform was imposed by the United States as an occupying military force following World War II. In Taiwan it was imposed by officials of the Kuomintang and their army as part of the process of consolidating their control after they occupied the island. In South Korea it followed a devastating war with North Korea that had decimated existing rural structures and involved substantial guidance from the United States. The current challenge is to achieve similar transformations elsewhere without war, armed revolution or military occupation.

17. While this framework generally assumes that the results of earlier stages should be in place before giving emphasis to activities of later stages, no assumptions are made here regarding the presumed phasing of activities within a given stage. Generally it is assumed that activities within a given stage will progress in tandem.

18. Corrupt judicial systems that provide justice only to the rich are a leading instrument for the harassment and exploitation of the poor in many Southern countries. The smart buyer in such countries does not hire a skilled lawyer, he hires the judge.

19. In too many settings, military personnel and even military units are available for private hire as a means of settling disputes. A friend who lived in the suburb of a major Asian city (not in the Philippines) once described arriving home one night to find a stand-off between several armed military and police units, some in full battle dress. His landlord was in a dispute with a land speculator who was trying to seize control of the property. Each had hired his own police and military units to intimidate the other, and the number of participants escalated daily. This particular dispute was ultimately settled without bloodshed, but there were some tense moments. It is not difficult to imagine the plight of the rural poor who have no money to hire their own police or military units to defend them from wealthy land-grabbers.

   The December 1989 coup attempt in the Philippines elements of the Philippine military were hired by opposition politicians seeking to establish themselves in power by force of arms. As the Philippines entered the final decade of the century, the central preoccupation of its loyal military leaders was with protecting the government from their own renegade units.

20. In a classic study, John D. Montgomery, "Allocation of Authority in Land Reform Programs: A Comparative Study of Administrative Processes and Outputs," *Administrative Science Quarterly,* March 1972, established that the success of land reform programs is greatly influenced by the administrative arrangements used in their implementation. The most successful ones have been those that are implemented through locally accountable organizations.

21. In allocating funds for infrastructure development priority is given to types and locations of new infrastructure that will create the greatest benefit measured in terms of additions to the incomes of households below or near the poverty line. This may be expected to result in quite different allocation decisions than the more conventional practice of placing such investments where they will produce the greatest impact in terms of stimulating increased returns industrial investments. The former approach is likely to result in infrastructure investments oriented toward the more remote and least served areas. The latter approach usually leads to a concentration of infrastructure in those few urban locations that already offer the fullest range of services.

22. Relative to building roads and supporting the necessary stock of vehicles, the telephone is an inexpensive and environmentally sound means of helping to break rural isolation and strengthen the free flow of information.

23. For a comprehensive review of these methods, their relevance to the current global situation, and an extensive bibliography see Michael Dover and Lee M. Talbot, *To Feed the Earth: Agro-Ecology for Sustainable Development* (Washington, DC: World Resources Institute, 1987).

24. In the Philippines one of the ways in which trading cartels maintain their monopolies is through their control over inter-island shipping. NGOs report that when farmer

owned cooperatives undertake to do their own marketing, the cartel-controlled shipping companies simply refuse to accept their shipments.

25. The dialogue on structural adjustment has stressed opening domestic markets to international competition. Far too little attention has been paid to the potential for increasing economic efficiency through the liberalization of domestic trade and markets. An important reality of many Southern countries is the existence of marketing cartels. Some are government founded and sanctioned. Others are created and controlled by mafia style syndicates that operate outside the law, though often with the connivance of corrupt officials. The World Bank notes that the liberalization of *domestic* trade was an important precursor of industrialization in Britain, many other European countries, the U.S. and Japan. *World Development Report, 1987* (Washington, DC: The World Bank, 1987), p. 55.

26. Domestic market development should not be confused with import substitution strategies. One of the most appropriate foci of a domestic market development strategy is the provision of basic goods and services needed by nonaffluent local consumers who lack the money to buy imported products. This may at times conflict with objectives of moving to higher valued uses of land and other local resources, however, expanding the consumption opportunities available to the poor is essential to a just development.

27. I do not know whether this is the case or not. Often the data will not be adequate to reach an empirical conclusion. In such cases it will be necessary to substitute judgment. In any event the more clearly stated the assumptions, the more readily they can be tested and the strategy refined accordingly as experience is acquired.

28. For a classic review of the advantages of small farm production units see Peter Dorner, *Land Reform and Economic Development* (Middlesex: Penguin Books, 1972).

29. See Dover and Talbot, *To Feed the Earth.*

30. These elements are rent seekers of the most pure and destructive type who seek to appropriate for themselves any available surplus from the rural areas, leaving the effort and risk to others, and making a mockery of the rule of law. In some areas the local barons are true warlords with private armies. Others simply hire elements of the military on contract to do their dirty work for them. For a detailed description of how the system works, see the cover story by John McBeth entitled "The Boss System," *Far Eastern Economic Review,* 14 September 1989, pp. 36-43. For a detailed personal account told by a Catholic priest of the consequences for the rural poor and their efforts to improve their lot through self-help measures see Niall O'Brien, *Revolution from the Heart* (New York: Oxford University Press, 1987). For a similar account of the corruption and violence that is depressing efforts to vitalize the rural areas of Bangladesh, see Bangladesh Rural Advancement Committee, "Unraveling Networks of Corruption," in David C. Korten (ed.), *Community Management: Asian Experience and Perspectives* (West Hartford: Kumarian Press, 1986), pp. 135–56.

31. It is estimated that in some areas of Peru more than 10 percent of deforestation results from the clearing of forests for coca and marijuana production, as well as from the dumping of kerosene and sulfuric acid used in drug production. *The Developing World: Danger Point for U.S. Security,* A report commissioned by Mark O. Hatfield, Matthew F. McHugh, and Mickey Leland (Washington, DC: Arms Control and Foreign Policy Caucus of the U.S. Congress, August 1, 1989), p. 67.

32. Wherever possible policies should encourage the development of this resource as a business opportunity by the poor. For example, in Indonesia the Institute of Technology in Bandung and the Lembaga Studi Pembangunan (LSP), an NGO, are organizing scavengers in Bandung and Jakarta to form trash collection and recycling cooperatives that work in decentralized "industrial estates" to completely recycle urban wastes, including the composting of organic materials. The result is improved trash collection, the complete recovery and recycling of trash for productive reuse, and substantially improved earnings and social status for the scavengers—who now consider themselves to be businessmen rather than outcasts. See Hasan Poerbo, Daniel T. Sicular and Vonny Supardj, "An Approach to Development of the Informal Sector: The Case of Garbage Collectors in Bandung," *Prisma,* published by LP3ES, Jakarta, Indonesia, No. 32, June 1984, pp. 85–100.

33. The argument that radical redistributive policies are politically infeasible has been offered as a major reason why official agencies have not been more forceful in addressing them. See Robert L. Ayers, *Banking on the Poor* (Cambridge, MA: The MIT Press, 1983), pp. 79–80. It is a real and serious dilemma. The rich who hold power are unlikely to voluntarily give up their power without a compelling reason and the fact that a lot of people are desperately poor has seldom proven to be an adequately compelling reason. What changes the picture at this stage in history is the threat of environmental collapse and pervasive communal violence—both of which produce a direct and serious threat to the wealthy, and cannot be resolved without resolving the problem of poverty.

34. For important studies focusing on people's self-help development initiatives of the type that must be the heart of a people's development movement see Robert Chambers, Arnold Pacey, and Lori Ann Thrupp (eds.), *Farmer First: Farmer Innovation and Agricultural Research* (London: Intermediate Technology Publications, 1989); Czech Conroy and Miles Litvinoff (eds.), *The Greening of Aid: Sustainable Livelihoods in Practice* (London: Earthscan Publications, Ltd., 1988); Bertrand Schneider, *The Barefoot Revolution: A Report to the Club of Rome* (London: Intermediate Technology Publications, 1988); and Alan B. Durning, "Action at the Grassroots: Fighting Poverty and Environmental Decline," *Worldwatch Paper 88* (Washington, DC: Worldwatch Institute, January 1989).

35. The first imperative of any bureaucracy is to maintain its budget, and this is ultimately the achilles' heal of any government bureaucracy. Threaten its budget and you get its attention. Some authoritarian regimes in the South have become more dependent on and accountable to their bankers than to their own people. In such cases the obvious strategy for international citizens' networks is to influence these regimes through the bankers who control their budgets. The World Bank is in its turn very sensitive to negative public press that weakens its case for increased financing from the legislatures of Northern democracies, which the environmental movement has effectively demonstrated.

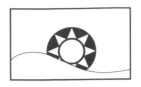

PART III

VOLUNTARY ORGANIZATIONS: DEVELOPMENT ROLES AND STRATEGIES

In most respects the equity-led sustainable growth strategy outlined in the previous chapter represents a confirmation of the existing commitments of many development-oriented voluntary organizations (VOs). These VOs have long been committed to empowering the poor through education and organization. Many are deeply concerned about asset control issues. Others work to help the poor control their fertility. Still others are working to increase rural productivity. Some of the more sophisticated ones define their task in terms of the democratization of society through the gradual reconstruction of the institutions that allocate power.

Such existing VO activities are all worthy and appropriate efforts consistent with people-centered development. The problem is that too many of these efforts are inconsequential in their scope and substance.

A LIMITED VISION

Most development-oriented VOs have suffered from a limited vision of their roles. They have accepted themselves as peripheral actors on the development stage, leaving the big issues to organizations that command far larger financial resources. They have been content to do good on a small-scale in a few localities, often limiting themselves to welfare activities that seek more to relieve immediate suffering than its underlying causes. There is no coherent sense of where the pieces of their activities fit into a broader national or global strategy. Individual VOs work in isolation from one another concentrating on implementing their projects in their "own" villages. There is seldom a clear distinction between those uses of time and resources that have a prospect of making a consequential long-term difference for many people and those that may help only a few in the immediate term so long as each can be justified as responding to an evident need.[1]

There is no attention to the implications of the policies being worked out between their own governments and the IMF, the World Bank and other multilateral and bilateral assistance agencies that shape the larger context of national and global development—and too often undermine the very work to which the VOs themselves are committed. Working without a clear strategic concept or development theory, some VOs may slip into reinforcing unjust structures,[2] even creating their own version of the enclave economy.[3]

A CRITICAL SELF-ASSESSMENT

The picture is changing, and the change is gathering new momentum with each passing day as increasing numbers of VOs re-examine their development roles and strategies.

A Global Dialogue

The Symposium on "Development Alternatives: The Challenge for NGOs" held in London in March 1987[4] helped set this process in motion. More than a hundred development professionals from forty-two countries met to examine the challenges facing development-oriented VOs.[5] Some of the world's most creative and influential VO leaders were among them, the majority from the South.

Pointing to the evident development failures of the 1980s—in particular the deepening debt crisis and alarming increases in absolute poverty throughout much of the world—participants in this meeting called for a fundamental re-examination of past development practices and policies, including a redefinition of the development roles of governments, donors and VOs. Participants concluded that the needed leadership for this re-examination was not being provided by either governments or the major international assistance agencies. These were seen as locked into old ways of thinking and acting that too often exacerbated a growing global crisis.

Greater leadership would have to come from VOs. VOs could no longer confine themselves to peripheral roles in providing relief to the worst victims of poverty and supporting scattered village development projects. They would need to interject new perspectives into decision making about the policies and institutions that set the directions for local and national development.

Participants from the South called on Northern VOs to re-examine their own roles; to recognize that the continued involvement of Northern VOs in field operations in Southern countries is an anachronism inconsistent with their espoused commitment to building local self-reliance. They also noted the impact of many policies of Northern governments and Northern-dominated international agencies regarding such matters as debt burdens and structural adjustment on the poor. They argued that Northern VOs should devote more of their attention to strengthening Southern VOs, to educating Northern constituencies to the realities of the role of the North in sustaining underdevelopment in the South, and to advocating for more enlightened policies.

The message articulated by the Southern VO representatives at the London Symposium carried such force that it was projected into countless subsequent forums—each of which has added new dimensions to the dialogue.[6] These meetings have dealt with the substance of the people-centered development vision, the new roles that VOs must assume, and the new capacities that VOs must develop.

Of particular interest was a meeting held in June 1989 under the joint sponsorship of the Asian NGO Coalition and the Environmental Liaison Centre. Thirty-one VO leaders from throughout the world met in Manila to discuss plans for regional VO consultations on people's participation in sustainable development. These consultations would engage people from a broad spectrum of organizations—including, government, business, education, people's organizations and VOs—in defining a people-centered development vision. Delegates to the Manila consultation produced the *Manila Declaration*, reprinted here in Appendix A, articulating the basic principles of a people-centered development vision.

From Vision to Action
Throughout the world, the dialogue continues in national, regional and local forums, continuously deepening understanding of the issues and expanding the consensus on necessary action. More and more VOs are taking on leadership roles in studying and taking positions on significant development policy issues, setting new directions for their own organizations, and joining in the formation of networks and coalitions in support of joint action, advocacy and educational strategies on critical local, national and international issues. In their local interventions, VOs are expanding the scale of their programming and joining forces with other VOs and with governments in an effort to achieve more comprehensive coverage of large populations.

Voluntary action takes a wide variety of forms, only one of which involves working within the framework of a formally constituted VO. The special concern of this volume, and particularly of the next two chapters, is with development-oriented VOs and their preparation for the challenges they must face during the current decade. These chapters are intended to provide the reader with basic conceptual tools to better understand the distinctive nature of the VO, its development role, and the strategic choices it faces.

In so doing, chapter 9 looks at VOs as defining a distinctive institutional sector, contrasting it with the government and business sectors. The chapter ends with an explanation of why voluntary action is so uniquely important to global society at this particular point in human history. Chapter 10 distinguishes among four "generations" of program strategies pursued by VOs.

NOTES

1. In the course of doing a strategic assessment, one international NGO became aware that as much as half of its actual field effort was being devoted to baby weighing. They preferred to call it "growth monitoring." But basically it involved weighing babies and recording the weight on a chart. The theory was that there would be follow-up with underweight babies. Occasionally there was, but it consisted mainly of giving a lecture on proper infant feeding to some poor mother who probably was already distraught about her inability to adequately feed her baby because she had no food to give it. Weighing babies and giving lectures is easier and a lot less politically sensitive than trying to get at the reasons why a poor mother cannot feed her baby.

2. One of the well-known international NGOs is quite proud of its extensive feeding program for malnourished children in Negros Occidental Province of the Philippines. Negros is a sugar growing area with large sugar plantations and the worst poverty in the Philippines. Contrary to a widely held international myth the children of Negros are not hungry because of depressed sugar prices. They are hungry because of a lack of land reform and agricultural diversification. In effect, though unintentionally, this international NGO was saying: "Don't worry. If the sugar estates chose to pay you a wage that is below what is required to feed your children, we will be here to make up the difference." Being a nonpolitical organization, this NGO did not concern itself with either land reform or with supporting unionization of the sugar workers so they could demand a living wage. It simply fed the children and gave their mothers nutrition education so that if their families ever were paid a living wage they would know what to buy to feed their children.

3. Consider, for example, the NGO in a Southeast Asian country that provides subsidized assistance to a village cooperative to grow coffee that the NGO then packages and exports to partner NGOs in Europe for sale through volunteer church groups. It is an attractive project, but it is wholly artificial, sustained by subsidies, foreign volunteers, and the charity impulse of the buyer who could buy essentially the same coffee more conveniently and at less cost in the supermarket.

4. For a proceedings of this important conference see the special supplemental issue of *World Development,* Vol. 15, Autumn 1987, on "Development Alternatives: The Challenge for NGOs," edited by Anne Gordon Drabek.

5. Terminology is a continuing problem in these discussions. The term actually used in most international fora is NGO. However, that term is too broad to be useful in serious discussions of NGO roles, because it embraces such a wide variety of dissimilar organizations that are appropriately oriented to an equally wide range of quite different roles. The focus of the discussion in the meetings cited is usually, implicitly at least, on the kinds of roles most naturally assumed by that subset of the larger NGO population that are defined here as voluntary organizations.

6. Over the intervening years, for example, the influence of the London meeting has resulted in completely reshaping the annual meetings of InterAction, the consortium body of U.S. NGOs. One of the most notable consequences has been that representatives of Southern NGOs have been invited to play an increasingly central role in setting and presenting the agenda for these meetings. In Asia, the Asian NGO Coalition has assumed a central role in expanding the dialogue. See, for example, Asian NGO Coalition, *NGO Strategic Management in Asia: Focus on Bangladesh, Indonesia, and the Philippines* (Manila: ANGOC, 1988).

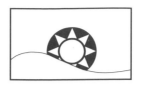

CHAPTER NINE

VOLUNTARY ORGANIZATIONS ARE DIFFERENT[1]

The widespread belief that development is primarily a task of government has legitimated authoritarianism and created a major barrier to true development progress in the South over the past four decades. The people have been expected to put their faith and resources in the hands of government. In return governments have promised to bestow on the people the gift of development. This promise has proven to be a chimera born of a false assessment of the capacity of government and of the nature of development itself.

One of the more positive advances of the 1980s has been a recognition of the essential development role of civil society. As a first step, private business and market forces were rediscovered. Equally important, but more recent, came an acknowledgement that nongovernmental organizations (NGOs) also have an important development role in their own right. Step-by-step we have moved to a recognition that government, business and voluntary organizations all have essential roles in development, as do organizations of what will be defined here as a fourth sector—people's organizations.

One problem that has been faced by those who work with and within NGOs in trying to define their legitimate development roles is the fact that, in common usage, any organization that is both non-governmental and nonprofit is generally considered to be an NGO.[2] This includes a bewildering variety of organizations that have little in common with one another. To speak meaningfully about the development roles of NGOs, it has become necessary to be more specific as to what type of NGO we have in mind. Reference was made to this problem in the introduction to this book and distinctions were noted among a number of different types of NGO: the voluntary organization (VO), the people's organization (PO), the public service contractor (PSC), and the governmental nongovernmental organization (GONGO). The present chapter delves into the differences and their implications.

As a point of departure in developing a framework for thinking about the differences among NGOs, we will look first at the differences among three types of *third*-party organization, i.e., those basing their social legitimacy on the premise that they exist to serve the needs of third parties—persons who are not themselves members of the organization. The three types of third-party organizations examined in this chapter are: government, business and voluntary. The resulting analysis generates a framework useful in understanding not only the distinctive nature of VOs, as one type of NGO, but also in understanding more fully the distinctive nature of other NGO types.

THE PRINCE, THE MERCHANT AND THE CITIZEN

In an essay exploring the distinctive nature of what he calls the "third sector," Nerfin contrasts the societal roles and orientations of the prince, who represents governmental power; the merchant, representing economic power; and the citizen, who embodies people's power. Each is essential to the functioning of society.[3] The prince maintains the public order. The merchant fills the need for goods and services. The responsible citizen, in association with other citizens, brings the autonomous force of people power to bear to demand the accountability of the prince and the merchant and to exercise the rights and responsibilities of citizenship.

The roles of each of society's three primary types of third-party organization—government, business and voluntary—parallel those of the prince, the merchant and the citizen. The legitimacy of each is based on the belief that it serves an essential function in meeting the needs of third parties, i.e., persons other than its own principals. For example, the legitimacy of government organizations is grounded in the theory that they serve the interests of the people who reside in their jurisdiction. Even the most self-serving and unrepresentative of governments will usually take great pains to justify its actions as being devoted to the interests of its citizens—in contrast to those of its politicians and bureaucrats.[4]

Similarly, the social purpose of business is to serve the needs of its customers.[5] The legitimacy and credibility of the VO is based on its functioning as an instrument of voluntary citizen action in the service of a social need neglected by the prince and the merchant.[6] This quality of having a legitimacy based on service to third parties is the common characteristic of the organizations grouped in these three sectors. There are, however, important differences among them.

Differences
Each of the three types of third-party organizations is distinguished by the degree to which it acquires resources primarily through threat power (the power of the prince), economic power (the power of the merchant) or integrative power (the power of the citizen).[7] While many, perhaps most, organizations use some combination of all three types of power, there is a tendency to specialize. The dominant source

of power of each sector has an important bearing on its organizations' distinctive nature, competence and societal role. For example:

- **Government:** Government specializes in the use of threat power derived from its ability to exercise legitimate coercion. Alone among the institutional sectors government has a recognized right to command resources through taxation and even expropriation—backing demands with coercion where necessary.[8] Because of its distinctive capacity to apply legitimate threat or coercion, government has a natural advantage among the three sectors in maintaining public order and security. It is also able to capture and reallocate existing wealth for such purposes as national defense, social welfare and infrastructure in ways that are beyond the capacity of either businesses or VOs. In making such allocations it tends to be most responsive to the perceived needs of those who possess political power, irrespective of the lip service it may give to populist rhetoric.

  Because of government's ability to command resources, government organizations are more able than businesses to insulate themselves from market forces. Thus they tend to be less efficient than the business sector in the production of goods and services. Because governments must cater to diverse constituencies with a wide variety of established and often conflicting interests, government organizations tend to be less innovative than organizations of either the business or voluntary sectors.

- **Business:** Business organizations specialize in economic power. They acquire their resources through exchange: producing goods and services for sale in the market. The more successful business organizations are highly responsive to market forces that represent the expression of consumer interests and provide incentives for productive efficiency. Their distinctive role is to create new wealth through value-added activities. Because of their orientation to market forces, they are most responsive to the wants of those who have the money that buys market power—including governments that may offer to buy under contract. The business sector is society's primary source of essential economic entrepreneurship.

  Businesses may be either for-profit or nonprofit. There are many nonprofit organizations that measure their performance primarily in financial terms and that are as market-oriented as any business in their approach to determining what products and messages will sell to both public and private donors.[9] Nonprofit organizations that are in the business of selling their services to private contributors and government agencies to implement public purposes as defined by those contributors or agencies are part of a sub-class of business organization known as *public service contractors* (PSCs). The customer in this instance is the donor.[10]

- **Voluntary:** Voluntary organizations (VOs) specialize in integrative power. They depend primarily on appeals to shared values as the basis for mobilizing human and financial resources. Citizens contribute their time, money and other resources to a VO because they believe in what it is contributing to society. They share in a commitment to the organization's vision of a better world. This value commitment is the distinctive strength of the VO, making it relatively immune to the political agendas of government or to the economic forces of the market place.

A healthy voluntary sector is characterized by a substantial number and variety of independent VOs, representing an array of distinctive and often conflicting commitments. Their small size, independence and focused value commitments give them a capacity for social and institutional innovation seldom found in either government or business. They serve as forums for the definition, testing and propagation of ideas and values in ways that are difficult or impossible for the other two sectors. Their commitment to integrative values, over political or economic values, gives them a natural orientation to the perceived needs of politically and economically disenfranchised elements of the population that are not met through the normal political processes of government or the economic processes of the market.

Complementarity

All three types of third-party organization have distinctive competencies essential to a dynamic self-sustaining development process. Development depends on mobilizing the competencies of all three in complementary ways. Conversely, excessive emphasis on any one to the exclusion of the others will seriously limit authentic development, as has the excessive emphasis on government over the past several decades.

Government, however, has a predominant capability within society to command the collective reallocation of a nation's available financial and physical resources to address otherwise unmet needs, and to set and enforce rules that limit the behavior of its citizens in order to preserve social order. These essential, but partial, capabilities define government's distinctive development role.

Development also needs capacity in wealth creation and entrepreneurship, and substantial inputs of creativity, innovation, self-direction and voluntary action. While these are inputs that governments can sometimes stimulate successfully, they do not represent its comparative advantage. It has been demonstrated throughout human history that, compared to the market, coercion is a severely limited means for creating new wealth. For wealth creation the predominant capability belongs to business. Similarly, the voluntary sector has the advantage in mobilizing voluntary social energy in the service of institutional and values innovation.

What gives the voluntary sector its natural advantage in stimulating social innovation? Governments depend for their function on a broadly-based political consensus fashioned through negotiation and compromise among numerous power holders and interest groups. The constituencies of individual VOs are much smaller, being by nature built around a more coherent values consensus. Thus VOs are able to define positions more clearly, to press for innovative solutions, and to experiment in ways that governments find difficult. This ability gives VOs a distinctive role as catalysts of system change in defining, articulating and advocating positions that are not in the established political mainstream and therefore not supported by existing public policy.[11] This ability contrasts with the necessary and legitimate role of public agencies in supporting and promoting only those public policies that have obtained broad endorsement through the political process.

In striking contrast to the government sector, which tends to define its strength in terms of the size and financial resources of its constituent organizations, the strength of the voluntary sector is found in the diversity of its constituent organizations and their capacity for independent action. VOs can reach out and form alliances more easily than other types of organizations, though these alliances are often by nature less stable than those between governments and businesses. Using this ability, VOs achieve scale and leverage through joining in ever shifting coalitions—constantly defining, elaborating and redefining social issues, expanding political constituencies supporting their agendas of choice, promoting experimentation and advocating political action. The cacophony of competing voices within a mature voluntary sector can be deafening. But in this type of process, it is numbers and diversity that give the voluntary sector its distinctive capacity to catalyze social innovation.

VOs perform particularly important roles in a democracy. In political roles, they supplement political parties as varied and flexible mechanisms through which citizens define and articulate a broad range of interests, meet local needs, and make demands on government. In their educational roles they provide training grounds for democratic citizenship, develop the political skills of their members, recruit new political leaders, stimulate political participation, and educate the broader public on a wide variety of public interest issues. In their watchdog roles they serve, along with the press, as checks on "...the relentless tendency of the state to centralize its power and to evade civic accountability and control."[12]

The government, business and voluntary sectors represent three mutually dependent, yet in some ways opposing, forces within society. Government is society's instrument for maintaining stability and for reallocating resources from one group to another for public purposes. Business is its instrument for mobilizing private entrepreneurship to produce and distribute goods and services in response to market forces. Voluntary action is its instrument for insuring a constant process of self-assessment, experimentation and change in accordance with the evolving values of the people. The society that lacks any one of the three is a deeply troubled society.

The major international assistance agencies have rightfully demand-ed that assisted countries stop using the power of the state to con-strain the essential development function of the business sector. It is equally important that they demand an end to the use of state power to constrain the development and effective functioning of the volun-tary sector in its unique role as social and political catalyst.

PEOPLE'S ORGANIZATIONS: THE FOURTH SECTOR

POs—because of their nature as first-party organizations and their distinctive ability to integrate the use of threat, economic and integra-tive power—represent a fourth organizational sector. They embody within a single organization the roles of the prince, the merchant and the citizen.[13] To qualify as a true PO an organization must possess three defining characteristics.

■ It must be a *mutual benefit association* that bases its legitimacy on the ability to serve its members' interests. In this sense it is a *first-party* organization, the critical feature that distinguishes it from government, business or VOs as defined above.[14]
■ It must have a *democratic structure* that gives members ultimate authority over its leaders.
■ It must be *self-reliant* in that its continued existence does not de-pend on outside initiative or funding.

Self-reliant cooperatives, landless associations, irrigator associations, burial associations, credit clubs, labor unions, trade associations, and political interest groups may all be examples of POs—to the extent that they meet the above standards.

A Mix of Power Competence

A common feature of POs that makes it necessary to classify them as a fourth organizational sector is their unusual ability to make effective use of all three types of power: threat, economic and integrative. While this makes them unusually complex and difficult to manage organizations, it also gives them a distinctive strength when these three forms of power are skillfully united.

This quality is illustrated by the cooperative business organization. The true member-owned cooperative fits the definition of a PO well. It also combines important elements of each of the three types of third-party organizations: government, business and voluntary. Of course the primary function of a cooperative is economic. Yet it is much more than a business. In the cooperative's governmental role, the members establish rules that they mutually agree to observe on threat of fines, expulsion or other sanctions. At the same time the members are bound together by shared values that may lead them to direct their business to the cooperative even when they might find better prices elsewhere. Their officers may contribute substantial time to the organization without compensation. The cooperative itself may also engage in community service activities purely for the community good, or it may assist the formation of other cooperatives as a public service, purely for the good of the cooperatives' cause.

Organizational Conversions

POs are of special importance to the people-centered development vision. A central commitment of most VOs in development is to recreate the institutional structures of society from the bottom up, turning more and more political and economic functions over to POs. This process involves creating new POs, strengthening existing ones and converting third-party organizations to POs.

There are numerous situations in which an organization of one of the first three sectors may be converted to a PO. For example, one goal of some NGOs is the development of local governments as POs. This involves making them truly elected representatives of the people, building their revenue base on locally levied tax revenues and developing strong direct citizen participation in their affairs. In this process, the organizational instrument of the prince becomes transformed into an organizational instrument of the citizen. Similarly, when the employees of a publicly owned corporation buy its shares and become owners through an employee ownership stock plan the corporation may become a PO—if the employees truly have ownership control.

A VO may also be converted to a PO. This is done by bringing the staff of the VO within the governance structure of a PO. For example, a VO may assist in the creation of a PO. As the PO develops to the point of being ready to become wholly self-managing and self-financing, it may still need a secretariat able to provide specialized administrative and technical services. One option is for the staff of the VO, previously an independent organization, to reconstitute itself as a paid secretariat of the PO, accountable to and financed by the members of the PO.

One might well ask why a people-centered development vision should favor POs over third-party organizations, since by definition the latter are supposed to be serving external constituencies. The answer is that irrespective of whom an organization is supposed to serve, there is a considerable tendency for the people who actually exercise control over an organization to put its resources to their own service first. Thus the more that people can be placed in control of the organizations that presumably exist to serve them, the greater the probability that those organizations will fulfill their true function.[15]

Importance

POs serve many functions in people-centered development. As noted above, they are instruments for distributing power within society by strengthening the economic and political power of the previously marginalized. They are training grounds for democratic citizenship and the institutional building blocks of democratization. They create demands for greater responsiveness to grassroots concerns, providing the collective bargaining power that can enable landless people, small farmers and urban squatters to negotiate on more equal terms with the representatives of government bureaucracies or wealthy private patrons or corporations.

PUBLIC SERVICE CONTRACTORS

The organizations we refer to here as PSCs are nongovernmental and often nonprofit. For this reason they are often classified as NGOs. They are third-party organizations, in that their avowed purpose is to provide services to third parties. However, they are driven by market considerations more than by values and therefore are more like businesses than VOs. PSCs often look much like VOs. They may have the same type of legal registration. Their mission statements may emphasize social agendas.

Overall, it can be difficult to tell the difference between a VO and a PSC, except when the organization is faced with a choice between social mission and market share.[16] At this point the true VO will opt for the former, while the PSC will opt for the latter. In particular, the PSC will be less likely than the VO to engage in advocacy on controversial issues, particularly when such action might upset current or prospective donors or risk favorable relations with host governments.

Consider the questions that sometimes face international NGOs:

- **Agency A** raises substantial amounts of money for child sponsorship. It comes to realize that the success of its fund-raising approach is based on appeals that create an inaccurate impression among its contributors of the nature and causes of poverty. It also has reason to believe that the program itself undermines the authority of the parent in the home, creates jealousies in the community, contributes to a welfare rather than a self-help mentality, does not touch on the underlying causes of poverty, and is costly in terms of the staff effort required to administer it. How does it deal with these contradictions?[17]

- **Agency B** has been involved in a range of community development activities, with an emphasis on self-help and self-reliance. A donor announces that it has major new funding available for three-year projects to deliver immunization, ORT and growth monitoring services intended to reduce infant mortality. This agency has reason to believe it could be successful in winning a grant that would increase its existing funding base by 50 to 100 percent during the three-year project period. In making a decision, how much weight does it place on the fact that taking on the activity would be contrary to its existing practice of not directly delivering services to the villages it is encouraging to become self-reliant?

These are complex choices that offer no easy answers. An organization cannot necessarily be faulted for making either choice, but the more its choice is conditioned by donor priorities and the availability of funds, in contrast to its own social mission, the more appropriate it is to classify it as a PSC.

It may be expected that during the 1990s there will be a substantial increase in demand from donors for legitimate, qualified public service contractors to manage large-scale implementation of social projects that government has proven incapable of handling. NGOs with the capacity to perform in such roles should seriously examine the implications of pursuing these opportunities. While both PSC and VO may serve important social needs, the nature of their roles and their contributions to the larger social agenda are likely to differ in important instances. It is difficult to be both a PSC and a social catalyst.

When donors talk about engaging NGOs as implementors of donor projects, they are usually looking for a PSC rather than a VO. There are good reasons for donors to seek the services of PSCs. The more competitive feature substantial technical competence, well developed management systems, and concern with cost efficiency. Where these organizations receive adequate funding, they may operate on considerable scale.[18] In Northern countries PSCs have become an important and popular means of meeting a wide range of service needs ranging from garbage collection to health delivery and are becoming important players in Southern countries as well.

There are constant pressures on VOs to become PSCs. These include the following:

- The fatigue of constantly existing at the margin of financial survival and the attraction of donor funding;
- The strain faced by more activist VOs who must constantly fight established interests, values and practices;
- The difficulty of maintaining the value consensus and commitment of the VO as the organization grows;
- A sense of moral obligation to provide job security for paid staff;
- The belief that contracting will bring in greater funding and make it possible for the organization to do more of those things it feels are truly important; and
- The pressure from donors and others to "professionalize" the staff by adding specialists who may not internalize the values of the organization.

The clearer the VO is regarding its distinctive nature and mission, the more effectively it can resist the pressures to become a PSC, and the more likely it is to consciously invest in maintaining the values consensus that is the essence of the organization.

It is important for donors, as well, to be aware of the distinction between the VO and the PSC. Donors are commonly most comfortable working with the PSC and are inclined, often without being aware of what they are doing or its implications, to support a conversion of VOs into PSCs. They thus tend to draw VOs away from system catalyst roles and into maintenance roles.

The purpose here is not to establish the superiority of either the VO or the PSC, but rather to stress that they both have important, but different, roles. Each brings distinctive strengths and has advantages in performing in its own distinctive social functions. The ability of the business organization to serve the market, as defined by the economic forces of the marketplace, is as important to the society as is the ability of the VO to resist market forces in the service of an independent mission. Where a donor wants a specific job done, the PSC is more likely than the VO to respond reliably to the donor's definition of needed problem solutions, and it is likely to find it easier to rapidly expand or contract staff as commitments require.

Dealing with growth is more complex for a VO than for a business organization, in part because of the difficulty faced in managing the values consensus that defines its distinctive nature. That difficulty increases geometrically as the organization grows. Consequently, VOs may be inherently ill-suited to large-scale program operations.[19] Rapid expansion or contraction of staff can also place inordinately severe strains on VOs because the employment may be based as much on value commitments as on a financial contract.

VOs and PSCs both are likely to have increasingly important roles in the 1990s. But it is important for both donors and NGOs to understand the differences and their implications.

HYBRID ORGANIZATIONS

While the distinctions among the organizational sectors are fairly clear conceptually, the reality of modern organizational life involves a degree of complexity that nearly defies classification. In fact, many organizations span the sectoral boundaries described here. While we will not dwell on this point, the following examples bear mention.

The GONGO
Many governments are troubled by the fact that major international assistance agencies are allocating funds to NGOs that would otherwise fund government projects. As direct confrontation on this issue might be poor politics, some of the more sophisticated governments respond instead by forming their own NGOs—to which they then direct those donors that indicate an interest in funding NGOs.

Generally these government creations have the outward appearance of being either POs or VOs. However, unlike true POs or VOs, they are most commonly channels for government patronage and control. Their existence depends on state sponsorship and resources, their leaders are subject to government appointment or approval, and ultimately they are accountable to the state rather than to their members or an independent board. For this reason they are known as governmental nongovernmental organizations or GONGOs.[20]

The Values-oriented PSC
Public funding for NGOs tends to blur the distinction between the VO and the PSC, because of the tendency of public funders to treat VOs much as they treat contractors. This draws the VO away from its own agenda and toward the implementation of the funder's agenda.

Many NGOs are quite unclear in their own minds as to whether they are primarily values-driven VOs or primarily market-driven PSCs.[21] Few NGOs engaged in international assistance work think of themselves as PSCs, yet the question of whether their organizations are really market-driven or values-driven leaves many NGO professionals quite uneasy. There is usually an instant recognition by NGO staff of the fact that many NGOs are driven more by the market than by a clear sense of their own values defined mission, and some recognize this quality in their own organization.

Many PSCs are in fact a legitimate sort of hybrid, combining a strong market orientation with a social commitment and high ethical standards. It should be noted that some of the more socially progressive for-profit businesses may at times also straddle the line between the business and voluntary sectors.[22] Such hybrids may be an important trend of the future.

THE DECADE OF VOLUNTARISM

While recognizing the complementary roles of all sectors, the central agenda of the decade of the 1990s is one of innovation and change: in values, institutions and technologies. Such change is the realm of civil society, but most particularly of the voluntary sector—of the citizen volunteer and of the organizations that are formed and led by citizen volunteers.

Our existing institutions are creations of our past, and the rewards they offer to shape our behavior serve more to tie us to our past than to propel us to the transformation that is our hope for the future. They have reasonably adequate internal mechanisms to support evolutionary changes within a broad framework of established assumptions, but not changes of the type outlined in chapter 12 that depend on challenging and rejecting many of the assumptions that form the very foundations of these institutions.

If transformation is to come, it must come as a consequence of voluntary action, an act of human commitment to collective survival driven by a vision that transcends the behaviors conditioned by existing institutions and culture. We must look to peoples' movements as the key to transformational change in the current era.[23]

By the end of the 1980s, the forces of voluntary action were gaining new respect in both East and West. Voluntary action was at the heart of the reform movements that swept the socialist countries of Eastern Europe. In the West, U.S. President George Bush was talking about a thousand points of light, the work of countless citizen volunteers, as the potential hope for a solution to America's social ills.

Global Learning and the Centrality of Integrative Power

There is no blueprint for the transformation of institutions and values called for by the people-centered development vision. The transformation can be achieved only through a global-scale social learning process that engages the creative energies of billions of people in a process of creative experimentation toward the recreation of our institutions to serve the needs of life on a living spaceship.

The organizational forms most conducive to social learning processes are based more on networks built on shared interests and the application of integrative power than on hierarchies sustained by threat and economic power. Hierarchy is the organizational mode of control, stability and bureaucratization. It inhibits the flow of the information and the creative voluntary energies on which rapid social learning depends. Networking is the organizational mode of lateral communication, self-direction, rapid adaptation and social movements. It frees the flow of creative and voluntary energies and unlocks the barriers to change imposed by hierarchy.[24]

Integrative power is the primary cohesive force of the just, sustainable and inclusive society. It is the foundation of people power and the driving force of transformation. The voluntary sector is, by definition, comprised of those organizations and individuals who specialize in the use of integrative power in pursuit of a values-driven social mission.

The Individual as Volunteer

Citizen volunteers come from all walks of life, including those of the prince and the merchant. They are those countless individuals who bring the spirit and action of committed citizenship to their communities and to the organizations in which they work—irrespective of the sector to which that organization belongs.[25]

The citizen volunteer may be a member of a legislative body, an officer of a government agency, a corporation executive, a school teacher, a military officer or an independent entrepreneur. In such jobs the volunteer spirit is actualized when the individual acts as a responsible values-driven human being in ways that go beyond, or even conflict with, defined bureaucratic roles. To the extent such behavior is not rewarded, or even sanctioned, by the organization, it is appropriate to speak of it as an expression of voluntary citizen commitment.

We have long been taught that we must learn to separate the role of loyal soldier who serves the organization by following orders when acting as an organizational functionary, and the role of private citizen with personal values and commitments when outside the organization. When we enter into our jobs within a public or private bureaucracy, we are expected to be good technocrats and bureaucrats, leaving our personal values at home and adhering to the organization's norms.

According to Louis Gawthrop, one of the leading theorists of American public administration, the values that sustain this bureaucratic orientation and the related bifurcation of the person present us with a serious handicap in dealing with the needs of contemporary society. It keeps our institutions in a straight jacket that limits the individual, debilitates the institution, and locks society into its current self-destructive course. Gawthrop argues that the truly responsible administrator is not the good soldier who simply follows orders. To the contrary, the responsible administrator is a full person, a citizen who is open to the conflicts, processes and values that shape societal growth and change, who brings to bear critical consciousness, not simply bureaucratic procedures, in carrying out his or her organizational duties.[26]

Peter Drucker, perhaps the foremost management guru of the industrial age, has written about the extraordinary ability of some VOs to attract enormous time and commitment, entirely for free, from professionals who hold high paying, responsible positions in business and government. Drucker observes that these VOs have innovative socially important programs backed by sound management practices that attract volunteers by providing a source of challenge and satisfaction many fail to find in their regular highly paid jobs.[27]

It is essential to our future that these same volunteers turn a part of their voluntary commitment and energy back into transforming the organizations that pay their daily wage. They have demonstrated that they are motivated by challenge and satisfaction. What greater challenge and satisfaction than to reorient the mega-organizations of modern society to make them more responsive to changing global circumstances. Those who do commit themselves to this challenge are among the most valuable members of the emerging people's development movement.

The Global Citizen
The distinctive quality of the responsible citizen is found in a commitment to integrative values and to the active application of a critical consciousness: the ability to think independently, critically and constructively, to view problems within their long-term context, and to make judgments based on a commitment to longer-term societal interests that are distinct from and, in fact, may conflict with short-term personal interests.[28] It is this critical consciousness that allows the responsible citizen to transcend institutional and cultural conditioning for the larger good of the society.

The voluntary organization is the instrument through which citizen volunteers establish an identity and legal recognition for their collective endeavors. It provides their organizational support system and their means for aggregating resources for endeavors that require more than individual action. The voluntary organization, in its purist expression, exists to project the social commitment of its citizen volunteers.

There are many levels of citizenship, depending on the boundaries of the individual's identity. We may speak of the *community* citizen, the *national* citizen, and the *global* citizen. It is the global citizen on whom the transformation depends and upon whose commitment to global responsibility the foundations of a peoples' development movement of the 1990s must be built.

What of the prince and the merchant? The prince and the merchant often pursue grand visions. However, the visions they are inclined to pursue in their traditional roles are seldom of the sort appropriate to the needed transformation. The vision of the prince is a vision of personal and national power and glory achieved by extending the state's domain through application of coercive power. The vision of the merchant is one of riches achieved by reaping the rewards of the marketplace through the application of economic power. Both prince and merchant are by nature conservative, seeking to conserve and enhance the sources of their power.

Only rarely do the prince and the merchant emerge as champions of dramatic change in the institutions that confirm their power. When they do, they assume the mantel of responsible citizen. Indeed, it is only by embracing the role and the critical consciousness of the citizen, and giving integrative values precedence over the drive to consolidate coercive or economic power, that prince or merchant becomes a true leader: the *citizen-prince,* the *citizen-merchant.* In the role of citizen, the prince and the merchant are positioned to release the constraints that authoritarian structures place on people's initiatives and thereby enable the release of the voluntary energy of the society. The critical historical role that a skilled citizen-prince can play in the transformation of history has been demonstrated in Eastern Europe. This will be discussed further in chapter 11.

NOTES

1. This chapter draws extensively on L. David Brown and David C. Korten, "Understanding Voluntary Organizations: Guidelines for Donors," WPS 258 (Washington, DC: Country Economics Department, The World Bank, September 1989).

2. For a comprehensive review of the nongovernmental, nonprofit sector and its role in U.S. society, see Michael O'Neill, *The Third America: The Emergence of the Non-Profit Sector in the United States* (San Francisco: Jossey-Bass Publishers, 1989).

3. Marc Nerfin, "Neither Prince nor Merchant: Citizen — An Introduction to the Third

System," *IFDA Dossier 56,* November/December 1986, pp. 3–29. Nerfin refers to people's power as

> an immediate and autonomous power, sometimes patent, always latent.... Some among the people develop an awareness of this [power], associate and act with others and thus become citizens. Citizens and their associations, when they do not seek either governmental or economic power, constitute the third system. Contributing to make patent what is latent, the third system is one expression of the autonomous power of the people. (pp. 4–5.)

4. Yet even in the most democratic states, if you ask an ordinary citizen, "Are you a member of the government?" the answer will usually be, "No, I am neither an elected official nor a government employee."

5. It is true that business is supposed to produce profits for its shareholders. However, it is rare for business to advertise that its primary business is enriching its shareholders. One exception was the famous claim: "What's good for General Motors is good for America." That pompous error has for decades been used with derision by those who sought to call into question the legitimacy of corporate America. Business maintains its legitimacy by stressing the good it does for society through its production of desired goods and services for its customers. It is this service that legitimates both its existence and the profits it provides to owners.

6. Nothing would result in a faster loss of its tax-exempt status than the charge that the VO is devoting itself to the self-serving interests of its contributors and staff.

7. See Kenneth E. Boulding, *Three Faces of Power* (Newbury Park, CA: Sage Publications, Inc., 1989). The three types of power defined by Boulding correspond to what David Brown and I have identified as the three basic ways in which organizations acquire resources: coercion, exchange or shared values. Brown and Korten, "Understanding Voluntary Organizations," pp. 5–6. Boulding's concept of integrative power encompasses legitimacy, respect, affection, love, community and identity.

8. The fact that government has a distinctive ability to acquire resources through coercion does not imply that it may not also engage in exchange transactions or even in the mobilization of voluntary action. But governments generally have demonstrated more consistent performance in the former. Similarly, governments may engage in some exchange or fee for service activities and may at times solicit voluntary contributions. But no government comes to mind that depends for resources primarily on the collection of fees for specific services rendered or on voluntary contributions from generous, public spirited citizens. On the other hand, legitimate governments exercise this coercion with the consent of the governed. This is the critical distinction between government and the protection racket of a mafia-type criminal organization. The mafia boss also acquires resources through coercion, but not with the freely given consent of the "governed." Authoritarian regimes that rule by force, without the consent of the governed, are essentially outlaw organizations that have more in common with mafia-style gangs than with legitimate governments.

9. These organizations are commonly grouped, together with voluntary and people's organizations, under the broad category of NGOs or private voluntary organizations. Berg has questioned the "voluntary" nature of many U.S. private voluntary organizations on similar grounds, noting that many of them are more "like large consulting firms only with higher ethical sensitivity and lower overhead rates." Robert J. Berg, *Non-Governmental Organizations: New Force in Third World Development and Politics* (East Lansing: Center for Advanced Study of International Development, Michigan

State University, May 1987), p. 33. Jon Van Til, *Mapping the Third Sector: Voluntarism in a Changing Social Economy* (New York: The Foundation Center, 1988), pp. 62–66, & 175–76 also discusses this phenomenon.

10. This is not a contradiction. The essential difference between a for-profit and a nonprofit organization is a technical, legal difference in tax status. Some "nonprofits" are as concerned with "profitability" as any organization legally classified as for-profit. Indeed one body of management opinion argues that nonprofits should be more concerned with profitability. See, for example, Paul B. Firstenberg, *Managing for Profit in the Nonprofit World* (New York: The Foundation Center, 1986).

11. VOs also have difficulties defining consensus. In this respect they tend to be rather volatile. When consensus cannot be reached within a VO, it is common for one or more factions to spin off and form another organization within which they can establish a consensus on the particular position that unites them. This is part of the dynamism of the sector. When such a split is attempted within government it is known as a civil war. However, it happens in the voluntary sector with the speed and relative ease of an amoeba dividing itself into new cells.

12. Larry Diamond, "Beyond Authoritarianism and Totalitarianism: Strategies for Democratization," *The Washington Quarterly* (forthcoming). As used by Diamond the term "voluntary associations" encompasses both voluntary and people's organizations as defined later in this book.

13. Such integration is natural at the micro-level, as in the family or household unit. It is, in many respects, an organizational idea to be sought wherever possible. On the other hand, integration is most readily achieved at levels where direct participation in decision making is possible. The further the organizational structure removes decision making from the individual and thus precludes individual participation, the greater the necessary reliance on a separation of powers in a system of checks and balances. This is partly a function of the structure of the organization. However, it is also a function of size. The larger the organization, the more difficult it is to achieve integration without a great risk of power becoming misappropriated by one individual or group at the expense of others. This reality is why socialist states, which try to maintain this integration without creating structures that insure a system of checks and balances, tend so often to become totalitarian.

14. Note that individuals who staff a PO serve in that capacity either as volunteers or as paid staff. They may be members of the organization also, but in their roles as staff they are second-party participants. They have an important stake in the organization, but the purpose of the PO is to serve its members, not the staff.

15. This concept has its limits. Majority rule can also create its own tyranny and thereby limit innovation. Actually pluralism is the key. There should always be a place for the individual or a group of individuals to create an organization to compete in both the economic marketplace and the marketplace of ideas. This may mean forming a business that competes with member-operated cooperatives. If the individual entrepreneur can provide a better service it is a good competitive prod to the cooperative. Within the voluntary sector, a distinction must be made between conventional service delivery organizations and those VOs that are primarily in the business of promoting social innovations. The former should probably move toward greater accountability to the persons served. The latter may inherently require greater flexibility and freedom to innovate and maneuver than may be found in a membership organization. Pluralism

is basic to a dynamic democratic society and is therefore essential to people-centered development.

16. It has been suggested that child sponsorship agencies are in fact in the business of selling or contracting children to affluent Northern families interested in adding an inexpensive and undemanding exotic child to their family circle. Such a characterization is surely unfair in most instances. On the other hand, those agencies involved in child sponsorship are often among the most articulate in describing their marketing strategies and the most aggressive in pursuing "market share." A good many Northern agencies have found child sponsorship to be a sufficiently profitable product line that they are understandably reluctant to drop as a fund raising tool.

17. World Vision is one international NGO that has been taking a hard and forthright look at these issues. See the special issue of their publication, *Together,* April–June 1989 on "Child Sponsorship: Getting to the Real Questions."

18. An excellent example in the international assistance field would be CARE's Food for Work Program in Bangladesh under which CARE provides contract services to the local USAID mission involving the distribution of food resources and the supervision of the public works that are built by the recipients of the food. The program operates on a significant national scale, contributes to the building or rehabilitation of nearly 10,000 kilometers of roads per year, and is a model of efficient management.

19. My experience with development-oriented NGOs suggests this conclusion. However, experience cited by Drucker from organizations such as the International Red Cross and the Salvation Army suggest the contrary. Peter E. Drucker, "What Business Can Learn from Nonprofits," *Harvard Business Review,* Vol. 67, No. 4, July–August 1989, pp. 88–93.

20. I believe this term was first coined by the Indonesian NGO community to make clear that not all NGOs in Indonesia are really nongovernmental.

21. Some international NGOs, when confronted with the reality that their fund raising seems unabashedly market-oriented, claim that they operate with two faces. The fund-raising face may function as a public services contractor competing for market share, but the program side operates as a VO driven by a distinctive social vision and commitment. It is difficult for an organization so bifurcated to maintain either that it is a responsible public services contractor or that it is true to its values as a VO. Such bifurcation has little place within the emerging vision of international assistance as a process of mutual empowerment based on people-to-people action that will be discussed in later chapters. If the message that is communicated to donors does not fit with the reality of the field action, there can be no pretense that the donor constituency is being informed and engaged as a development partner. Furthermore, the ambiguity and confusion between the orientations of these two roles must surely undermine the capacity of the organization to do either well.

22. Many VOs and PSCs share another important point in common that sets both of them apart from conventional business organizations. In a conventional business the consumer of the good or service it produces also pays for that good or service. This provides the basis of market discipline, establishing a direct link between the real service the organization renders and its prosperity and survivability. Presumably the customer will only pay if he or she finds the product worth the price demanded. For nearly all VOs and many, if not most, PSCs this relationship does not hold. They commonly find themselves dealing with two different clientele. The one who puts up

the money is not the direct beneficiary of the product. Indeed it is not uncommon that there is no connection whatever between the funder and the presumed beneficiary. The person, organization or government agency that makes a contribution to an NGO to deliver relief services in Ethiopia may never have had any direct contact with Ethiopia or have any idea whether the product is ever delivered.

23. The basis for this argument is well established in contemporary history. As observed by James P. Grant:

...we have had a remarkable amount of structural change in the past 30 years. ...most of this change has been brought about by public pressure, with people ahead of governments.... The outstanding example is the national liberation movements, which have all been against governments. The civil rights movement in the US was another case of people being ahead of the government and forcing change. And the environmental and women's movements....

"Achieving Social and Economic Goals for the Year 2000," *Compass,* No. 8, January–April 1981, p. 1 as cited by Marc Nerfin, "Neither Prince nor Merchant," p. 26.

24. Jessica Lipnack and Jeffrey Stamps, *The Networking Book: People Connecting with People* (New York: Routledge and Kegan Paul, 1986).

25. For a review of the critical role of voluntary action in the development of the United States, see Susan J. Ellis and Katherine H. Noyes, *By the People: A History of Americans as Volunteers* (Philadelphia, PA: Energize, 1978).

26. Louis C. Gawthrop, *Public Sector Management, Systems, and Ethics* (Bloomington, Indiana: Indiana University Press, 1984), pp. 137–62.

27. Drucker, "What Business Can Learn from Nonprofits."

28. See Gawthrop, *Public Sector,* for discussion of the concept of critical consciousness in public sector management.

CHAPTER TEN

FROM RELIEF TO PEOPLE'S MOVEMENT

> If you see a baby drowning you jump in to save it;
> and if you see a second and a third, you do the
> same. Soon you are so busy saving drowning babies
> you never look up to see there is someone there
> throwing these babies in the river.
> —*Wayne Ellwood*[1]

The programs of those voluntary organizations (VOs) that style themselves as development organizations represent a variety of strategic
orientations. Some deliver relief and welfare services to alleviate
immediate suffering. Some engage in community development interventions to build capacity for self-help action. Others seek to change
specific institutions and policies in support of more just, sustainable
and inclusive development outcomes. Still others may facilitate broadly-based people's movements driven by a social vision. Each one aims
to right a perceived wrong, but implicitly works from different assumptions regarding the nature of the development problem.

This chapter looks at the strategic choices that face nongovernmental organizations (NGOs), and VOs in particular. It also examines
the forces that tend to move NGOs away from addressing problem
symptoms and toward an attack on fundamental causes.

IMPORTANCE OF A DEVELOPMENT THEORY

Tim Brodhead argues that it is impossible to be a true development
agency without a theory that directs action to the underlying causes of
underdevelopment.[2] In the absence of a theory, the aspiring development agency almost inevitably becomes instead merely an *assistance*
agency engaged in relieving the more visible symptoms of underdevelopment through relief and welfare measures. The assistance agency
that acts without a theory also runs considerable risk of inadvertently
strengthening the very forces responsible for the conditions of suffering and injustice that it seeks to alleviate through its aid.[3]

Without a theory, the assumptions underlying the organization's choice of intervention are never made explicit. Therefore they cannot be tested against experience, essentially eliminating the possibility of experience-based learning.

For the same reasons, an organization cannot have a meaningful development *strategy* without a development theory. To maintain that an organization has a strategy is to claim that there is a well thought out logic behind the way in which it positions its resources. This logic must make explicit the organization's assumptions regarding the forces that sustain the problem condition it is addressing, and the points of system vulnerability at which an intervention will create a new and more desirable equilibrium of forces.

Without a theory, the organization can only proceed to scatter its resources in response to immediately visible needs. This may have been an adequate approach to programming when VOs were mainly interested in providing humanitarian relief to the poor and suffering. However, the more immediate the need that the assisting agency is addressing, the less likely it is that the intervention is truly developmental, i.e., the less likely the intervention will remove the conditions that prevent the sufferer from meeting that need through his or her own efforts.

Our present concern is with the threefold global crisis of poverty, environmental destruction, and social disintegration. These are symptoms of the malfunction of our institutions and values. The more we focus our attention directly on the symptoms, rather than on transforming the institutions and values that cause them, the more certain we can be that the crisis will deepen for lack of appropriate action. Under the circumstances, the need for a theory of the causes of the breakdown is of more than academic relevance. It is a condition of survival.

THREE GENERATIONS
OF VOLUNTARY DEVELOPMENT ACTION

My own insights into the strategic choices facing NGOs began to take shape in 1985 while I was working with the U.S. Agency for International Development (AID). I had been looking primarily to the large donor agencies to serve as instruments for the institutional changes required to support the community-based management of development resources. In 1985 I came to the conclusion that the large donors were not the answer to this need. Their competence was in transferring large sums of money to central governments, not in facilitating complex social and institutional change processes.[4]

The need for more basic institutional change remained as real as ever. If the large donors could not address it, then who would? Colleagues in AID who were also struggling to answer this question suggested that we should look more closely at the potential of NGOs to assume this role. As I began to look at the experience of NGOs in development from the perspective of this need, I was struck that there seemed to be a definite pattern of evolution within the community away from more traditional relief activities and toward greater involvement in catalyzing larger institutional and policy changes.

This pattern seemed to reflect the learning that many of these organizations had derived from the critical self-examination of their own experience. The pattern seemed to involve three identifiable stages or generations of strategic orientation, each moving further away from alleviating symptoms toward attacking ever more fundamental causes. I decided to identify these stages as *generations*.

The resulting framework, which is presented in this chapter, attracted a considerable interest among those who felt it was confirmed by their own experience. Many said they found it a useful tool for considering the strategic choices facing their organizations.[5]

Since the framework was first formulated, many NGO leaders have been contributing ideas toward its further evolution, including a suggestion that a fourth generation strategy must be added to the scheme to make it complete. Consequently this chapter defines the fourth generation strategy, in addition to updating established statements on the first three generations. See Table 10–1 for a comparative summary of the four generations.

Generation One: Relief and Welfare

First generation strategies involve the NGO in the direct delivery of services to meet an immediate deficiency or shortage experienced by the beneficiary population, such as needs for food, health care or shelter. During an emergency such as a flood, an earthquake or a war this may be correctly characterized as humanitarian assistance, to distinguish it from development assistance—which it is not. The assisting NGO relates directly to the individual or the family and the benefits delivered depend entirely on the funds, staff and administrative capability of the NGO.

First generation strategies grow out of a long history of international voluntary action aimed at assisting the victims of wars and natural disasters, and providing welfare services to the poor. Religious groups commonly have been at the forefront of these efforts.

In 1647, Irish Protestants sent food to North America to aid settlers who were victims of wars with the Indians. Throughout much of the 17th and 18th centuries, private British charities provided assistance to America to support missionaries and schools for Indians, Negroes and poor whites, as well as colleges and learned societies for the affluent.[6]

In 1793, private groups in the United States provided voluntary assistance to refugees who fled revolutionary turmoil in Santo Domingo. In the 1800s, several international relief and missionary societies were established in Europe and America, including the Red Cross.

World War I saw a substantial increase in private international
initiatives, with the value of food supplies contributed to Europe by
U.S. charities during World War I reaching $250 million a year.[7] The
oldest of the British international assistance charities, Save the Children Fund, was founded in 1919.[8]

Many of the contemporary international NGOs were originally
established to help victims of World War II in Europe. These include
Catholic Relief Services, CARE, OXFAM UK and the Danish Association for International Co-operation.[9] As recovery progressed in Europe, these organizations turned their attention to Southern countries.
Particular attention was given to assisting refugees from political
conflicts in China, India, Korea and the Middle East.[10]

The history of the development of NGOs indigenous to Southern
countries followed patterns similar to those of NGO assistance from
the North. For example, charitable activities in the South were often
church- or mission-related and commonly depended on funds and
commodities from the North. Until the mid-1960s, NGO activities in
Latin America, especially those connected with the Catholic Church,
were substantially oriented to charitable welfare actions.[11]

Churches and missionary societies were important in Africa
throughout the colonial era, as colonial governments left the provision
of basic education and health care largely to church-related organizations.[12] Efforts to respond to the needs of victims of war and national
disaster account in large measure for the flowering of indigenous
NGO activity in Bangladesh.

NGOs that have undertaken first generation strategies in the name
of development have implicitly assumed, perhaps as a result of their
experience with short-term emergency relief efforts, that with a little
short-term assistance the people assisted would be able to get themselves back on their feet. Or perhaps it was an assumption that the
work being done by government and the large donor agencies to
stimulate the economy would provide the assisted populations with
new opportunities. At least in the early stages of such efforts, NGOs
rarely theorize about why the assisted people have unmet needs. If
people are hungry they obviously lack food and should be fed. So the
NGO attempts to feed them. Theories of development seem far removed from the reality.

In the first generation strategy the NGO responds to an immediate
and visible need. The NGO is the doer, while the beneficiary is passive. The management capability required by the NGO is primarily a
capability in logistics management. Efforts to provide education on
development issues to the general public from whom private donations
are solicited are generally synonymous with fund raising appeals. They
focus on dramatized presentations of starving children appealing from
magazines and TV screens with sad and longing eyes for a kind person
to help them by sending money to the sponsoring NGO.

Table 10-1: Strategies of Development-Oriented NGOs: Four Generations

	GENERATION			
	FIRST *Relief and Welfare*	**SECOND** *Community Development*	**THIRD** *Sustainable Systems Development*	**FOURTH** *People's Movements*
Problem Definition	Shortage	Local Inertia	Institutional and Policy Constraints	Inadequate Mobilizing Vision
Time Frame	Immediate	Project Life	Ten to Twenty Years	Indefinite Future
Scope	Individual or Family	Neighborhood or Village	Region or Nation	National or Global
Chief Actors	NGO	NGO plus Community	All Relevant Public and Private Institutions	Loosely Defined Networks of People & Organizations
NGO Role	Doer	Mobilizer	Catalyst	Activist/Educator
Management Orientation	Logistics Management	Project Management	Strategic Management	Coalescing and Energizing Self-Managing Networks
Development Education	Starving Children	Community Self-Help	Constraining Policies and Institutions	Spaceship Earth

Relief efforts remain an essential and appropriate response to emergency situations that demand immediate and effective humanitarian action. A substantial portion of NGO effort continues to be directed to this need. However, relief and welfare assistance offer little more than a temporary alleviation of the symptoms of underdevelopment and should not be confused with development assistance.[13] It was this realization that led many NGOs created to serve as relief organizations to redirect their attention to what are described below as second generation strategies.

Generation Two: Small-scale, Self-reliant Local Development

Second generation strategies focus the energies of the NGO on developing the capacities of the people to better meet their own needs through self-reliant local action. Because of their attention to sustainability, true second generation strategies are developmental in concept, and are often referred to as *community development* strategies. Commonly the activities involve such village level self-help actions as the development of health committees to carry out preventive health measures, introduction of improved agricultural practices, formation of community councils, digging wells, building feeder roads, etc. It is the stress on local self-reliance, with the intent that benefits will be sustained by community self-help action beyond the period of NGO assistance, that distinguishes first from second generation strategies.[14] Often the intervention is described as an attempt to "empower" the village people.

Some of the NGOs engaged in second generation strategies have done so since their founding. However, a more common pattern has been for NGOs working with the poor in Southern countries to begin with first generation strategies. Gradually their experience leads them to question the validity of relief and welfare activities. Yes, they are meeting immediate needs, but the needs substantially exceed their capacities. Furthermore, charity creates dependence, which for many NGOs is contrary to their own values.[15]

Thus many NGOs have come to see the need for a more developmental approach. The welfare versus development debate became quite active in the late 1970s. John Sommer's book *Beyond Charity* substantially influenced the thinking of many NGOs.[16] Community development seemed to provide them with a response to a need that was developmental and yet fit with their small size and limited financial and technical capabilities. Increasingly dependent on government financing from agencies that had come to favor project funding, NGOs began to package their activities as village development projects, fitting the time frame of their efforts to the project funding cycles of their donors.[17]

Second generation strategies focus on groups, usually either a village or some sub-group within it, such as women, or landless agricultural workers. The work assumes a partnership between the NGO and the community, with the latter expected to contribute to both decision making and implementation.

Second generation strategies involve an implicit theory of village development that assumes local inertia is the heart of the problem. According to this theory the potential for self-advancement rests within the village community, but remains dormant because of the inertia of tradition, isolation and a lack of education and proper health care. The theory suggests that this inertia can be broken through the intervention of an outside change agent who helps the community realize its potentials through education, organization, consciousness raising, small loans and the introduction of simple new technologies.

The implementation of second generation strategies calls on the NGO to be more a mobilizer than an actual doer. Since the interventions are commonly funded in part by public donors who like to package their money as projects, the NGO comes under pressure to develop a capacity in project management.

Since most international NGOs depend on a combination of public and private funding, they also face a need to communicate with private contributors in the North. Efforts to educate the general public on development issues remain closely tied with private fund raising appeals. For many Northern NGOs the focus has remained on starving children on the theory that they have more appeal to potential contributors than stories of self-help village action.[18] Others have felt that their public messages must be consistent with their actions irrespective of the impact on fund raising. Thus their messages are likely to tell of how with a little help from outsiders the poor can get themselves on their feet and meet their own needs through self-help action.

Second generation strategies differ in the extent to which they focus on human resource development or empowerment as the central issue. While second generation strategies almost universally involve a substantial focus on education, the human resource development tradition assumes that the problem lies exclusively in the individuals' lack of skills and physical strength. Develop the economic resource value of the person, and the economic system will provide the needed opportunities for gainful employment. The rallying cry of the human resource development group has been the ancient oriental proverb: "Give a man a fish, and you feed him for a day; teach him to fish, and you feed him for a lifetime."[19]

Unfortunately, in practice, many second generation program interventions are little more than handouts in a more sophisticated guise. Too many of these interventions give little more than lip service to self-reliance and, in fact, build long-term dependence on the assisting NGO.

More militant NGOs view the problem in somewhat more complex terms, usually combining education with organizing techniques oriented to political confrontation of local power elites, as inspired by the teachings of Saul Alinsky. They assume that the problem results from a combination of a lack of development of the individual *and* patterns of exploitative relationships at the local level. These NGOs are prone to point out that villagers who live near the water already know a great deal more about fishing than do the city kids that NGOs send out as community organizers. The more substantial need is to insure the access of the poor to the fishing grounds and markets that local elites control.

Second generation strategies are developmental in concept, but it has become increasingly evident that their underlying assumptions are often overly simplistic—even those of groups that attempt to confront local power relationships. Even NGOs engaged in more empower-ment-oriented local organizing that acknowledges the political dimen-sion of poverty, commonly assume—at least by implication—that village organizations of the poor, by their own initiative, can mobilize suffi-cient political resources to change the relevant power structures. It has become evident to many such NGOs that local power structures are maintained by protective national and international systems against which even the strongest village organizations are relatively powerless. The empowerment-oriented organizing efforts of most NGOs are too limited and fragmented to make any consequential or lasting impact on these larger structures.

Generation Three: Sustainable Systems Development

Third generation strategies look beyond the individual community and seek changes in specific policies and institutions at local, national and global levels. The decision to pursue a third generation strategy often grows out of frustration with the limitations of second generation strategies based on a growing realization that: 1) the benefits generat-ed by its village interventions depend on a continued NGO presence and the availability of donor subsidies; and 2) acting on its own, the NGO can never hope to benefit more than a few favored localities. Self-reliant village development initiatives are likely to be sustained only so long as they are linked into a supportive national development system. Since existing systems tend to be hostile to, rather than sup-portive of, such initiative, it is essential that such systems be changed. Because NGOs are often the only consistent advocates of such change, they must accept a substantial leadership role in catalyzing them.

Third generation strategies may involve the NGO in working with major national agencies to help them reorient their policies and work modes in ways that strengthen broadly-based local control over re-sources. These strategies may also involve the creation of new insti-tutions of significant size to provide essential local services on a sus-tained, self-financing basis. Examples include the following.

■ In India, Samakhya and the Multi-Coops Association carried out an extensive state and national campaign involving use of the courts, media, lobbying and public demonstrations to force the Government of Andhra Pradesh State to restore free elections to cooperatives throughout the state.

■ In Indonesia the Institute for Social and Economic Research, Education & Information (LP3ES) has assisted the Ministry of Public Works in the development and implementation of a policy to convert government managed irrigation systems into independent, farmer owned and operated systems.

■ In Bangladesh, the Bangladesh Rural Advancement Committee is establishing a bank as a self-managing, self-financing institution to provide credit on a sustained basis to landless associations.[20]

■ In Sri Lanka, Helen Keller International assisted the government in introducing to the national public health system a primary eye care and cataract surgery program with a rural outreach capability.

■ In the Philippines the Ford Foundation assisted the National Irrigation Agency in developing a national capacity to strengthen and support local irrigator groups.[21]

■ In Bangladesh, Savar Gonoshasthaya Kendra established its own drug company to break the price fixing cartels maintained by the pharmaceutical industry through undercutting their prices in the market. It also provided leadership in helping government write a new policy for pharmaceuticals that eliminated useless and harmful drugs from the market and focused production on essential drug products.[22]

Third generation strategies focus on creating a policy and institutional setting that facilitates, rather than constraining, just, sustainable and inclusive local development action. The underlying theory of third generation strategies is grounded in an assumption that local inertia is sustained by structures that centralize control of resources, keep essential services from reaching the poor, and maintain systems of corruption and exploitation. Creating the necessary changes often depends on working simultaneously to build the capacity of the people to make demands on the system and working to build alliances with enlightened power holders in support of action that makes the system more responsive to the people. The third generation strategies of Southern NGOs often benefit from financial and technical assistance, and political pressures provided by partner NGOs from the North.

The more fully the NGO embraces third generation program strategies, the more it finds itself working in a catalytic, foundation-like role, rather as an operational service provider. It may find that it intervenes in complex national-scale institutional systems comprised of many different organizations from both the public and private sectors.[23] It will need to develop in-depth knowledge of the system. It will also need to develop relations with the system's key players and the necessary technical competence to establish its credibility with them. It must learn to manage strategically, positioning and repositioning its own limited resources where they have the best prospect of shifting system dynamics in the desired direction. If the NGO engages in development education appropriate to its strategy, it will seek to build public awareness of the need and potential for the transformation of critical institutions.

Which NGOs?
The generational framework deals with NGOs in the aggregate, without addressing the question of whether it applies equally to each of the four different NGO types identified in chapter 9. The generational framework does not apply equally to all types of NGOs. Its underlying logic assumes that the NGO will be led by the lessons of its own experience to focus its resources increasingly on more fundamental determinants of the problem it seeks to address. The extent to which this movement does occur is likely to depend on the extent to which the NGO:

- Is clearly focused on trying to make a sustainable difference in the lives of the people it is assisting;
- Has attempted to make explicit the theory underlying its intervention aimed at improving their lives; and
- Engages in the regular and critical assessment of its own performance.

These are essentially the preconditions for social learning: a focus on a problem or goal, an intervention theory, and a critical ongoing self-assessment.

It cannot be assumed that an individual VO or people's organization (PO) will have an explicit theory of action that guides its interventions toward underlying problem causes. However, VOs and POs are more likely to have such a theory than either the public service contractor (PSC) or the governmental nongovernmental organization (GONGO)—because they have a need for it. In any event, they are much more likely to be focused on the problems experienced by the people—the VO because of its value commitment to the people and their cause, and the PO because the people themselves are making the decisions. This is likely to lead them into an assessment of problem causes.

The PSC and the GONGO are less likely to perceive such a need. For the PSC it is up to the donor to define the need. The stronger its market orientation, the more it will be focused on what is popular with donors and the less need it will have for its own theory of poverty. Its strategic orientation will change with changes in donor preferences. The GONGO, being a creature of government, will likely define the problem in whatever terms the government uses. Its strategic orientation will therefore change in response to changes in government policy.

As a general rule, donors and governments are more interested in supporting NGOs in relief and welfare interventions to relieve immediate suffering than in efforts aimed at fundamental structural change. Thus it is rare to find either the PSC or the GONGO moving beyond the relatively noncontroversial human resource development type of second generation strategy. Both will tend to shy away from controversy and to concentrate on activities that avoid challenges to existing structures.

VOs do not necessarily start out with a commitment to structural change. Nor do they necessarily seek controversy. However, if their value commitment is genuine, they will feel more keenly the contradictions that they encounter between their commitment and the reality of what their experience tells them to be true. The more the VO is focused on the assisted people and their problems, rather than on the preferences of donors, the more likely it will be in the first instance to move toward politically oriented empowerment interventions and to seek to build community capacity to stand up against local injustice. This same commitment will tend to lead it increasingly toward third generation—and ultimately to fourth generation—strategies.

THE FOURTH GENERATION

Third generation strategies seek changes in specific policies and institutions. The achievement of just, sustainable, and inclusive development outcomes depends on accomplishing such changes across nearly every sector in every nation. It is an essential, but tedious process that must be replicated hundreds of thousands, even millions, of times to achieve the needed transformation of the institutions of global society. Furthermore, each individual step toward transforming a policy or institution is subject to reversal by the still larger forces generated by backward looking national and international institutions and an invalid development vision.

The critical deficiency of the third generation strategy parallels at the macro-level the deficiency that the second generation strategy displays at a more micro-level. The second generation strategy's critical flaw is that it requires countless replications in millions of communities, all within a basically hostile political and institutional context. It is much the same with third generation strategies, only at a more macro-level.

Thus it is not surprising that almost since the first workshop in which I articulated the concept of the third generation strategy, thoughtful colleagues have suggested that something is missing. There had to be a further step, a fourth generation.

Isagani R. Serrano of the Philippine Rural Reconstruction Movement (PRRM) is among those who have struggled with this issue. Arguing that the unequal distribution of power and wealth at national and international levels carries major responsibility for the multiple crises gripping Southern countries, he wrote a paper suggesting that third generation strategies are only a partial answer.

Where do NGOs go from here? (from the third generation)....

Development theorists and practitioners must think beyond "repair work" addressed to the components of interdependent systems although they can build up from there. Their efforts at re-examination should help enable the whole international NGO community to effectively promote what the watershed NGO conference in London called the Alternative Development Paradigm.[24]

Serrano suggests that this should be the central concern of a fourth generation NGO development strategy.[25]

Social Movements and Global Change

There is a need to energize decentralized action toward a people-centered development vision on a much broader scale than is possible with the more focused interventions of either second or third generation strategies. This is the challenge that currently faces those VOs that are committed to achieving people-centered development on a global scale. They must become facilitators of a global people's development movement.

Within the past three decades people's movements have reshaped thought and action on the environment, human rights, women, peace and population. Though these are all wars yet to be won, the progress—from an historical perspective—has been rapid and pervasive. These experiences demonstrate the power of people's movements in driving social change.

Social movements have a special quality. They are driven not by budgets or organizational structures, but rather by ideas, by a vision of a better world. They move on social energy more than on money. The vision mobilizes independent action by countless individuals and organizations across national boundaries, all supporting a shared ideal. Participants in successful movements collaborate in continuously shifting networks and coalitions.[26] They may quarrel over ideological issues and tactics. But where they have been successful, their efforts have generated a reinforcing synergy.

The power of people's movements has largely been ignored in the field of development. Attention has been focused on money rather than social energy as the engine of development. The irony is that the surest way to kill a movement is to smother it with money.

A Legendary Development Movement

One of the most durable of development legends concerns an intervention built on the energy of a people's movement. This is the legend of Dr. Y. C. James Yen and the literacy movement he energized in China in the 1920s and 1930s. It involved some hundred thousand volunteers teaching an estimated five million illiterate workers. The effort engaged scholars, statesmen, shopkeepers, military officers, students and others in a national commitment to eradicate illiteracy. The effort started with an idea—that every person has a right and an obligation to be literate, an appropriate technology, a simplified set of a thousand basic Chinese characters that covered the minimum vocabulary required by a literate person, and a budget of $1,000.

The Mass Education Movement was launched with massive parades and large banners bearing slogans such as "An Illiterate Man is a Blind Man." Classes were arranged wherever space could be found: in Buddhist temples, Christian churches, private residences, police stations, storefronts and wherever else space was available. Groups such as the YMCA were mobilized to recruit students, and the teachers received only a small transportation allowance. There were songs and chants. A general steering committee of some seventy leading businessmen, college presidents, editors, officials and labor leaders was formed. Mass meetings of shopkeepers, teachers and students were held. Funds came entirely from voluntary contributions.

Copies of the texts were used and reused. Unauthorized printings appeared in provinces and towns throughout the country, and not even James Yen knew how many classes were in fact being taught or how many schools were operating. In a more conventional project or program these conditions would have been a sign of poor management. In a true movement it is a sign of the vitality of an idea with the power to spread by its own momentum, wholly beyond any central control or monitoring.[27]

Population as a People's Movement

One of the most dramatic global policy reversals in human history was achieved by a small group of dedicated individuals who mobilized a world population movement under the banner of the International Planned Parenthood Federation (IPPF). IPPF was founded in 1952 by eight national family planning associations (FPAs) to stimulate development of FPAs in other countries and to promote family planning policies and programs worldwide.

At its inception IPPF functioned as a dynamic network of dedicated volunteers who traveled around the world, often at their own expense or with funds raised from friends, to help other committed individuals form local FPAs. This network included most of the early leaders of the global family planning movement. A tiny staff receiving token remuneration worked round the clock out of a small office in London to provide support.

The network offered mutual inspiration, political support, and exchange of experience and technology. Many FPAs engaged in family planning service delivery, but often primarily as a tactical measure aimed at influencing governments to take up the service delivery task by demonstrating its technical and political feasibility. The more dynamic FPAs defined their roles as catalysts and policy advocates. The effort was a major contributor to one of human history's most extraordinary public policy reversals, as family planning was moved from a forbidden topic to a global public policy priority.[28]

To Kill a Movement
True movements are the purest of voluntary phenomena. Perhaps the surest way to kill them is push them toward bureaucratization by drowning them in money. The problem is demonstrated by both the Chinese Mass Education Movement and the IPPF experiences.

James Yen's movement attracted increasing public financial support, culminating in the creation of the Chinese-American Joint Commission on Rural Reconstruction (JCRR). The JCRR had a budget of US$27.5 million, funded by the American and Chinese governments for projects in agriculture, irrigation, cooperative organization, public health, literacy and land-tenure reform.

As a result of this good fortune, the qualities of a truly voluntary movement gave way to the features of a publicly funded and centrally administered program with a large budget, formalized organization, accounting systems and a professional staff. The final implications will never be known because only about $4 million of the new JCRR's budget had been spent when the Communists took over Mainland China.[29]

In 1966 Sweden made the first government grant to IPPF, quickly followed by others, including AID—which rapidly assumed a dominant funding role.[30] The budget climbed from $11,600 in 1953/54 to $48 million in 1978, with 353 persons on the central IPPF payroll. By 1987 the budget had risen to over $55 million, almost entirely from government sources. As public donor funding grew, so too did the administrative and auditing requirements. More and more energy was directed to bureaucratic procedures.

As funding increased, paid staff took over functions from the volunteers. Given the increasing complexity of the organization and the need for advanced technical capabilities some shift from volunteers to paid staff was probably inevitable. But attention increasingly focused on the management of financial allocations to the affiliates, with less emphasis on advocacy and pioneering innovation. The pioneers died or drifted away. The dynamism was gone. IPPF had become an expensive and lethargic international bureaucracy.

A few affiliates have retained their activist, catalytic roles. But most FPAs have become dependent on paid staff engaged primarily in the routine delivery of IPPF funded services. With IPPF effectively neutralized as catalyst and advocate at the international level global priorities have since shifted dramatically away from family planning, even as the population problem becomes more ominous by the day.[31]

There is no necessary reason that success should lead a movement to lose its vitality. I cite these examples as a cautionary note both to social activists, and to the donors who share their cause.

Facilitating People's Movements

Fourth generation strategies look beyond focused initiatives aimed at changing specific policies and institutional sub-systems. Their goal is to energize a critical mass of independent, decentralized initiative in support of a social vision. Here we speak purely of VOs and POs. The entry of PSCs and GONGOs into a people's movement is a strong indication that the movement has spent its force and become an establishment institution concerned with the protection of its own interests.

Active social movements may be supported by individual VOs with paid staff, but the role of such personnel is to support the volunteers who provide the real energy in any social movement. The staff must share the spirit and commitment of the volunteers, even though they may depend on the organization for their livelihood.[32]

The theory of action that informs the fourth generation strategy points to an inadequate mobilizing vision as the root cause of our development failure. It calls for imbuing the public consciousness with an alternative vision adequate to mobilize voluntary action on a national or global scale. The focus is on the communication of ideas and information through the mass media, newsletters, recorded media, school curricula, major media events, study groups and social networks of all types to energize voluntary action by people both within and outside their formal organizations in support of social transformation.

The VO with a fourth generation strategy is essentially a service organization to the people's movement it supports. While it must be a master at the strategic positioning of its resources, the management skills required go well beyond those normally associated with strategic management. The job of the fourth generation VO is to coalesce and energize self-managing networks over which it has no control whatever. This must be achieved primarily through the power of ideas, values and communication links. To the extent the VO is truly successful in these efforts, most of the resulting action will be beyond its range of vision. Thus it must learn to deal with partial data, while becoming highly sophisticated in gathering appropriate types of feedback where they are available.

VOs pursuing fourth generation strategies require a strong sense of the nature of self-directing and motivating volunteer activated social systems: What makes them coalesce? What activates them? How can integrative power be used to sustain and focus their commitment? These VOs involve themselves in the broader movement of which they are a part as social and political activists. Their effectiveness depends on working from a well articulated philosophy or vision.

It is difficult to identify VOs in the development field that have specific experience with fourth generation strategies. Development has generally not been viewed as a movement. VOs with this orientation are more commonly found working in support of women's, peace, human rights, consumer affairs or environmental movements. It is, however, becoming clear that there is a need to mobilize a people's movement around a people-centered development vision, and there is evidence that such a movement is emerging.

Nurturing this movement will call for a new kind of voluntary action by a type of development-oriented VO that bears little resemblance to the more conventional NGOs that have traditionally concerned themselves with the problems of the poor.[33] The VOs that accept this challenge will be well advised to move rapidly in building alliances with other people's movements that deal with related elements of the global crisis.

NOTES

1. From *Generating Power: A Guide to Consumer Organizing* (Penang, Malaysia: International Organization of Consumers Unions, 1984), p. 38.

2. Tim Brodhead is President of the Canadian Council for International Cooperation, the Canadian consortium of development NGOs. This observation was made at a seminar for NGO leaders held in Boston by the Institute for Development Research. This same point is underlined by Robert L. Ayers, *Banking on the Poor* (Cambridge, MA: The MIT Press, 1983), p. 75.

3. Take, for example, the case of the organization that is concerned with the deplorable conditions of street children. Seeing that the children are often forced onto the street to earn income for their families, the most obvious response is to provide them with more pleasant and remunerative ways of earning a living. This, of course, makes it more attractive for desperately poor families to send their children onto the street to contribute to the family's income rather than sending them to school. It may also result in an increase in the numbers of street children. If the opportunities are adequate, the family may even decide to have more children in order to increase its income earning potential. These problems are avoided if the focus is on helping the adult members of the household increase their income so they can provide adequate support for their children.

4. For further discussion, see the report on a seminar with David Korten titled "Practical Problems of Project Design and Implementation" in *Institutional Development: Improving Management in Developing Countries*, A Report on a Series of Seminars Conducted by the American Consortium for International Public Administration (ACIPA) under a Grant from the United States Agency for International Development, 1986, pp. 7–17, available from ACIPA, 1120 G Street N.W., Suite 225, Washington, D.C. 20005; and David C. Korten, "Third Generation NGO Strategies: A Key to People-Centered Development," *World Development,* Vol. 15, Supplement, Autumn 1987, pp. 153–4.

5. The diversity of NGO experience seems to defy precise classification. The scheme gained substantial currency, however, even before it was formally published. It was evident that a consequential number of people related to the world of NGOs found it meaningful and useful. The first statement of this framework was in a brief informal paper I prepared for PACT on August 1, 1985, titled "Private Voluntary Development: Toward the Third Generation." Several subsequent versions of the paper were distributed informally through various NGO networks, using what I call the Xerox Press. The first "published" version was a working paper titled, "Micro-Policy Reform: The

Role of Private Voluntary Development Agencies," released by the National Association of Schools of Public Affairs and Administration on January 14, 1986. An abstracted version titled "Private Aid Enters Third Phase," was published in *Development Forum*, in June 1986. The full paper, "Micro-Policy Reform: The Role of Private Voluntary Agencies" was published as a chapter in David C. Korten, *Community Management: Asian Experience and Perspectives* (West Hartford: Kumarian Press, 1986), pp. 309–18. By the time an expanded and updated version was published as "Third Generation NGO Strategies: A Key to People-centered Development," *World Development*, Vol. 15, Supplement, 1987, pp. 145–59, the "three generations" terminology had come into common usage by NGOs in many parts of the world. An NGO in Thailand even named itself Third.

Some critics have noted, quite correctly in my view, that few NGOs fit purely in one generation or another. Many have a variety of programs, some of which may be first generation, others second generation, and still others third generation. It is generally more useful to classify an individual program strategy according to the scheme than to attempt to classify an entire NGO as having a generation specific strategy.

Another criticism has been of the use of the term "generation" on the grounds that it implies that some strategic orientations are better or more advanced than others. Critics argue that there is a need for all three types of program, and that a scheme for classifying alternative program strategies should not carry an implicit value judgment. I have responded by stressing that each generation meets an important need and has its place within the NGO family, much as the generations in a human family. I have not, however, given up using the generational terminology. In truth I *am* partial. I do believe that the future of development, perhaps of global society, depends on many more VOs engaging boldly and effectively in the third and fourth generation type strategies discussed in this chapter than is currently the case. The reasons will be further elaborated in subsequent chapters.

6. John G. Sommer, *Beyond Charity: U.S. Voluntary Aid for a Changing Third World* (Washington, DC: Overseas Development Council, 1977), p. 17.

7. *Ibid.*, pp. 17–18.

8. OECD, *Voluntary Aid for Development: The Role of Non-Governmental Organizations* (Paris: OECD, 1988), p. 18.

9. *Ibid.*, pp. 18–19.

10. *Ibid.*

11. Leilah Landim, "Non-Governmental Organizations in Latin America," *World Development*, Vol. 15, Supplement, Autumn 1987, pp. 31–2.

12. Michael Bratton, "The Politics of Government — N.G.O. Relations in Africa," *World Development*, Vol. 17, No. 4, April 1988, pp. 569–87.

13. This realization not withstanding, Brian H. Smith, "U.S. and Canadian PVOs as Transnational Development Institutions," in Robert F. Gorman (ed.), *Private Voluntary Organizations as Agents of Development* (Boulder: Westview Press, 1984), pp. 118–22, observes that the bulk of the resources of U.S. PVOs is still devoted to delivery of food, clothing and medicine to alleviate immediate suffering.

14. In India, much of the NGO movement was born out of the call by Mahatma

Gandhi in the 1920s and 1930s to young Indian men and women to work among the rural poor and scheduled castes (untouchables and tribals). These efforts emphasized constructive self-help action. Rajesh Tandon, "The State and Voluntary Agencies in Asia," in Richard Holloway (ed.), *Doing Development: Government, NGOs and the Rural Poor in Asia* (London: Earthscan Publications, Ltd., 1989), pp. 12–29.

15. For a case study of how one NGO, the Bangladesh Rural Advancement Committee (BRAC), moved from a first to a second generation strategy through its own learning process see David C. Korten, "Community Organization and Rural Development: A Learning Process Approach," *Public Administration Review*, Vol. 40, No. 5, September–October 1980, pp. 488–90.

16. See Sommer, *Beyond Charity*.

17. The pernicious consequences for village development projects of donor insistence on projectizing their funding are described at length by Bernard J. Lecomte, *Project Aid: Limitations and Alternatives* (Paris: Development Centre of the OECD, 1986).

18. World Vision USA has reported that it tested this widespread assumption by presenting a TV special featuring a more developmental theme than did its usual presentations. It reportedly drew more contributions than any of their previous TV specials. Hopefully the public is becoming ready to respond to more sophisticated appeals. It makes sense. You give each year and the result seems to be there are more hungry people than the year before. What's the point? The public needs to hear that there is hope for people to actually overcome their problem.

19. OECD, *Voluntary Aid*, pp. 20–21.

20. David C. Korten, "Bangladesh Rural Advancement Committee: Strategy for the 1990s," (Boston: Institute for Development Research, July 19, 1989). Publication by Private Agencies Collaborating Together, New York is forthcoming.

21. A breakthrough in my own thinking about NGO's serving as institutional change catalysts in third generation roles came when I realized that the Ford Foundation, which is often thought of as a development donor, has more in common with VOs than it does with the large public development assistance agencies. For further discussion of this point see Korten, "Third Generation NGO Strategies," pp. 152–54. I then realized that VOs can and do assume roles similar to that undertaken by the Ford Foundation in its work with the Philippine National Irrigation Administration (NIA). The Ford/NIA experience represents a classic, but unfortunately all too rare, case in the development field of a successful effort to transform a national bureaucracy into a strategic development organization. This experience and the methods involved are documented in detail in Frances F. Korten and Robert Y. Siy, Jr. (eds.), *Transforming a Bureaucracy: The Experience of the Philippine National Irrigation Administration* (West Hartford: Kumarian Press, 1988).

22. Juan Miguel Luz and Ernesto D. Garilao, "The NGO as Advocate: Savar Gonoshasthaya Kendra, Bangladesh." A case written for the APPROTECH V, Organizational Strategy Planning Workshop, Manila, October 20–21, 1985.

23. One of the most serious barriers to expanding the development roles of NGOs may be the difficulties they face in working with one another. Jealousies among them are often intense, and efforts at collaboration too often break down into internecine warfare that paralyzes efforts to work together toward the achievement of shared pur-

poses. Ironically, it at times seems easier for some NGOs to work with government than with other NGOs.

24. Isagani R. Serrano, "Developing a Fourth Generation NGO Strategy." Informal working paper (undated *circa* 1989) available from the Philippine Rural Reconstruction Movement, Manila, Philippines.

25. While many people have contributed to the definition of the fourth generation, I also owe a particular debt to F. Stephen, the Director of SEARCH, an important NGO support organization located in Bangalore, India, and to the staff of SEARCH. Much of the fourth generation part of the strategies' matrix was first worked out during a most stimulating strategic assessment workshop with this group as part of their effort to define a strategy relevant to SEARCH. Serrano's definition of the fourth generation strategy ties it to the promotion of "the Alternative Development Paradigm." As Alicia M. Korten called to my attention in reviewing an earlier draft, to be consistent with the larger generational framework it should be clear that any NGO that engages in movement facilitation as a major program strategy is appropriately classified as engaged in a fourth generation strategy irrespective of whether the alternative development paradigm defines the central idea of the movement. Since Serrano and I are both interested primarily in the alternative paradigm, my discussion of fourth generation strategies and their implementation is focused specifically on fourth generation strategies in support of the alternative paradigm.

26. See Jessica Lipnack and Jeffrey Stamps, *The Networking Book: People Connecting with People* (New York: Routledge & Kegan Paul, 1986); and Jessica Lipnack and Jeffrey Stamps, *Networking: People Connecting with People, Linking Ideas and Resources* (New York: Doubleday and Co., 1982).

27. For the story of this remarkable visionary and his work see James B. Mayfield, *Go to the People: Releasing the Rural Poor Through the People's School System* (West Hartford: Kumarian Press, 1985).

28. Based on Dolores Foley, *Non-Governmental Organizations as Catalysts of Policy Reform and Social Change: A Case Study of The International Planned Parenthood Federation,* University of Southern California Ph.D. Dissertation, May 1989.

29. From Mayfield, *Go to the People.*

30. Some years later, under pressure from anti-abortion forces in the U.S., AID demanded that IPPF withhold financial support from any organization that provided abortion assistance. IPPF refused to comply, and all AID funding was stopped. Other donors quickly filled the gap and IPPF continued to grow.

31. Volunteers retain a titular role in IPPF's governance and policy direction, but few have the day-to-day involvement in family planning as a cause that characterized the early activists. Twenty-one percent of the Secretariat budget continues to be allocated for volunteer "support," mainly for travel to international meetings, as an "incentive" to maintain volunteer interest. Foley, *Non-Governmental Organizations as Catalysts.*

32. The addition of the fourth generation to the three generation scheme raises some serious conceptual issues. The description of the first three generations was arrived at inductively through the observation of experience. While there is nothing that says an organization must begin with first generation program strategies and move to more sophisticated strategies, there does seem to be such a tendency. The fourth generation,

as it relates to development agencies, represents more of an emerging concept or goal than a description of reality. While I could name some organizations that are developing incipient fourth generation strategies, I could not at the moment name any *development* VOs that are engaged in a predominantly fourth generation strategy. Also there is no empirical basis as yet for assuming that the emergence of fourth generation strategies will involve a movement from third to fourth generation strategies by the NGOs in question. To the contrary, the examples of fourth generation strategies that have been cited here all involve organizations or initiatives that began as fourth generation. In fact the weight of the evidence seems to suggest that the more common pattern is for a group of volunteers to engage in a movement-oriented fourth generation strategy and then move almost directly into a bureaucratized first generation type of program, as in the cases of James Yen and the IPPF. These issues will need considerably more examination as experience is gained.

33. One of the most interesting of the U.S. VOs concerned with development is a relatively new organization called Results, a volunteer development movement with chapters throughout the United Sstates and in a number of other Northern countries. Its sole concern is with volunteer-led advocacy and education. It has done what other U.S. groups have said is impossible—it has engaged Americans in development issues. I spoke to the annual membership meeting of Results in June 1989. At that meeting I learned about the potency of voluntary energy in mobilizing political action through meeting hundreds of volunteers who were far more deeply engaged in the intelligent examination of basic development issues than are many of the paid development workers I know. They were also highly committed to making a difference in the world through their educational and lobbying efforts. It was truly inspiring.

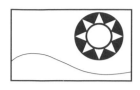

PART IV

THE 1990s:
FROM GROWTH TO TRANSFORMATION

As we approach the 21st century, global society finds itself between the proverbial rock and a hard place. A major portion of the world's population lives below minimal tolerable standards for a civilized human society. The current wisdom says that to address these most basic of needs we must accelerate worldwide economic growth. Yet the environmental burdens created by current levels of production are at or near the limits of tolerance of the earth's ecosystems.

We cannot sustain continued growth, at least as it is conventionally defined without risking the collapse of the ecosystem on which both rich and poor depend. Does this mean that the poor are doomed to eternal misery? Hopefully not. It does mean, however, that the priority of the current decade must be the transformation of our values, technology and institutions—in both North and South—as a prelude to setting a new pattern for the restoration of growth consistent with justice, sustainability and inclusiveness. Transformation, not growth, defines the essential global development priority for the 1990s and the only path to resolving the crisis.

- We must transform our *definition of the quality of life* to place less emphasis on material consumption and give greater attention to our social, mental and spiritual development.
- We must transform our *technologies* to increase the contribution made to human well-being achieved from any resource for which we depend on nature—whether a nonrenewable physical resource or a resource such as air or water that depends for its availability on the natural recycling capability of the environment. We will refer to these jointly as *environmental resources.*
- We must transform our *institutions* to simplify our lifestyles and insure the just distribution of the benefits of environmental resource use. This means that we, the over-consumers of these resources, must defer in our resource demands to satisfy our ever increasing *wants* to the efforts of the under-consumers to meet their basic needs. This need not necessarily involve a reduction in the *quality of our lives,* but it surely will involve a reduction in the *quantity of our consumption.*

The following chapters elaborate on the transformation agenda and its implications for voluntary action.

Chapter 11 makes the case that there is no lifeboat in which a fortunate few may escape the consequences of the global crisis. It suggests that all people, in both the North and South, must work together in a process of mutual empowerment aimed at transforming society's institutions and values.

Chapter 12 outlines the case for democratization and considers the implications for the South of the forces that are bringing an end to the dominance of the state over civil society. Chapter 13 outlines a citizen's agenda for the transitional period of the 1990s toward a just, sustainable and inclusive society.

Chapter 14 returns to the voluntary sector and the critical roles that the citizen volunteer and the voluntary organization must assume in support of transformation. It also discusses the new competencies and relationships that effective performance in these roles will require.

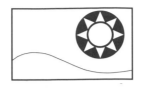

CHAPTER ELEVEN

A SPACESHIP HAS NO LIFEBOAT

> If you have come to help me you can go home
> again. But if you see my struggle as part of your
> own survival then perhaps we can work together.
> — *Australian Aborigine Woman*[1]

Many years ago Garrit Hardin published a controversial article entitled "Lifeboat Ethics."[2] He argued that the people of the world who live in affluence are in a situation much like the occupants of a lifeboat cast off from a sinking ship. The seas are filled with survivors struggling for a place on the lifeboat. Unfortunately the lifeboat is full. Either its occupants must beat off those who are clinging to its sides or the boat will be swamped, and all will perish.

The analogy was intended to drive home the point that the affluent of the world, the chosen few, have essentially filled the available ecological niche for excessive consumption. There is no more room.

Hardin was making an important point, but his analogy was wrong in one fundamental respect. We live on a spaceship, not an ocean liner. A spaceship has no lifeboat. Its occupants either prosper or perish together.

The world is simply too interdependent and its boundaries too permeable for the wealthy to protect their privileged position behind any form of fortification. We see daily reminders of this reality in the flow of economic and political refugees and migrant laborers from South to North, the vulnerability of the North to terrorism, the growing numbers of Southern countries with chemical and nuclear weapons and long range missiles[3], and the dependence of the North on Middle Eastern oil and other Southern resources. It is also evident in the potential of the South to accelerate global warming and its disastrous consequences through forest destruction and the increased release of carbon dioxide and other greenhouse gases.[4]

We had best get on with figuring out how to accommodate the long-term needs of everyone in our shared habitat. A reassessment of our approach to international assistance offers one starting point.

WHY INTERNATIONAL ASSISTANCE?

There has long been a tendency within public policy circles to solve problems by throwing money at them in ways that are consistent with bureaucratic convenience. This tendency has long plagued international assistance efforts. Generally there has been a strong preference for dispensing money in short-term bursts packaged as projects that fit nicely with the donor's budgeting cycle and auditing requirements. Each project is treated by its sponsoring assistance agency as a monument to the agency's wisdom and generosity, discrete unto itself and a priority above all others. Special incentives attract talented personnel away from permanent agencies to staff short-term project offices that vanish with the end of donor funding. New construction is substituted for maintenance. Opportunities to improve the utilization of existing national resources are neglected. Local initiative is undermined.[5]

All too often what remains is a landscape littered with over designed, overly expensive, often unusable or under-utilized physical structures—and the debt from the loans used to finance them. Meanwhile, policy advice of every strip and persuasion is offered as the new panacea, much of it, on balance, self-serving of the interests of the advising countries.

Official government-to-government assistance has almost always been linked in one way or another to national political and economic interests.[6] In fact, a great deal of the failure of international assistance efforts can be traced to a narrow, short-term definition of national self-interest on the part of the assistance providers.[7]

For nearly three decades, until surpassed by Japan at the end of the 1980s, the U.S. government had consistently been the largest single national foreign assistance donor. The United States has also been among the most outspoken of donors in citing its own national security interests, specifically the threat of spreading communism, as the primary justification for its foreign assistance program. That focus led to important contradictions.

Was the focus of U.S. assistance to be on winning the favor of the elites who controlled the military and political power that kept communist insurgents in check? This could be accomplished through military assistance and measures to increase economic growth and thereby the wealth and power of these elites.

Or was assistance to be directed to increasing the well-being of the poor to weaken the appeal of communist revolutions? This almost invariably required fundamental institutional changes in direct conflict with the interests of the elites whose use of power represented the single most important barrier to improving the conditions of the poor.

There was a considerable tendency to deny the reality that these were competing demands representing interests in fundamental conflict. To acknowledge that the way in which social institutions allocate power and wealth is one of the primary causes of poverty would have been tantamount to confirming the Marxist theory of class conflict, which the United States and other Western countries were loathe to do. Instead they held firmly to the myth that development is primarily a matter of money and technology.

Forced to deny a fundamental reality of Southern development, the West consistently opted for short-term perspectives and avoided the tough choices. As a consequence, much of the task of transforming the institutions that lock Southern nations into self-defeating patterns of unjust, unsustainable and non-inclusive development still remains ahead of us.

By the 1980s the "bulwark against communism" argument had worn thin with the U.S. public. The communist threat was beginning to seem more remote, and there was little to indicate that international assistance had proven much of a bulwark in any event. So self-interest was taken a step further. In line with the prevailing free market ideology and the orientations of the "me-first" generation of the 1980s, the argument was put forward that U.S. international assistance was creating vibrant new markets for its goods and could reverse America's balance of payments deficits. The argument had a rather hollow ring as well. Among other things it conveniently ignored the fact that the United States had major negative trade balances with those very countries—Taiwan, South Korea and Japan—being touted as the leading examples of development success that it was supposedly helping others to emulate.[8] We of course were also urging other countries to concentrate their efforts on export-led growth, targeted primarily to U.S. markets.

There is an obvious need to define the self-interest of the North more broadly in relation to foreign assistance. However, the need for a broader definition is only a part of the problem. Our whole approach to development assistance is a product of the growth-centered development vision. We not only need a new rationale; we need to fundamentally rethink the approach as well. Simply pumping more money through the existing foreign assistance system will only worsen the problems the assistance is ostensibly intended to solve.

OFFICIAL ASSISTANCE: MORE THAN MONEY

A first step toward reform is to acknowledge that the provision of financial assistance to poor countries is not the same as helping poor people. Neither does it necessarily translate into development by any meaningful definition. Relief, trade credits, counter-insurgency campaigns, operating costs of recipient governments, recurrent costs of social services, the rental of military facilities, patronage systems, international political alignments, and United Nations votes have all been funded under the rubric of development assistance. These seldom help the poor. Even more rarely do they leave behind enhanced capacity to manage national resources. However, since loan financing is often involved, debt burdens are increased—though these activities seldom if ever generate foreign exchange to support repayment.[9]

Some development assistance has been targeted to the poor, and specifically, to land reform and the development of small farmers and small business, but this has been the exception more than the rule. A major study conducted for a consortium of donor countries, which took a highly sympathetic view of aid performance, concluded that:

> In Africa only a small proportion of aid—much of it rather unsuccessful—has gone into small-scale agriculture or livestock investment, and aid for research on food crops has been relatively neglected, compared with cash crops. ...the record of almost all aid is least satisfactory where good performance is most urgently needed: in the poorest countries, particularly in sub-Saharan Africa.[10]

Indeed, rather than helping the poor, it is not uncommon for international assistance to work directly against their long-term interests. The anti-developmental consequences of international aid can be demonstrated for each of the three major categories of official assistance: military, humanitarian and development. While each of these three types of assistance is of a distinctly different nature, they all share one important characteristic—increasing the level of expenditure *can* lead to important anti-developmental consequences, particularly in relation to the interests of the poor.

Military Assistance

Military assistance encourages a distortion of the priorities of many of the world's poorest countries toward the build-up of large military establishments. The greater the military power they control, the less the pressures on authoritarian leaders to be responsive to the needs of their people and the more prone they become to engage in regional power plays. Production of military equipment makes demands on natural resources for purposes that in the aggregate[11] make a negative contribution to human well-being.

The more sophisticated and deadly the available weapons, the greater the intensity and, thereby, the suffering inflicted by regional and internal conflicts. In many Southern countries military personnel and units are for sale to the highest bidder for land grabbing and other illegal activities, even the overthrow of democratically elected governments. They may, as well, play a major role in illegal logging and fishing operations, gambling and drugs.

Conventional warfare between nations has become all but obsolete. Increasingly, military units serve mainly to control civil unrest, or in other words, to prohibit the expression of dissent among populations alienated from their governments by the unjust use of state power. In too many countries the army is the primary enforcer of injustice. Furthermore, to maintain the loyalty of the military, the astute head of state often feels compelled to extend privileges to the military's leaders that exacerbate the injustice.

Global de-militarization should be a high priority on any agenda for the 1990s. Systematic reduction of international military assistance and arms sales is an obvious and important starting point. Indeed, it may well be that *reductions* in military expenditures and in the size of military forces would contribute more to sustainable human well-being throughout the world than would comparable *increases* in expenditures for development assistance.

Humanitarian Assistance

Humanitarian assistance addresses the symptoms of system failure by attempting to relieve the worst suffering of its victims. It meets a particular need at a specific moment in time. Sometimes the need, as in the face of a natural disaster, is truly temporary and a brief period of emergency assistance will help the victims re-establish themselves.

In other cases the need is chronic, and a short-term welfare intervention cannot be expected to provide more than temporary relief. Here the welfare intervention does not contribute to the person's ability to meet the need in the future with his or her own resources. In many cases he or she has no resources. That is the problem. Unfortunately humanitarian assistance seldom draws attention to this reality. More likely it draws attention away from it, while creating a dependent reaction on the part of the recipient and ultimately reducing prospects for eventual self-reliance.

Where the needs are chronic, rather than temporary, increasing the amount of humanitarian assistance, especially food aid, is likely to exacerbate the problem. All too often, the consequence is to drive down farm prices, adding to the impoverishment of local farmers and reducing the incentives for increased domestic production.

Development Assistance

When used well, development assistance leaves behind enhanced capacities to generate new sustainable flows of justly distributed benefits to people.[12] While it is widely recognized that development assistance often fails by this standard, the extent to which it all too often *reduces* capacities for sustained self-reliant development is less widely recognized. The following examples are illustrative.

- At a November 1988 OECD meeting on nongovernmental organizations (NGOs), one participant told of a study from Latin America that compared a region of a recipient country that had received a major injection of foreign project assistance with one that had not. The aid-receiving area had built up the staffing of its public development agencies and prospered so long as the assistance funding flowed. However, once the foreign-funded project terminated, overstaffed bureaucracies sat idle waiting for someone to send more money. The other region, spurred by creative local leadership, had undertaken its own development initiative based on the mobilization of local resources. Having learned effective self-reliance it continued to progress without special outside funding.

■ Studies in one Asian country compared local irrigation systems in contiguous communities. In each case one system had been assisted by government under a foreign aid project while the other had been financed, constructed and managed by the community with its own resources. The facilities in the unassisted systems were more often functional, operating costs were lower, maintenance was better, and performance reliability was higher.

■ An NGO tells of a livestock project it was promoting based on a village self-help breeding program. Another NGO entered the area and started handing out animals to anyone who wanted them. The self-help program was completely disrupted and the animals received as handouts were soon sold off.

■ A U.S. PVO engaged in constructing nearly fully financed village water systems found that when it began requiring villages to finance system construction the interest of the villagers increased and subsequent maintenance improved.

More is not necessarily better, especially when the more is a gift from a foreigner. One reason, as indicated by the examples above, is that external aid has a way of creating expectations within the community that development will come as the gift from an outside agent rather than through people's own efforts. A second reason is found within the aid giving agencies themselves.

Aid officials commonly describe their jobs as being to "move money." It is an apt description. The image comes to mind of workers shoveling coal to fire the boiler of an old steam driven locomotive with the expectation that the faster they shovel, the faster the train will move.

It seems to be an iron law of development assistance that the more money an assisting organization has to move, the more its energies are consumed by the imperative to insure that the funds are obligated[13] on schedule according to whatever procedures the agency mandates. This focus leaves little time to apply the money in ways that increase local capacities for sustainable, self-reliant development.[14]

The conflict between moving money and building capacity becomes particularly critical at this point in history when the transformation of institutions must be the central agenda. The more the assistance money that is poured through existing agencies without a clear strategy of using the money to support a transformation of resource management systems, the more those agencies are likely to resist substantive reform.

An objective assessment would likely establish that up to a point all three types of international assistance have the potential to produce human benefits. But beyond that elusive point, which may vary substantially with the individual situation, the consequences of increased assistance are quite likely to be negative—irrespective of whether it is used for military, humanitarian or development purposes. Thereafter, the more money transferred, the less the future capacity of the assisted countries and people to mobilize and manage their own resources.

PRIVATE VOLUNTARY ASSISTANCE: MORE THAN RELIEF

As a general rule, nonofficial, private voluntary international assistance has been motivated predominantly by humanitarian and religious concerns. It is therefore natural that it has gone primarily to relief and welfare efforts, even though the NGOs involved now tend to style themselves as development organizations.

NGOs as Relief Organizations
One of the major weaknesses of the framework for classifying the four generations of NGO strategic orientation (see chapter 10) is that the framework suggests a greater shift has occurred from first to second or third generation strategies than is actually the case. A substantial amount of NGO activity that on the surface appears to belong in the category of second generation community development is in fact more accurately classified as little more than relief and welfare with a face lift. Far too often even NGO efforts that are intended as second generation interventions do not result in empowerment and self-reliance. On the contrary, they often create a long-term dependence on the NGO and the services it provides.[15]

Given the importance of the distinction, it is striking that official statistics on NGO funding only rarely make an attempt to distinguish between expenditures for humanitarian assistance (relief and welfare) and those for development. This includes the statistics compiled from its member governments by the OECD, which monitors all international assistance from Western countries.

OECD figures for 1983 do, however, indicate that for seven reporting countries, plus the European Economic Commission, 44 percent of official development assistance funding channeled to NGOs was for food aid and relief activities.[16] In 1986, 52 percent of the $1.06 billion in official contributions channeled by the American government to private international assistance agencies consisted of donated food, related transportation and excess property—which are predominantly relief and welfare assistance.[17]

Even indicative figures are lacking regarding the division of private contributions between welfare and development assistance. However, the fund raising appeals that generate these funds are heavily oriented to relief and welfare, especially the appeals of U.S. organizations.[18] There are no comparable figures or estimates for Southern NGOs. However, the fact that a considerable portion of their total funding comes from Northern NGOs and governments suggests that probably a consequential portion of their total effort is also devoted to relief and welfare.

There are constant pressures on the NGOs of both North and South to focus on humanitarian assistance rather than development. The former produces more immediate and visible (though less sustainable) benefits to the poor than does true development assistance and is therefore easier to justify to donors, whether public or private. It is easier to administer and requires less technical expertise. It is popular with farm groups in Northern countries as it increases their markets and creates upward pressure on prices for their output. Serious development assistance to the poor, on the other hand, demands attention to political and economic empowerment. Dealing with this reality almost inevitably infringes on established interests, creates political resistance, and is likely to prove offensive to some donors.

NGOs with long traditions of delivering charitable and technical assistance have particular difficulty coming to terms with the fact that the conditions with which they are concerned are a result of the maldistribution of power and require major institutional change. This is especially true for groups that work internationally. Political activism carries inherent risks, especially in countries with dictatorial regimes and raises ethical questions when working in a country other than one's own.

Yet in our contemporary world, no organization can simply choose to ignore the political dimension of poverty and still consider itself a serious development agency. Furthermore, those that choose to maintain their more traditional focus may soon face a terrible dilemma.

The Terrible Dilemma

Unless effective action reverses current global trends, we must expect the demands for humanitarian assistance, particularly food assistance, to grow significantly during the 1990s as the number of victims of our collective failure increases at an accelerating rate. NGOs engaged in relief efforts will find they have a growing market for their services.

Unfortunately, the resources required to provide humanitarian assistance to the victims of system failure are almost certain to decline as the crisis deepens, due to a combination of compassion fatigue and declining food surpluses. The *per capita* declines in worldwide food production experienced in the mid- to late-1980s are likely to continue. Paying customers with hard currencies will almost certainly receive priority in the allocation of available supplies as the U.S. struggles under its massive and growing foreign debt. This will be a harsh reality for NGOs that have built major portions of their programming around distribution of food commodities—and for the people they assist.

"Temporary" Responses to Long-Term Problems

In the international community we like to maintain the myth that humanitarian assistance consists primarily of temporary relief interventions. We fund it accordingly, with short-term contributions or project funding. It would be more accurate, and perhaps more helpful—though certainly not politically popular—to admit that in most instances we are maintaining a massive welfare system to meet needs that are not only chronic, but also increasing at an alarming rate.

Even "natural" disasters are taking on a new quality. There is an important distinction between the victims of truly natural disasters that have been with us since the beginning of time and remain beyond human influence, such as earthquakes, typhoons and droughts; and the victims of "unnatural" disasters—properly called *human* disasters because they are the direct result of collective human folly.[19] The former represent true short-term emergencies for which temporary humanitarian assistance is appropriate in order to restore people to their former self-sustaining status. The latter represent chronic situations that are a direct result of human action—war, environmental destruction, lack of access to productive resources and employment, and political repression—and can be resolved only through difficult institutional and behavioral changes.

While assisting the victims of system failure, we must be clear that such humanitarian assistance does nothing to remove its causes, or even to slow the rate at which it generates new victims. Thus, to the extent that humanitarian assistance is given precedence over corrective action, our capacity to render the necessary assistance will inevitably be overwhelmed by the growing demand.

We must conclude that the substantial majority of NGO efforts loosely described in official gazettes as development assistance is in reality humanitarian assistance, addressed to relieving the suffering of the victims of our global crisis, not to eliminating its causes. A comprehensive transformation is needed, not only in the thinking and roles of a large number of NGOs, but also in the whole development assistance system of which they are a part.

FROM PUBLIC HANDOUTS TO MUTUAL EMPOWERMENT

Conventional approaches to development assistance are based on two myths long treated almost as holy writ: the productive investment myth and the benevolent state myth.

- **Productive Investment Myth:** Development is a function of capital investment and technology transfer from wealthy countries to poor countries through concessional aid programs. The productive investment of transferred funds produces a continually increasing stream of useful economic outputs that strengthens economic self-reliance, raises living standards and eliminates poverty. Consequently, the best indicator of a Northern nation's concern for the world's poor is found in the percentage of its GNP transferred as development assistance.[20]

- **Benevolent State Myth:** Unlike all other societal institutions, which each represent special interest groups, governments represent the objective best interests of all the people. Therefore, it is appropriate to look to government as the final arbiter in allocating development resources to their economically and socially most productive uses.[21]

Together these two myths have long provided the logical foundation of the framework for most official development assistance transfers from the North to the South. They confirm the pre-eminent role of the state in development and contribute to the exclusion of people from participation in decisions that have important consequences for their lives. Yet all the major elements of these myths are false.

- The heart of development is institutions and politics, not money and technology, though the latter are undeniably important.
- Only a small percentage of foreign assistance funds are invested in ways that produce a continuing stream of useful benefits.
- Governments almost invariably represent the interests of power holders. The more that power is concentrated, the narrower the interests that government represents. External financial assistance placed in the hands of these governments generally serves these interests.

The validity of these counter assertions is so obvious that one might argue that to articulate the two myths is to create a straw man. The fact remains, however, that the structure and administration of our existing system of official international development assistance have logical validity only to the extent that what I have labelled as myths are in fact valid. Otherwise, our system of official international development assistance represents a fundamental contradiction.

International Development Assistance: A Financial Transfer System

International development assistance has been developed around systems of financial flows intended to translate money into benefits for the needy of recipient countries.

- **Approach 1: Parallel Public–Private Systems.** Traditionally there have been two parallel systems of international assistance flows. One has featured official government-to-government assistance channeled through either bilateral or multilateral agencies. The other has featured flows of private assistance channeled through NGOs. Both systems were designed to achieve the transfer of money, or of those things that money will buy, from the citizens of wealthy nations to those of poor nations. One, however, dealt exclusively with public funds and the other exclusively with private funds. One channeled assistance through recipient governments.

The other went directly to the people. This is illustrated in Figure 11-1, Approach 1.

Until the end of World War II the international financial assistance flows through the private system substantially exceeded those through the public system. Once official international assistance became a global priority, however, the balance between private and public assistance was rapidly reversed, with the public system becoming by far the more significant of the two in purely financial terms.

Within the public system, governmental agencies, including the multilaterals, transfer resources to the recipient government, most often for defined projects. Agencies of the receiving government, in theory, then convert these resources into investments and/or goods and services that are expected ultimately to benefit the poor. In fact, the benefits are more often absorbed by the government officials who administer the project, the cronies they employ as contractors, and the foreign suppliers and consultants hired at the donor's insistence.

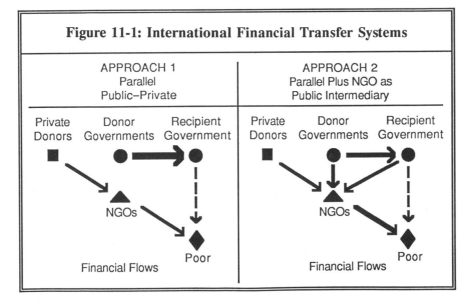

Figure 11-1: International Financial Transfer Systems

■ **Approach 2: Parallel Systems Plus NGO as Public Intermediary.** The persistent failure of international assistance extended through governments to benefit the poor has led to increased donor interest in channeling a portion of their assistance through NGOs, either directly or through the host government.[22] See Figure 11-1, Approach 2. In this approach the NGO serves as a conduit for both private and public assistance to the poor. NGOs serving in this role are commonly and accurately referred to as intermediaries, a term that reflects the relief and welfare orientation of much of this assistance.

Approach 2 retains a heavily top-down, welfare-oriented perspective in that it provides one way flows of money, commodities, services and technical assistance to address donor and government defined needs. The introduction of the NGO as intermediary in the delivery of the assistance increases the likelihood that assistance will be received by the poor, but in itself contributes little or nothing to removing the underlying causes of their poverty.

When international assistance is approached primarily as financial flows, both development and humanitarian assistance become primarily welfare programs—irrespective of whether implemented through governments or NGOs. The critical difference is that the beneficiaries of the *development* assistance are more often the middle and upper classes who carry out the "project implementation." The beneficiaries of the *humanitarian* assistance are more likely, though not necessarily, to be the needy. Neither variant addresses, with any consistency, the political and structural issues that are fundamental to just, sustainable and inclusive development. There is a clear need to move beyond *international assistance* to a new concept of *international cooperation* based on a fundamentally different set of assumptions.

International Cooperation: A System of Mutual Empowerment
Some international NGOs are exploring a concept of international development cooperation toward the mutual empowerment of people and governments to transform local, national and global institutions. This concept involves people-to-people, government-to-government, and people–government cooperation in solving the problems that people and nations throughout the world increasingly share in common. See Figure 11-2. Through cooperation and information-sharing, progress is made toward increasing individual and collective capacities to make better use of available resources to meet the people's self-defined needs on a finite planet.[23]

This approach has a number of distinctive elements.

- The primary resource around which assistance relationships are developed is information, not money, and the flow is two-way. The focus is on people helping one another make better use of their own resources to create the foundation on which the use of supplemental external assistance resources can build.
- Most development issues are addressed as shared or joint problems, recognizing that most contemporary development problems know no North or South, East or West. See Table 11-1.
- Mutual assistance relationships are established at both government-to-government and people-to-people levels—within and among countries, between people's organizations (POs), voluntary organizations (VOs), and central and local governments on a South/-

South, North/North, South/North and North/South basis.
- Substantial attention is given to establishing vertical communications linkages, commonly called micro-macro linkages, through which the people can contribute to setting national and international development agendas, provide feedback to governments and international donors on the consequences of government and donor programs and policies; and through which government and donors can provide feedback to the people on the collective consequences of their individual and collective behaviors at the local level.[24]

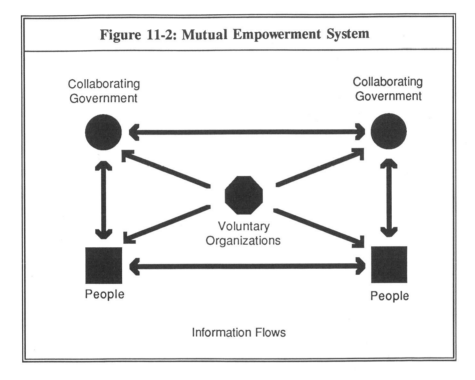

Figure 11-2: Mutual Empowerment System

- Serious priority is given to *global* education that: 1) analyzes development issues within the context of global interdependence; *and* 2) seeks to develop new values, and behaviors consistent with contemporary human realities within all elements of society, North and South, rich and poor.
- Voluntary organizations are expected to play important roles as catalysts, mobilizers, feedback facilitators, analysts and advocates.

The mutual empowerment approach views international assistance not as a government project so much as a people's movement. Government plays an important role, but as an instrument of the sovereign people to serve them in those functions that fit government's competence. Much of the real action and leadership is centered in voluntary and people's organizations.

Table 11-1: Problems Without Borders

An increasing number of development problems do not recognize either North-South, or East-West distinctions. The needs that North and South, East and West increasingly share in common include:

- Restoring depleted soils.
- Conserving and allocating scarce water resources.
- Reducing air pollution.
- Preserving and strengthening the small farm.
- Reducing chronic unemployment.
- Insuring the preservation of human rights.
- Making credit available for micro-economic activities.
- Achieving arms reduction and demilitarization.
- Controlling global warming.
- Providing housing for the homeless.
- Meeting needs for bilingual education.
- Reducing hunger, illiteracy and infant mortality among difficult to reach populations.
- Reducing teenage pregnancy.
- Managing population growth and distribution.
- Increasing citizen awareness of global development issues.
- Improving preparedness for natural disasters.
- Facilitating reconciliation to reduce regional tensions based on racial, religious and ethnic differences.
- Eliminating acid rain.
- Treating AIDS victims and controlling spread of the disease.
- Resettling refugees.
- Controlling drug trafficking and abuse.

This is only an illustrative sample of the needs shared by countries throughout the world in all regions and at all levels of development.

PUBLIC FUNDING OF VOLUNTARY ACTION

VOs and POs perform their distinctive role as instruments of democratic social process, in part, by testing and challenging mainstream public policies. It is rare, however, for international VOs and POs that receive funds from conventional foreign assistance agencies to serve as independent voices challenging the conventional wisdom of the foreign and development assistance policies of their own governments.[25] Yet such challenges are essential. Consequently, this failure should be of substantial concern to the legislative bodies of the donor countries.

We now have a need, as never before, for independent voices to enrich the policy debate on foreign and international assistance policies that are seriously in need of thorough rethinking. It is in the public interest for Northern governments to encourage the engagement of a wide range of VOs in this debate as people-to-people catalysts, advocates, innovators and educators.

Independent Public Foundations

Providing this encouragement and financing is not a task well suited to the official development agencies of most donor countries. These agencies are too burdened by administrative and audit procedures, too locked into established relationships with conventional mainstream NGOs, too closely tied to their foreign affairs ministries and their official policies, too closely scrutinized by legislative bodies and too sensitive to the possibility of media criticism to take the risks involved in supporting true independent citizen action.

Channeling public funds for more innovative activities, including advocacy and public education, in support of people-to-people development cooperation is a function more appropriately carried out by independent publicly funded foundations that have considerable procedural flexibility and the freedom to operate independently of official foreign policy.

There are numerous examples of such public foundations. One of the better known is the Inter-American Foundation (IAF) created and funded as a public corporation by the U.S. Congress.[26] The Netherlands and Norway also channel funds to NGOs through public foundations.[27] Other Northern donor nations that do not have such funding mechanisms would be well advised to create them.[28]

Beyond Mainstream International Assistance NGOs

In many instances the work of voluntary women's, environment, civil rights, consumer affairs and peace organizations addresses more fundamental development issues and provides greater focus on people-to-people cooperation than does the work of most mainstream international assistance NGOs.[29] To date there has been all too little recognition among official Northern donors of the development relevance of these groups. These groups should be given greater support and encouragement in their international activities to the extent that they feature true people-to-people cooperation. Public support should be concentrated on programs that have strong private support and feature active voluntary commitment.[30]

Particular consideration should be given to providing public support for international cooperation among citizen groups with broadly-based membership.[31] Donors must, however, be alert to the fact that funding the professionally staffed secretariat of a citizen membership organization does not necessarily result in broadly based citizen involvement in international cooperation efforts. Often the programs so funded are indistinguishable from those of any other professionally staffed development organization. Both funding agencies and NGOs should re-examine these programs with the intention of recreating them as true people-to-people cooperation programs.

On a spaceship there is neither lifeboat nor fortress. Ultimately we share a common destiny. People of all nations must rethink and transform the relationships that join and divide them, seeking greater cooperation and innovation at all levels—government-to-government and people-to-people—in shaping that destiny for the good of all.

NOTES

1. From "The Manila Declaration on People's Participation and Sustainable Development." See Appendix A of this volume.

2. Garrett Hardin, "Lifeboat Ethics: The Case Against Helping the Poor," *Psychology Today,* Vol. 8, September 1974, pp. 38+. An expanded and revised version was published as Garrett Hardin, "Living on a Lifeboat," *BioScience,* Vol. 24, No. 10, October 1974, pp. 261-79.

3. According to a U.S. Congressional study, thirteen Southern countries possess chemical weapons and or the capability to produce them. Five Southern countries are considered to possess nuclear weapons or the ability to produce them and two more are in the development stage. Nineteen have or are developing ballistics missiles, including all of the countries that possess nuclear weapons. A number of the countries that possess such weapons have histories of hostile relations with one another, including: Israel and Syria, India and Pakistan, and Egypt and Libya. *The Developing World: Danger Point for U.S. Security,* a report commissioned by Mark O. Hatfield, Matthew F. McHugh and Mickey Leland (Washington, DC: Arms Control and Foreign Policy Caucus of the U.S. Congress, August 1, 1989), pp. 56–57. Much of the violence in the South has far deeper roots than the ideological conflict between East and West. The nuclear and chemical holocaust that seems to have been avoided in the North could possibly become a reality in the South, with the North becoming the fallout victim. Imagine an Idi Amin with a few dozen nuclear weapons and ballistics missiles.

4. This is in no sense intended to imply that the South is responsible for global warming. As discussed elsewhere in this book, the North carries by far the major responsibility. However, under current circumstances to the extent that the South seeks to equal the North in its release of greenhouse gases through its push for growth, the incremental additions from the South could have disastrous consequences for everyone in a system already strained beyond its natural limits.

5. A study conducted by a team of international experts under the aegis of an intergovernmental task force of aid giving countries reported that according to the end of project evaluations of assistance projects carried out by the funding agencies, between two-thirds and three-quarters are judged to be satisfactory by rate-of-return criteria. It was specifically noted that the reported success rate is somewhat higher for World Bank projects. Reported by Robert Cassen, the study team leader, in "The Effectiveness of Aid," *Finance & Development,* March 1986, p. 12.

What this study failed to note is that these evaluations are normally done at the time of project completion, and their results are heavily dependent on assumptions regarding whether the benefits anticipated by the designers of the project eventually will be achieved and sustained. Actual performance often proves these assumptions to be highly optimistic and self-serving of donor interests. A less publicized study done by the Operations Evaluation Department of the World Bank represents an important step toward a more realistic, self-critical examination. This study looked at twenty-five World Bank funded projects from four to ten years after project completion to assess *actual* economic performance. This sample included *only* projects that at the time of project completion had been rated as successful with good long-term prospects. The study concluded that only twelve of the twenty-five "successful" projects had been able to sustain an acceptable level of economic performance. The recalculated average rate of return on the thirteen unsatisfactory projects was only 2.7%. Reported by Michael M. Cernea, "Farmer Organizations and Institution Building for Sustainable Development," *Regional Development Dialogue,* Vol. 8, No. 2, Summer 1987, pp. 1–19. (Published by the United Nations Centre for Regional Development, Nagoya, Japan.)

For more detailed critiques documenting the reasons for such failures, see Cheryl Payer, *The World Bank: A Critical Analysis* (New York: Monthly Review Press, 1982); Guy Gran, *Development by People: Citizen Construction of a Just World* (New York: Praeger Publishers, 1983); Judith Tendler, *Inside Foreign Aid* (Baltimore, MD: Johns Hopkins University Press, 1975); and Bernard J. Lecomte, *Project Aid: Limitations and Alternatives* (Paris: OECD, 1986).

6. At times the efforts to deny the obvious with claims of humanitarian concern reach ridiculous extremes. Among the most blatant was the provision of "humanitarian assistance" to the Nicaraguan Contras by the U.S. government. The more common examples involve the ill-disguised use of foreign assistance primarily to promote the national trade interests of the "donor" country. The Japanese use of aid to promote Japanese business is legendary, but few countries are exempt. British NGOs recently called on their government to end the policy of tying its aid to British procurement. *Britain and the Brundtland Report: A Programme of Action for Sustainable Development* (England: International Institute for Environment and Development, *circa* 1989), p. 22.

7. According to Douglas Ensminger, "Agriculture, Food and Employment: Agenda for the Coming Century," *Kidma,* Vol. 10, No. 2, 1988, p. 21, the proportion of Third World people who live in a culture of poverty and malnutrition is approximately the same today as it was when the colonies gained their independence: 52 to 54 percent for rural areas and 32 to 37 percent for urban regions. To the extent that one purpose of foreign assistance has been to reduce the incidence of poverty, we have failed.

8. Given the narrow arguments presented in support of foreign assistance and the checkered history of foreign assistance performance, it is little wonder that foreign assistance has so little public support in the U.S., even though American citizens have made clear in poll after poll that they are concerned about the plight of the poor of the world and want to see more done to help them. Nick Eberstadt, "The Perversion of Foreign Aid," *Commentary,* Vol. 79, No. 6, June 1985, p. 19. The U.S. public has consistently backed its concern for global poverty with substantial contributions to private voluntary organizations engaged in international assistance. In 1986, they made voluntary contributions totaling $1.8 billion to these organizations. This was more than 50 percent of the private contributions made to NGOs in that year by all citizens of the member countries of the Development Assistance Committee (DAC) of the OECD, the club of industrial nations. Based on statistical tables reported in OECD, *Voluntary Aid for Development: The Role of Non-Government Organizations* (Paris: OECD, 1988). Furthermore, Americans are consistently above the average for the DAC countries in the percentage of their GNP that is donated to private international assistance organizations (OECD, *Voluntary Aid,* p. 152).

Yet Americans also indicate with equal consistency in public opinion polls that they favor reducing official foreign aid. Eberstadt, "The Perversion of Foreign Aid," p. 19. This lack of public support is reflected in the fact that the United States is next to last among the eighteen DAC-member countries in the percentage of GNP it allocates to official foreign assistance. OECD Development Cooperation Report 1988, as cited in "Report of the Task Force on Foreign Assistance to the Committee on Foreign Affairs, U.S. House of Representatives," (Washington, DC: U.S. Government Printing Office, 1989), p. 7. Americans are not known for their sophisticated understanding of

international affairs. Yet they are aware of and concerned about the poor of Southern
nations. They also seem to be aware that official foreign assistance has done a great
deal more to help the wealthy than to help the poor of Southern countries. It should
not be surprising that arguments for a foreign assistance program geared primarily to
restoring colonial-type trade and investment patterns has had very little appeal to
them. If this is true for Americans, it is presumably even more true for the citizens of
other more globally sophisticated and compassionate Northern countries. Perhaps if
international assistance were truly addressed to a serious attack on poverty it might
capture widespread public support.

9. See Eberstadt, "The Perversion of Foreign Aid," pp. 19–33.

10. As summarized by Robert Cassen, the study team leader, in "The Effectiveness of
Aid," p. 11.

11. Balance of power advocates will argue that failure to provide military assistance
creates power imbalances that invite the use of force by the more powerful player.
This is why I have used the term aggregate here. I am not arguing the individual case.
I am suggesting that the net effect of all international military assistance is on balance
contributing to system breakdown. It most certainly is not helping the poor of the
South.

12. A fundamental premise underlying development assistance efforts is that there is
a need to augment existing resources to expand the investment base available to
generate economic growth. While never stated explicitly, there is an implicit premise
that existing resources are being used well, but are too limited in quantity. Surely it
would be irrational for a foreign donor to augment existing resources with additional
concessional resources if existing domestic resources are not being productively used.
There is no basis for assuming that an individual, organization or nation that fails to
use its own resources productively will make any better use of resources provided by
a foreigner as gift. Yet this is exactly what a great deal of foreign assistance assumes.
   Many years ago Robert Chambers introduced me to a simple, but profound reality
that has been fundamental to my thinking and work in the intervening years. Even in
the poorest rural areas of Southern countries, if one totals the numbers of government
staff and the aggregate budgets of the various government agencies working in any
given jurisdiction the numbers are usually substantial relative to the results that are
produced. Pouring in more money simply increases the waste. The first priority in any
development undertaking should be to improve the effective utilization of already
available resources.
   Another key point made by Chambers is that most of the funds and staff managed
by government come under operating budgets, not development budgets. If you really
want to make a difference, focus on improving operations and pay a lot less attention
to the funds allocated to special "development" budgets. These insight come from
Chambers' classic *Managing Rural Development: Ideas and Experience from East Africa*
(Uppsala: Scandinavian Institute of African Studies, 1974), pp. 29–30. This gold mine
of practical and timeless insights into development management has been reprinted by
Kumarian Press.
   In a study of a desperately poor tribal *taluka* in India, Ranjit Gupta, "The Poverty
Trap: Lessons from Dharampur," in David C. Korten and Felipe B. Alfonso (eds.),
Bureaucracy and the Poor: Closing the Gap (West Hartford: Kumarian Press, 1983), p.
120, estimated that not counting the police and the staff of the public works and
electricity departments, there were over 1,000 paid government functionaries, including
school teachers, public health staff and employees of the Forest Department assigned
to the area supported by a budget of 20 million rupees a year.

Transforming a public bureaucracy to make it truly effective in using its own resources to help local communities mobilize and manage their own resources is no small undertaking. However, it can be done and it costs relatively little. It does require large amounts of commitment and creative human energy. A classical case study of a successful transformation of this type is reported by Frances F. Korten and Robert Y. Siy, Jr., *Transforming a Bureaucracy: The Experience of the Philippine National Irrigation Administration* (West Hartford: Kumarian Press, 1989). See also John C. Ickis, Edilberto de Jesus, and Rushikesh Maru (eds), *Beyond Bureaucracy: Strategic Management of Social Development* (West Hartford: Kumarian Press, 1987); and Samuel Paul, *Managing Development Programs: The Lessons of Success* (Boulder: Westview Press, 1982).

13. In the donor vocabulary this means that formal budgetary commitments had been made by the donor according to established bureaucratic proceedures.

14. Stephen Hellinger, Douglas Hellinger, and Fred M. O'Regan, *AID for Just Development: Report on the Future of Foreign Assistance* (Boulder: Lynne Reinner Publishers, 1988), p. 6, conclude that "If the appropriate institutions cannot be funded or if they cannot operate freely the poor will generally be served best by no aid at all. Only when the fixation on the quantity of aid disappears can the quality of aid begin to improve." This is as true for PVOs as for major public donors.

15. This is evident from the fact that very few NGOs working in community development have been able to leave an assisted village with a reasonable assurance that the benefits provided during their stay would be sustained beyond their departure. In Bangladesh and India, many NGOs have become more or less permanent fixtures in the villages in which they work, serving as conduits for the distribution of foreign funded charities.

16. OECD, *Voluntary Aid*, Table 8, p. 154. This includes $24 million in U.S. assistance for ocean freight reimbursement and refugee assistance as food aid and relief.

17. Calculated from a table compiled by the U.S. AID Office of Private Voluntary Cooperation.

18. Many studies of NGO activities make no distinction between humanitarian and development assistance, erroneously labelling both as development assistance. Brian H. Smith, "U.S. and Canadian PVOs as Transnational Development Institutions" in Robert F. Gorman (ed.), *Private Voluntary Organizations as Agents of Development* (Boulder: Westview Press, 1984), pp. 115–64, notes that the predominant emphasis of U.S. NGO effort is on relief, though the official mission statements commonly emphasize long-term development.

19. Actually a part of our current reality is that it is becoming increasingly difficult to distinguish between true natural disasters and unnatural, human caused disasters. Floods were at one time considered a natural disaster. While Bangladesh has long experienced floods, the extreme flooding and consequent destruction now being experienced is greatly exacerbated by deforestation in the Himalayas. This deforestation, and the resulting consequences for Bangladesh are human creations. Droughts used to be natural disasters caused by decreased rainfall. Some still are, but we have reason to believe that human action makes even the natural ones worse.

20. Many Northern NGOs have also bought into this myth. They assume that the larger the amount of the funds they collect and transfer, the more good they are

doing. To the extent they are engaged primarily in humanitarian assistance there may be some validity to this assumption. For many organizations their perspective on this issue may reflect their historical roots as relief agencies. An important difference in the assessment of humanitarian and development assistance is that optimal efficiency in humanitarian assistance is 100 percent return on expenditure. Perfect performance consists of getting the full pound of donated rice into the belly of a hungry child. It is therefore appropriate to measure the performance of a humanitarian assistance effort in terms of the amount of financial resources transferred, if the aid in fact gets to the targeted individuals. However, for a development program 100 percent return consti-tutes failure. A successful *development* intervention must have a *multiplier* effect. The intervention is successful only if the pound of rice offered as assistance translates into a farmer's capability to produce several pounds of rice each year for an indefinite period of time. Increasing the amount of external resources applied in a development effort may actually undermine this result by reducing the incentive to become self-reliant. This represents an important difference between humanitarian and develop-ment assistance programs that is inadequately recognized either by public or private agencies.

21. The reader may note the strong current emphasis on market forces in policy thinking. However, this has done little to change the basic pattern that official devel-opment assistance flows to governments in response to government determined priorities.

22. There are a number of variants on this model. Commonly the intermediary NGO is an international group or of the same nationality as the donor. Other times the funds may go directly from a foreign donor to an indigenous NGO. Or they may go from the donor to an NGO of its own nationality to then be allocated to indigenous NGOs that become the ultimate service providers.

23. One person can never empower another. However, people can collaborate in a process of mutual empowerment.

24. Under the old approaches to international assistance it was uncommon for either governments or donors to have any real idea how their programs and projects affected the lives of the people they were supposed to help—particularly if those people were poor.

25. Ironically, when viewed from this perspective, there appears to be a much healthier relationship between the international voluntary community and the World Bank than between most development NGOs and their own national public development assis-tance agencies. A number of international VOs have posed serious challenges to selected Bank projects and policies. The Bank has responded with an attempt to strengthen constructive dialogue with these organizations as an opportunity to improve its own programming.

26. Other examples in the U.S. include Appropriate Technology International and the African Development Foundation. Though they have a private charters, the Asia Foundation and the Foundation for the People's of the South Pacific are funded primarily with public money and serve similar functions.

27. Hellinger, *et al., Aid for Just Development,* pp. 114-15.

28. This is not to suggest that bilateral donors should discontinue their existing pro-grams of support for NGOs in favor of providing public funding for these activities

exclusively through public foundations. The direct contact with NGOs is valuable to these agencies and they should be encouraged to maintain these relationships. It is probably appropriate, however, for the bilateral agencies to concentrate their support on those NGOs that operate more in a public service contracting mode responsive to agency agendas. Presumably an increasing focus of these efforts might be on implementing large-scale programs. The public foundations should be oriented more toward true VOs that have more independent catalyst oriented agendas. Any activities of a relief nature should be funded entirely under the bilateral assistance agencies. The public development foundations should be concerned exclusively with development efforts and avoid mixing humanitarian assistance and development agendas.

29. See Robert J. Berg, *Non-Governmental Organizations: New Force in Third World Development and Politics* (East Lansing: Center for Advanced Study of International Development, Michigan State University, May 1987), p. 32.

30. It is common practice among public donors to require the NGOs they assist to provide a private counterpart contribution to the funding of individual projects. This is intended to insure that the activities involve a private commitment and are not simply a response to public funding. While the intent is sound, the actual result is exactly contrary to what is intended. There is a strong tendency for the private, untied money of the organization to become absorbed in meeting co-financing requirements on government approved projects. As a consequence, the NGO that receives government funding often finds that it no longer has funds available for those activities that are not government approved. All its funds become allocated to government endorsed activities and are subject to government audit. This results in a pernicious, generally unintended, co-optation of the organization and a loss of its capacity for independent action. It is perfectly reasonable and appropriate to require that some defined portion of an NGO's total budget be from private sources. However, requirements for private counterpart contributions to specific projects should be eliminated as contrary to the public interest in maintaining a strong and independent voluntary sector.

31. Much of the assistance that the Swedish government provides to NGOs is channeled through consortium bodies of NGOs affiliated with church, labor or other membership based civic organizations. The U.S. Congress established and funds the National Endowment for Democracy, which functions as a public foundation to support the international involvement of groups affiliated with U.S. labor unions, the U.S. Chamber of Commerce, and the two major political parties. AID itself gives special attention to supporting the overseas activities of the U.S. cooperatives movement though it is sometimes difficult to tell the extent to which the assistance provided to Southern cooperatives by the U.S. cooperatives movement is really aimed at strengthening the economic power of the poor or at advancing the economic interests of powerful U.S. cooperative businesses.

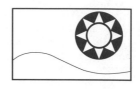

CHAPTER TWELVE

END OF THE DOMINANT STATE

Throughout much of the 20th century, the state gained ever increasing prominence, in both North and South, as society's problem solver. In the Northern industrial democracies, the state did a tolerable job in this role, largely because it was assisted and held accountable by a strong civil society. Where the state has been able to dominate a weak civil society, it generally has done a less competent job as problem solver. Under such conditions the individuals who control state power face overwhelming temptations to use it for their own narrow advantage, suppressing the free flow of ideas, monopolizing the control of resources and enervating all societal institutions that they do not control. The power of the state to expropriate existing wealth is used to build vast personal fortunes, the incentives to create new wealth are undermined, the civil sector atrophies, and the people feel alienated from their own society.

PEOPLE POWER AND THE CITIZEN-PRINCE

Recognition throughout Eastern Europe of the limitations of the dominant state as an engine of national development has led to a rapid and turbulent transformation of the institutions that control power. Brzezinski argues that these countries have finally faced the fundamental contradiction between the regimentation and bureaucratization of the Marxist state, and the participation and individual incentive required to advance a society beyond the phase of industrialization into the more dynamic era of information-based technologies.[1] Addressing the Communist Party Central Committee in February 1990, Mikhail Gorbachev called for a break with outmoded concepts that "...kept the socialist countries in isolation from the general flow of civilization."[2] State dominance is simply incompatible with human progress in the contemporary world.

The Eastern European experience demonstrates the speed with which human institutions can be transformed when the prince (in this instance Mikhail Gorbachev) opts for the role of global citizen and the people are prepared to seize the opportunity to recreate their political and economic institutions in a new image.

There are important lessons here. Neither Gorbachev nor the people of Eastern Europe could have brought about these changes without the other. The people created the pressure. The prince responded as a citizen to enable the people to pursue a new vision. The people seized the moment. It proved a powerful combination. The East suddenly made a transition in the Western mind from being a feared and hated enemy to being a friend and neighbor worthy of respect and assistance.

As a result of his action as a global citizen, Gorbachev earned high praise from people throughout the world. Who would have dared to predict that a day would come when loyal citizens of North American and Western European countries would hail a head of the Soviet Union as a champion of democratic reform and give him higher opinion poll ratings than their own elected leaders? When a people gain freedom, there is rejoicing throughout the world and a veneration of freedom's heroes.

LESSONS FOR THE SOUTH

The same limitations of the dominant state have been conclusively demonstrated in the South, where the efforts of the state to control all aspects of human activity in the name of development have stifled the innovation, human initiative and local resource generation essential to development progress. The strengthening of civil society to allow the people to mobilize and apply social energy to the improvement of their futures, with an accountable government assuming an enabling role, is one of the central themes of the people-centered development vision. The people, by right and by necessity, must be both the architects and the engines of development.

Loss of Political Leverage

The South now faces its own moment of truth. While East and West embrace as members of an estranged family reunited, and the possibilities for cooperation and mutual progress strain the imagination of the most creative idealist, the South is all but forgotten. The political competition between East and West has been a major force behind Northern interest in the South. As competition turns to cooperation, the South is losing an important source of political leverage over the North. The implications may be most painful for Southern tyrants who skillfully played on the East-West division as a means of sustaining their own power. They had only to proclaim themselves either anti-Communist or anti-Capitalist to win certain support from the side of their choice. Such declarations are likely to attract less attention during the 1990s.

We may take heart in the fact that the way is now open to establish a new and more positive basis for North-South relations. The leadership in this change must come from the South much as the leadership for changing East-West relations has come from the East. The South must take the first step toward shedding its own self-imposed limitations that leave it an easy mark for exploitation by the North.

Setting a New Direction

The prevailing Northern image of the South is one of persistent poverty, corruption, environmental degradation, terrorism, oppression and exploitation. It is neither a positive nor a hopeful image. The combination of pity, scorn, fear and hopelessness it provokes provides a poor basis for serious partnership.

The pragmatic reality is that the balance of power between North and South strongly favors the North. Current events in Europe will only add to this imbalance. The progress of the South depends on the sympathetic support of the North. While the long-term future of the North depends on the South in almost equal measure, the interest of the South in changing existing relationships is more immediate and self-evident. Thus it falls to the South, as it has to Eastern Europe, to take the initiative toward change. The South must act to project a new image that captures the imagination of the North with a sense of creative possibilities for human progress. The potentials have been convincingly demonstrated. The West's image of Eastern Europe changed almost overnight. The North's image of the South could easily change as dramatically and abruptly.

The North's image of the Philippines was changed in the wink of an eye by the Philippine people-power revolution. This triumph over the corrupt Marcos dictatorship electrified the world, instantly winning the hearts and inspiring the admiration of people everywhere. For a brief historical moment the people of the world were one with the Filipinos and their cause. Filipinos stood tall and proud, and the world felt ennobled by their strength and pride. Cory Aquino, a humble housewife who had risen from the martyrdom of her husband's death to lead her people to freedom, became an inspiring symbol to both North and South. People from throughout the world were drawn to the cause, not out of pity or charity, but out of a true sense of human solidarity and a desire to contribute to an ennobling accomplishment.

In a similar way the Chinese students who demonstrated for democracy in Tiananmen Square also captured the global imagination and for a brief moment gave the North a new image of their country. As these events took shape, the pity evoked by the images of the South's starving children and the outrage elicited by tales of corruption and oppression were displaced by a shared pride in images of courageous people seeking the opportunity to create a better future for themselves and their nation.

Unfortunately the aura of the Philippine revolution dulled all too quickly as it became evident that the country's politics continued to be dominated by unrepentant elites and military adventurers bent on restoring the factional politics, corruption, family favoritism and disregard of human rights that has for so long characterized the country.[3]

The violent repression by China's aged rulers of the voices of freedom had an even more chilling impact on the world's changing view of that country. Whether these are temporary or permanent setbacks remains to be seen. The potentials remain.

The ultimate potentials of the South are far greater than those of Eastern Europe, but they will be realized only if key individuals who hold political and economic power in the South assume the mantel of global citizenship and allow the state to be transformed, through nonviolent democratic processes, from the protector of their own privileges to enabler of the people's self-development. Such action would position Southern countries to engage as full partners in shaping global transformation.

NATIONAL SOVEREIGNTY AND THE GLOBAL CITIZEN

In chapter 11 we noted that the myth of the benevolent state was one basis for the broad acceptance during the past several decades of government as the final arbiter in the allocation of development resources.[4] Two increasingly outmoded concepts of national sovereignty have also contributed to this acceptance, the ideas that: 1) sovereignty resides in the state as the legitimate representative of the national interest; and 2) what a nation decides to do within its own borders is exclusively its own business. The people-to-people dimension of international cooperation proposed in chapter 11 gains its legitimacy from a recognition of the people's sovereignty and the realities of global interdependence.

The Principle of People's Sovereignty

Many traditional concepts of national sovereignty have become hopelessly out-of-date and appropriately rejected as bases for contemporary action. Under the modern concept, sovereignty originates in the people, not in the state. This principle is clearly established in the Universal Declaration of Human Rights[5] and is the essential foundation of effective people-to-people international cooperation.

The principle of people's sovereignty establishes the basic human right of the people of any country to organize, access information, undertake development activities of their own choosing on their own initiative, express views on policies, participate in international exchange, and receive financial and other assistance from foreign and domestic contributors of their choice. It also establishes the right of one people to assist another in seeking the realization of their democratic aspirations. The basic argument is well articulated by Larry Diamond:

True sovereignty resides not with the regime in control of the state of a country, but with its people, and when the people clearly indicate their rejection of the ruling regime, democratic governments and organizations are justified in offering them assistance to realize their political aspirations. This is not a carte blanche for democracies to overthrow regimes they fear or dislike, but rather an argument for popular legitimacy as the fount of sovereignty, and for reading unambiguous signals of the illegitimacy or delegitimation of an authoritarian regime as due cause for no longer according it the full respect and privileges of sovereignty.[6]

In line with this principle, Diamond has noted the important role of NGOs in aiding the development of democratic organizations and movements in authoritarian or newly democratizing countries:

Aid [in supporting democratization] that comes from non-governmental organizations is less likely to be politically tainted or suspect, and more likely to create enduring bonds of democratic cooperation across countries along functional lines: between journalists, intellectuals, bar associations, human rights organizations, women's organizations, student and youth groups, independent trade unions, business associations, and political parties of broadly similar orientation.[7]

This basic principle should apply in other areas of shared international concern as well. It is the right of any people to forge collaborative links with other peoples across national boundaries for the nonviolent exercise of what are recognized to be universal human rights.[8]

The Principle of Global Interdependence
Conventional concepts of national sovereignty were established during an era in which nation-states were substantially self–contained fortresses. What a nation-state decided to do within its borders was considered to be its exclusive concern as long as it did not intrude on a neighboring state.

We now live in a different world in which a great deal of what goes on within the borders of most states is of considerable and rightful concern to other states and their citizens. AIDS, drugs, acid rain, ozone depletion, transnational corporations, the greenhouse effect, financial flows, computer communications, refugees and much else—exhibit little regard for national boundaries and have largely passed beyond the control of individual governments. Trade and monetary policies affect the global economy and the viability of the international financial system. Political suppression and economic inequality create political and economic refugees that demand relocation. Any state that neglects attention to balancing its population with its environmental resources will generate new claims for international welfare assistance and additional flows of economic and environmental refugees.

The decision of some nations not to regulate aerosol sprays increases risk of skin cancer in all countries. Industrial pollution in the United States destroys forests in Canada. Actions by a Middle Eastern state may provoke or support acts of terrorist violence that infringe on the security of all people who happen to be at a particular location at a particular time, irrespective of nationality. The denuding of forest lands in Nepal and the management of river flows in India exacerbates the periodic flooding of Bangladesh—with large-scale loss of life and property.

Interdependence does not justify one state or people imposing its will on another. But it does create a situation in which countries and citizens have legitimate interests in the affairs of one another and a right to seek to influence those affairs that goes well beyond what would be sanctioned under more traditional concepts of national sovereignty.

The rediscovery of the role of civil society as a primary agent of development is long overdue. Hopefully, the era of the dominant state is behind us, and none too soon. People throughout the world must now join hands in the spirit of global citizenship to define and implement an agenda for social transformation.

NOTES

1. Zbigniew Brzezinski, "The Crisis of Communism: The Paradox of Political Participation," *The Washington Quarterly*, Vol. 10, No. 4, Autumn 1987, pp. 167–68.

2. As reported in "Gorbachev Reforms Facing Easy Approval," *The Manila Chronicle*, February 7, 1990, p. 2.

3. It is important to note that the Philippines remains perhaps the most open and democratic country in Asia. Unfortunately, however, the vision of the potential for a better future dims by the day as the unreconstructed traditional elite power holders demonstrate the continued strength of their hold on the society.

4. There is no stronger indication of this myth than the common donor practice of treating project planning documents as privileged and available only to donor staff and members of government. There is an assumption that the public has no right to be informed of, or to participate in, the decisions being made by assistance agencies and governments in their name. There are some signs of movement, partly under pressure from NGOs. The World Bank is now considering the possibility of requiring public hearings as a condition of loan approval on projects that may have detrimental environmental impact. This step would be an enormous positive advance. The significance of the question of whether government has the sole right to determine the use of international assistance within its own borders becomes particularly salient when dealing with NGOs. Does a government have the arbitrary right to prevent a legally constituted voluntary association from receiving funds from abroad simply on the grounds that these funds rightfully belong to government and it does not find the activities of the association sufficiently supportive of its own plans and interests?

5. The Universal Declaration of Human Rights of the United Nations, Article 21,

Section 3, states, "The will of the people shall be the basis of the authority of government; this will shall be expressed in periodic and genuine elections which shall be by universal and equal suffrage and shall be held by secret vote or by equivalent free voting procedures." In the absence of a democratic mandate, a government cannot rightfully claim legitimate authority.

6. Larry Diamond, "Beyond Authoritarianism and Totalitarianism: Strategies for Democratization," *The Washington Quarterly* (forthcoming).

7. *Ibid.*

8. These rights are spelled out in the Universal Declaration of Human Rights formulated by the United Nations in 1948. Article 19 specifically states that "Everyone has the right to freedom of opinion and expression; this right includes freedom to hold opinions without interference and to seek, receive and impart information and ideas through any media and regardless of frontiers."

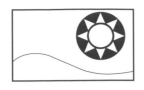

CHAPTER THIRTEEN

AGENDA FOR A SOCIETY IN TRANSITION

Countless individuals and organizations throughout the world are currently engaged in the development and actualization of an agenda for social transformation. It is an agenda with many dimensions, and the speed with which it is being advanced defies monitoring and documentation.

The most dramatic manifestations of changes supportive of the transformation agenda are found in the events reshaping the political structures of Eastern Europe. As this chapter was being drafted, what was unthinkable only weeks before happened. The Berlin Wall, the universal symbol of human tyranny, crumbled. The Soviet Union reduced travel restrictions on its citizens, and democracy swept through Eastern Europe. A few weeks later the Communist Party of the Soviet Union voted to relinquish its monopoly on power, and South Africa released Nelson Mandela, a political prisoner for twenty-seven years, paving the way for a possible end to apartheid.

Surely there will be setbacks. Hopefully there will also be new breakthroughs. Either way, there can be no doubt that we are in a period of profound historical change. Seemingly impossible historical events are occurring almost daily. What other such events are on the horizon? The possibilities challenge the imagination.

With these events as the backdrop, this chapter looks at key elements of a global transformation agenda for the 1990s. Voluntary action has a critical role to play in mobilizing citizen action in support of each.

RECONCILIATION AND DEMILITARIZATION

Writing in the World Vision journal *Together,* Tom Houston said, "The main problem in the world today is conflict, and the greatest need is for reconciliation in these conflicts."[1] There is no greater contributor to human suffering and no more significant barrier to effective development action than the violent conflicts that are tearing apart communities and societies throughout the world in Ethiopia, Lebanon, Sri Lanka, Nicaragua, Colombia, Peru, India, Laos, Palestine, El Salvador,

South Africa, Angola, Chad, the Philippines and others. Since 1945, 120 armed conflicts in Southern countries have killed at least twenty million people, roughly the equivalent to the toll of World War II. During the 1950s, 52 percent of those killed in these conflicts were civilians. In the 1980s, 85 percent were civilians, many of them the victims of war related famine.[2]

As discussed in chapter 1, war between nations has become rare. It has been replaced by war between people who share a common nationality, the product of growing communal tensions, and an unraveling of the social fabric. In the prevailing climate of fear and tension military budgets continue to grow, individual citizens build up personal arsenals in the name of protecting themselves and their families, and national armies are turned by governments against their own citizens.

In the end the use of force to contain communal violence only escalates it. The underlying tensions themselves must be resolved through reconciliation, not repression, through forgiveness, not gunfire.

Global demilitarization and the reallocation of military resources to alleviate poverty and to convert the global economy to sustainable modes of production must be at the top of the agenda for the 1990s. The momentum of East-West detente must be sustained, translated into disarmament of the super powers, and projected into demilitarization in the South.[3] Military assistance should be limited to helping Southern nations achieve small, disciplined, military forces committed to the principles of democratic civilian rule.[4]

LIFESTYLES AND TECHNOLOGIES

One of the most difficult, yet essential, challenges of the decade will be to redress the balance between the interests of the world's under and overconsumers. The basic problem is straight forward.

Limits to Conventional Growth
Every human being places some demand on the earth's ecosystem to provide at least the minimal supply of oxygen, water, energy, food and waste disposal required to sustain life. The demands of a few, mainly those living in the North, are enormous. There is a limit to the total capacity of the ecosystem to sustain these demands. Beyond this limit the system begins to break down and its overall life support capability declines. The more the demand exceeds the natural capacity of the ecosystem, the faster we may expect that decline to be.

There is increasing evidence that we are now at or near this limit, if indeed we have not already exceeded it in many essential areas. Even if we have not there is little cause for rejoicing. A real growth rate of only 4 percent a year throughout the 1990s will increase total world economic output by 48 percent by the 21st century. Unless there is a truly fundamental restructuring of the composition of that growth to reduce the related burden placed on the environment, the ecology's limits of tolerance will surely be exceeded by the turn of the century, and corrective action will become increasingly painful.

The Overconsumers
There is no question regarding who bears responsibility for the environmental burden. In 1984–85, four countries—the United States, the Soviet Union, Japan and West Germany—with 14 percent of the world's population accounted for 53 percent of the worlds consumption of commercial energy and a comparable share of important metals. For the rest of the world to equal the per capita consumption standards of these four countries, total world energy production and resource extraction would have to increase more than 250 percent.[5]

In terms of environmental loading, it has been estimated that carbon dioxide buildup in the atmosphere accounts for approximately 50 percent of the global warming that threatens a dramatic change in climatic patterns, agricultural productivity and the flooding of coastal cities. The main contributor to carbon dioxide buildup is the combustion of fossil fuels.[6] In 1988, according to the World Resources Institute, the United States, with roughly 5 percent of the world's population, was responsible for generating nearly 24 percent of worldwide carbon dioxide emissions and its emissions are growing at a rate faster than those of the rest of the world.[7]

Dramatic reductions in carbon dioxide emissions in the North, particularly in the United States and the Soviet Union, are as important to the future of global weather patterns as are similar reductions in the rates of tropical forest destruction in the South. Furthermore, only through reduced carbon dioxide loading in the North can excess recycling capacity be freed up to allow the Southern poor to achieve the minimum levels of energy use necessary to raise their poor from dehumanizing poverty—without disastrous ecological consequences.

Reality versus Politics
Action in three areas seems essential. Citizen groups are playing an active role in each.

■ The world's overconsumers of environmental capacity, irrespective of whether they reside in North or South, must reduce the per capita demands their lifestyles place on the environment. In part this can be accomplished through economic incentives that encourage the application of more environmentally sound technologies. In part it may require changes in lifestyles and the definition of the good life, with less emphasis on the material and greater emphasis on the social, intellectual and spiritual quality of life. The overconsumers, whose lifestyles set the standard for the aspirations of the underconsumers, must take the lead in redefining those standards, communicating through their own example the possibilities of living well *and* responsibly.[8]

- The underconsumers of the world should be assisted in mastering and applying environmentally sound technologies as the basis for future improvements in their well-being. Improvements in their well-being based on replicating the environmentally unsound technologies of the overconsumers would be both wasteful and self-destructive. In the end we may expect that the underconsumers may have a great deal to teach the overconsumers regarding environmentally appropriate technologies and the values of a less materialistic lifestyle.
- Population growth must be brought under control as rapidly as possible using the broadest range of incentives, educational approaches and technologies consistent with basic principles of free choice. Nothing casts a greater shadow over prospects for the world coming to terms with the limits of our planet's ecosystem *and* insuring that all people are able to attain an acceptable standard of living than does continued explosive growth of the world's population. While it may be accurate to argue that most of the people added to the population will be too poor to make a consequential demand on the ecosystem, such logic condemns the majority of human society to perpetual poverty and runs contrary to the principle of justice.

Each of these three areas presents an awesome political challenge, particularly the need to achieve dramatic reductions in the burdens placed on the ecosystem by the overconsumers. Even the much heralded Brundtland Commission Report, *Our Common Future,* deftly sidestepped the question of whether continued economic growth is feasible in an environmentally finite world. To the contrary, it optimistically forecast a "new era of economic growth" with global economic activity growing five to tenfold in the coming half-century. Furthermore, it listed "reviving growth" as the first of several "critical objectives for environment and development policies that follow from the concept of sustainable development." While the report also calls for a change in the "quality of growth" it says little about the environmental feasibility of continuing to give growth, rather than transformation, top priority. The rationale given by the report for a strong emphasis on growth is that this is the key to raising the world's poor above the poverty line.[9] Of course, it is assumed that the rich will increase their own incomes proportionately in the process, which means that the absolute gains of the rich will exceed those of the poor by many times. Possibly this may be good politics, but it certainly is weak ecology, a classic example of the perennial false promise of the growth-centered development vision.

Encouraging Initiatives

Fortunately there are encouraging indications that difficult and truly consequential changes are possible. The United States, by far the world leader in total energy consumption, reduced per capita energy consumption by 12 percent from 1970 to 1984 and reduced the energy required to produce $1 of gross national product by 32 percent.[10]

In 1983 the Scandinavian countries presented a proposal to the U.N. Economic Commission for Europe calling for a 30 percent reduction in sulfur dioxide emissions by each member country by 1993. Originally blocked by the United States, the United Kingdom and others, the proposal was not adopted. It led, however, to the formation of an informal "30 percent club" comprised of those nations that were willing to commit themselves to this target. By 1986, ten countries had met or exceeded the goal. Four countries committed themselves to a 70 percent reduction.[11] In 1987, twenty-four nations signed the Montreal protocol, which committed them to a 50 percent reduction in ozone damaging chlorofluorocarbon production by 1999.

The Natural Resources Council has called on the Unites States and the Soviet Union, together responsible for nearly 50 percent of carbon dioxide buildup in the atmosphere, to each cut their releases in half over the next twenty-five years.[12] Given the implications and the needs of less prosperous countries that seems a modest goal. Dramatic increases in energy efficiency, far beyond those already achieved, are an important key to achieving such reductions.[13]

Further Steps

An effort must be made in nearly every aspect of product design and packaging to reduce physical and energy input requirements, increase product life, and facilitate recycling of component materials. Various citizen advocacy groups are calling for actions such as:

- Restructuring agriculture to apply the concepts and technologies of agro-ecology or regenerative agriculture as a means of reducing dependence on resource depleting inputs and environmental contamination, and restoring soil fertility and water tables.
- Greater use of electronic communication as a substitute for physical movement of people.
- Improving public transportation systems—particularly high speed, energy efficient rail lines—to reduce dependence on the personal automobile.
- Reducing or eliminating subsidies, such as depletion allowances, that encourage the use of new resources and substituting incentives favoring the use of recycled materials.
- Restructuring tax and regulatory systems, especially in the United States, to eliminate the predatory corporate raiders and junk bond artists that press corporate management to mine the assets of their companies, including natural resource holdings, to maximize short-term profits.[14]
- Changing existing systems of economic accounting to distinguish between forms of economic activity that are harmful to people and the environment and those that are beneficial.[15]

SPIRITUAL DEVELOPMENT

Questions relating to the uses of power, values, love, brotherhood, peace and the ability of people to live in harmony with one another are fundamental to religion and to the role of church in society. Some more perceptive religious writers and thinkers point out the essential relevance of religious teaching in addressing poverty and injustice.

According to Charles Elliot, most structural theories of the determinants of poverty and injustice fail to take an essential additional step. Unjust structures are the creation of people and are products of the greed and egotism that are deeply imbedded in human nature. The human spirit must be strengthened to the point that greed and egotism play a less dominant role.[16] This is perhaps the most central of religious missions, and a far worthier challenge for religiously oriented voluntary development organizations than the distribution of charity to the victims of the failure of spiritual teaching.

This leads to a sobering realization. The elimination of unjust structures depends on the emergence of an alternative human consciousness. This consciousness must view power not as a club to be used in the service of personal aggrandizement, but rather as a gift to be held in stewardship to the service of the community and the human and spiritual fulfillment of all people—especially the powerless.[17]

More realistic than seeking to eliminate power holders, as communist revolutions have implicitly presumed and consistently failed to do, are efforts to increase the likelihood that power will be used in ways that take responsible account of the interests of the weak. This is partly a function of structures that establish checks and balances among power holders and increase their accountability to the people on whose lives they are in a position to influence. It is partly a function of the political consciousness of the otherwise disempowered. It is also, however, a function of the values of the power holder.

Consequently, raising the consciousness of power holders of the nature and consequences of power relationships to impress upon them their stewardship responsibility is as important as carrying out consciousness raising exercises among the powerless that help them discover the sources of their own inherent strength.[18] Only those power holders who are conscious of their privilege and its consequences for those not so endowed can be expected to embrace their obligation to be responsible stewards.

This has long been the essence of all great religious teaching. Progress in realizing the ideal of stewardship, even within formal religious establishments, does not give much reason for hope that the necessary progress can be made during the new decade ahead. Never before, however, has there been such urgency or such overwhelming evidence that it is in our immediate self-interest to do so.[19] This presents a special challenge for religiously oriented NGOs.

Another way to state the need for a transformation in consciousness might be in terms of a shift from the dominance of traditional masculine consciousness to the dominance, or preferably a melding into the dominant culture, of critical elements of traditional feminine consciousness. Growth-centered development institutionalizes the masculine ideals of competition, empire and conquest. It is intrusive and individualistic. It seeks symbols of dominance and power over others and nature. People-centered development depends on a realization of traditionally more feminine ideals of a nurturing family and community, place, continuity, conserving, reconciliation, caring and reverence for nature and the continuous regeneration of life.

Thus perhaps the key to a necessary transformation in social consciousness is the rapid advancement of women into positions of leadership, not simply as a matter of equity, but rather because of the need to bring their distinctive values and orientations to bear on a wide range of social problems. Few of the programs concerned with women in development have addressed this issue. More commonly they have either dealt with women in purely traditional homemaker roles, or have sought to prepare them to participate more effectively as producers and consumers in the service of a masculinized vision of economic growth. This is a serious limitation that overlooks the essential contribution that women with a well developed feminine consciousness must bring to development as transformation in the 1990s.

THE FAMILY

There has been another serious weakness of efforts during the 1980s to deal with the special deprivations and exploitation that have been experienced by both women and children living under conditions of poverty. Though only a beginning, important advances were made in legislative changes and the provision of targeted services. Similarly, attention was drawn to the terrible struggle a substantial portion of the world's children face in surviving the first few months and years of life. Steps were taken that may make it easier for more of them to survive.

These are all positive advances, as far as they go. The negative side has been that in the effort to focus attention on these especially neglected members of society there has been a tendency to lose sight of the fact that ultimately the well-being of women, children—and men as well—depends on their being able to function as members of family and community.

The Family: Protector and Oppressor
The family is the most basic social unit of human society. It is the building block that is essential to the construction and maintenance of strong integrative social structures. A strong family provides enduring bonds that are the individual's most important sources of economic

and psychological security. The family unit is essential to the healthy development and functioning of any society.

Unfortunately, the family is often a mechanism of suppression and subordination, particularly for women and children. In some societies that has been one of its predominant roles. Where this is the case, the family joins the list of human institutions that are candidates for significant transformation. Given the failure of the family in many settings, it is not surprising that well intentioned programs have tended to focus on women and children as discrete entities in isolation from the family.

Separating Women from Family

Women's programs commonly have focused on breaking the dependence of women on the family, more specifically on their husbands. This is accomplished in part by improving their education and also by increasing their income earning opportunities. In some settings, such as in Bangladesh and Pakistan, these are essential steps toward the transformation of family relationships and women's roles in society. On the other hand, it is essential to recognize that the goal is to transform family relationships, not to separate the woman from the family—with the disastrous consequences this brings for men, women, and particularly children.

The problem is perhaps most tragically demonstrated in those African societies where women, though they face many forms of economic discrimination, are financially independent by necessity, in the sense that the men commonly accept little or no financial responsibility for family maintenance. This is a central problem in many African countries for both women and children. It cannot adequately be resolved until men are able to establish a constructive role for themselves within the family.

Separating Children from Family

The central and essential role of the family in improving children's welfare would seem to be self-evident. Yet the campaigns of child advocacy groups sometimes almost seem intent on separating the child from the family. One manifestation of this is the popular slogan, "Children First." This is a logical contradiction of the reality that the well-being of the child is derivative of the welfare of family and community—as it places the child apart from both.

The pernicious consequences of taking such slogans seriously is found in programs for street children that focus exclusively on improving their situation to the exclusion of concern for the family and community context. The resulting child-centered actions focus almost exclusively on reducing the unfavorable consequences of being a street child by providing them, for example, with improved educational and income earning opportunities. Measures to reduce the number of street children by attempting to strengthen and restore the disintegrated family units and ability of the parents to provide for themselves and their children are neglected. By treating the symptom of the problem, rather than its cause, such programs may actually increase the incentive for families to send their children into the streets to gain the benefits that well-intentioned programs for street children provide.

The 1980s exposed the special problems facing women and children. Work on them must continue in the 1990s. Serious attention must also be given to the needs of those women and children who by circumstances have no family and no hope of being restored to a family unit. However, the social agenda of the 1990s should be built more around the family as the focal unit of analysis and action—giving attention to restoring and strengthening it in ways that increase equality, love, mutual respect and responsibility.

POLITICAL DEMOCRATIZATION

More than 50 percent of the people of the South, including China, live under nonelected governments and thereby are deprived of the most basic political freedoms. Only 22 percent live under full democracies. The remainder live under partial democracies that still lack a functioning judiciary, a free press and civilian control over the military.[20]

Costs of Authoritarianism
Countries with authoritarian governments are severely handicapped in dealing with the issues of the global agenda. Their governments have too little contact with the grassroots level where the burden of environmental destruction is most acutely felt. Their rulers are too dependent on maintaining the support of a small group of exploitative elites whose primary interest is in mining as much of the resource base as possible to build up foreign bank accounts while they have access to state power. The dominance of the state suppresses the creative social energy of the civil society.

The problem of conflict is also directly related to the issue of democratization. There is strong evidence that civil conflict *increases* as political freedoms *decrease*. There were twenty-three conflicts in which more than one thousand people died in either 1987 or 1988. Of these only three involved invasions by an outside power, and two of these, Afghanistan and Cambodia, also had a strong element of civil war. The other twenty were primarily civil conflicts. What is most striking is that only one of these, in India's Punjab, occurred in a country ranked as a full democracy.[21]

A Commitment to Democratization

People throughout the world are finding increasing courage to send a message to dictators, who maintain their personal rule through force, that their authority is not accepted as legitimate. They are exposing the lie of nonelected rulers who claim to represent the views and interests of the people. Human rights are universal, and acting to protect these rights for those to whom they are denied is a universal human obligation that knows no nationality. Open and honest elections, an independent judiciary and a free press are purely internal national matters only to the extent that the people of a nation have freely chosen to renounce their own liberties—a rare event in human history. Otherwise they are appropriately viewed as universal concerns of all people.

Too often international assistance—whether military, humanitarian, or development—has served to strengthen authoritarian rule. The cold war created its own logic for democratic governments of the North to support authoritarian rule in the South. That logic is rapidly evaporating. An argument can now be made that future international assistance should be guided by two principles.

- Aid should be provided to nonelected governments only when applied in ways that clearly and directly contribute to the strengthening of democratic institutions. Support for economic growth under authoritarian rule based on the argument that growth leads to democratization is a convenient, but not a sufficient, rationale.[22]
- Other aid intended to benefit people living under authoritarian governments should be extended primarily through nongovernmental channels to make clear that the aid is intended for the people, not for the ruling dictator.

There is little justification for giving aid in the name of development or humanitarianism to a government that imposes its rule by force to enrich its cronies. There is even less justification for strengthening the ability of such a government to apply force.[23] Why should citizens of democratic countries pay taxes to assist governments that suppress the rights of their own people to freely form associations of their choice to carry out self-help development initiatives and to provide voluntary service to the poor? In fact the international community regularly provides assistance to countries that do exactly that. Suppression of the rights to free association and expression is in clear violation of the Universal Declaration of Human Rights. Such suppression establishes the offending government as anti-democratic and anti-people and calls into question the legitimacy of its claim to international support.

Perhaps it is time for the global NGO community to take the initiative of preparing a universal bill of rights for voluntary and people's organizations. Such a bill would be based on existing international legal documents, including the Universal Declaration of Human

Rights and other instruments of international law, and would set forth universal standards by which governmental compliance might be assessed by monitoring bodies.

The cry for freedom is being heard loudly and clearly from citizen's groups around the world. It is an important and timely cry, because freedom is nearly a precondition for achieving the other elements of the transformation agenda. A demonstrated commitment to guaranteeing the rights and freedoms of its people should be a basic precondition for international recognition of, and support to, any government in a post-cold war world and is an issue to which the international NGO community should give increasing attention.

ECONOMIC DEMOCRATIZATION

Economic democratization seeks the just distribution of economic power, primarily through broad participation in the control of productive assets and the exercise of collective bargaining power. It goes hand in hand with political democratization as the foundation of an equity-led sustainable growth strategy.

There are many measures that support economic democratization, including land reform, aquarian reform (the reform of rights to fisheries), the formation of member-owned and controlled cooperatives, the implementation of employee stock ownership plans that give employees a strong voice in management and a share in profits, policies that favor a strong small business sector, and guarantees of the right to unionize. The goal is to create economic structures that will insure broadly-based participation in growth and its benefits.

Broadly distributed local control of productive assets also creates incentives to use available resources in ways that are at once productive and sustainable. The absentee-owner is more likely than a local resident to make decisions regarding the disposition of assets that take into account only short-term financial returns. When persons own property near their residence and depend on it for their own future livelihood, they are likely to be concerned with maintaining its value and with the consequences of its use for the beauty and well-being of the community.

At their foundations, both of the two major economic ideologies, capitalism and socialism, profess a commitment to the ideal of broad participation by people throughout the society in controlling productive assets.[24] Socialism and capitalism, in practice, have both failed seriously in this regard. Socialism has concentrated productive assets in the hands of those who control state power, though these people are neither owners nor workers in any meaningful sense. In a parallel fashion, capitalism has concentrated control in the hands of financial managers, and particularly investment bankers, who leverage large sums of other people's money to gain control over corporate assets for their personal benefit. As in the practice of socialism, these people are neither owners of the capital they control nor are they workers who depend on this capital to produce useful outputs.

Economic democracy is an agenda item of immediate relevance to North and South, East and West. Though a great deal remains to be done, we now see dramatic steps being taken in Eastern Europe toward economic democratization through privatization. There is increasing interest in the West in employee stock ownership plans, which, though too often abused, represent a positive step away from absentee ownership and financial manipulation by the rent collecting speculators who have come to dominate corporate America.[25]

The question of who controls productive assets remains central to current policy debates, but not as the question has been defined by traditional socialists and capitalists. The current need is to achieve true economic democracy based on meaningful participation in the ownership and control of productive assets for reasons of equity, productivity and environmental responsibility.

TRADE AND INVESTMENT RELATIONS

As discussed in chapter 6, the dynamics of the international trade and investment system are geared more to the maintenance and exploitation of enclave economies in the South for the benefit of Northern consumers and investors than to development of integrated economies that serve local producers and consumers. Southern countries that have become dependent on this system find themselves struggling ever harder to earn sufficient foreign exchange to meet their bills to purchase high-value manufacturing goods from the North and repay international debts. To earn this exchange they come under increasing pressures to mine their nonrenewable resources, cut their forests, commit their agricultural lands to export commodities, offer substantial concessions to foreign investors, and maintain low domestic wage rates. Excess supplies of the resulting commodities depress prices, increase pressures for more rapid extraction and encourage wasteful use of new materials, while discouraging conservation and recycling.

Increasing Self-reliance
Effective progress toward justice, sustainability and inclusiveness depends on breaking this cycle of international dependence. To do so, priority must be given to the development of domestic resources to meet domestic needs, particularly those of the poor.

Contemporary development wisdom, as elaborated in earlier chapters, works in exactly the opposite direction. It focuses the attention on foreign financial resources. The more loans and foreign investments a country accepts, the greater the obligations it incurs for repayment in foreign currencies.[26] Meeting such repayments depends on the generation of foreign exchange through exports. This means diverting resources away from meeting the needs of its own citizens to meet the needs of foreign consumers and businesses. This serves the interests of the international bankers and corporations who advocate such policies.[27] It may also be satisfactory for economies that are already meeting the basic needs of their own people. It is not acceptable for countries in which substantial portions of the population live at subsistence levels or below and have a desperate need to use these resources to meet their own most basic needs.[28]

For these reasons increases in international investment and trade cannot be considered universally positive. On the contrary, some economists argue that for the above reasons the incentives built into economic systems should give a clear, though by no means exclusive, preference to local investment and trade, as these are more likely to serve the long-term interests of the community.[29]

Tariffs and Subsidies

Northern countries have been strongly outspoken in appeals for eliminating barriers to free trade—especially by others. In a world of protected markets this demand is unrealistic, and perhaps inappropriate—particularly for nations that are trying to develop competitive domestic markets based on competitive small-producer output. The North should begin the appeal for free trade with an examination of its own trade practices, particularly those that work against the poor and the environment.

For example, agricultural export subsidies provided by Northern governments to their own agricultural producers suppress farm prices and production in the South, with the impact being greatest on the small farmer. To the extent that Northern countries are truly concerned with helping Southern countries advance in ways that preserve their environmental resources, Northern tariff policies should discourage low value imports that have a high environmental resource content and give preference to high value-added products with low environmental resource content.[30] This would require substantial economic statesmanship as it works directly against the narrower economic interests of the importing country. It may, however, be a more appropriate way of transferring financial resources than through conventional foreign aid.

Realigning Terms of Trade

There has been much discussion of the unfavorable terms of trade that prevail between Northern and Southern countries. We cannot appreciate how truly unfavorable these terms are until we recognize that the export earnings of Southern countries are heavily dependent on exporting environmental resources, which cost them dearly in future productive potentials. These earnings are used then used to pay for imports from Northern countries that derive their value from non-depleting information inputs. Not only do these tend to have a very low environmental content, trade in these products tends to strengthen the dominance of Northern countries in control of the information-based technologies that are the key to future prosperity.[31]

Adding insult to injury, environmental resources tend to be sold at bargain basement prices, while products with a high information content command exclusive boutique prices. These are truly unfavorable terms of trade that in no way reflect the long-term costs and benefits to the producing country.

It is hypocritical for the Northern nations—the primary overconsumers of environmental resources and the owners of the world's information resources—to demand free market competition in the sale of primary resources and the granting of monopoly ownership rights to holders of intellectual properties. The logic of a sustainable development would argue for quite the reverse. Environmental resources should be carefully protected and their prices maintained at high levels. Information resources, which by nature are nondepleting, should be freely shared.[32]

We should be seeking to sharply reduce or eliminate those international trade and investment practices that transfer environmental costs from one country to another. Since the open market grossly undervalues non-renewable resources, the sale of these resources must be regulated to insure a floor price that discourages their use in favor of greater use of labor and information resources. From this perspective, organizations such as OPEC that force up the prices of nonrenewable environmental resources are making an important positive contribution to global environmental policy.

Conversely, steps should be taken to limit monopoly rights to intellectual properties, in particular the protection of patent rights to those information-based technologies that make it possible to obtain substantially greater use values from a given unit of an environmental resource. While it is essential that incentives to encourage investments in the development of such technologies be maintained, we must at the same time recognize that the broader public interest demands that competitive forces must be allowed to work to make the application of these technologies as widely and cheaply available as possible. When viewed from the perspective of long-term global interests we cannot afford open market competition in the exploitation of natural resources. Similarly we cannot afford monopoly control of information resources.

Exporting Environmental Costs
There is an important element of existing trade and investment practice that essentially represents the successful effort by one country to pass the environmental costs of its consumption and capital accumula-

tion to another country. Japan has been a particular target of such charges. For example, Japanese VOs have pointed out that while Japan has strict policies to preserve its own forests, it is the world's largest consumer of tropical timber; more than 50 percent of its timber requirements being met through imports, primarily from Southeast Asia. To insure the sustained flow of this timber, the Japanese government, according to one VO, has financed "development" projects in the exporting countries that actively promote harmful and unsustainable forest management practices.[33] Japan has also been accused of exporting pollution by locating its pollution generating industrial plants in Southeast Asia.

Among the most scandalous examples of abuse in international trade relations has been the export by Northern countries of their toxic wastes to Southern countries. In this instance the receiving country is directly selling its environment to protect Northern consumers from the consequences of their own life-styles. Even more pernicious is the export sale by producer countries of harmful chemicals, such as pesticides and drugs that have been banned or severely restricted in the producing country. Here the importing country is literally paying for the destruction of its environment and the health of its people. Equally unconscionable is the active promotion of harmful substances, in particular tobacco, to Southern consumers, using advertising and promotion practices that are banned in the North.[34]

International Investments
A similar differentiation should be made in assessing foreign investments. To speak of the "development" of a nonrenewable resource is a contradiction. A non-renewable resources can be exploited or expropriated. It cannot be developed. Development must, at least by a people-centered definition, be sustainable.

When an investor proposes an investment project that is aimed at creating an enclave to mine a country's nonrenewable resources or clear cut and export its forests, the proposal should be assessed for what it is, a scheme to relieve the country of its capital stock of a critical environmental resource for the primary benefit of foreign investors and those who are in a position to capture the fees paid for extraction rights. Both national and international public opinion should be rallied to block such proposals.

But this is not to suggest that all foreign investment is anti-developmental. For example, a foreign investor might propose the transfer of technical knowledge in support of a sustained yield forestry project that would supply materials to local industries to meet domestic market demands in return for an investment share. Such a project might be built around small-holder tree farms and the development of vertical linkages that contribute to the growth of a diversified, integrated local economy. The proposal might include provision for employee participation in the ownership of the processing facilities, all under the umbrella of a marketing cooperative controlled by the tree producers and the worker-owners of the factories. A share of the production might be designated for export to compensate the investor for the technology transfer services provided.

The extraction of mineral resources is by nature nonsustainable. Such extraction should be approached with special care to insure the maximum contribution to building a sustainable local economy able to survive the exhaustion of its mines. Proceeds should be invested in developing the local labor force and local suppliers, with an eye to how their capabilities may be redirected once the mine is exhausted. Royalties from the mine should be used to establish other local economic activities that are not mining dependent. First priority in use of the yield from the mine should be to supply domestic industries. If the extraction is assisted by a foreign investor, the project should contribute to development of domestic capacities to manage similar projects.

Foreign investors who are willing to participate in local projects on such terms should be welcomed. An equally warm welcome should be extended to foreign investors who propose to transfer advanced information based technologies in areas such as electronics, materials science and bio-engineering.[35]

Regulation of Product Labeling and Use
To limit the exploitative export of consumer abusive labeling and trade practices from North to South, the regulation of product labeling and use should be internationalized. More of the necessary testing and standard setting should be done on an international basis, with recommendations issued globally for implementation by individual national governments. Voluntary consumer organizations throughout the world are taking the lead in creating the political demand for enforcement of these standards. Their efforts deserve broad support.

Countries that ban or severely restrict the use of toxic chemicals or of harmful or useless pharmaceuticals should prohibit the export of such products except to countries that have a known commitment and capacity to properly regulate their use. Exports of such products should be a matter of public record, and this information should be widely disseminated through global networks of consumer protection organizations. International corporations should be required to meet the minimum labeling standards of their country of registration on all of their products, irrespective of the country of sale. For example, British or American tobacco companies should be required to include warning labels on their products and advertising in the Philippines and Costa Rica just as they would in Britain or the United States.

The export of toxic and other hazardous wastes from one country to another, especially to countries whose citizens lack the education, political voice or economic power to refuse them, should be prohibited by international law. The country that generates such wastes should bear the hazards involved.

Trade Balances

Strong international pressures should be brought to bear on all nations to maintain a reasonable balance between their total imports and exports. This is essential to maintain a balance of economic power within the international system. Countries, such as Japan, that consistently maintain strong positive trade balances are gradually increasing their economic power over those, such as the United States, that are living beyond their means in the short-term by foreign borrowing and the sale of their own productive assets. The former engages in the expansion of absentee ownership and weakens local control and ownership. The latter undermines economic discipline and mortgages its future and its resources. Each works to undermine economic democracy and responsible environmental stewardship.[36]

The Underlying Vision

The above recommendations are based on application of the basic principles and concepts of a people-centered development vision outlined in chapter 7. They focus on the development of just, sustainable and inclusive local communities as the building blocks of a just, sustainable and inclusive global society. Each such community features a diversified local economy that is relatively self-reliant in meeting basic needs and controls its productive resources and technologies. Each local economy is expected to conserve its resources for the long-term benefit of its people and their children in perpetuity. Likewise it is expected to absorb its own wastes.[37]

The application of the people-centered vision would seem to turn much of the conventional thinking about trade and investment on its head. This is not entirely true. The intent is not to stop international trade and investment, but rather to moderate and restructure it in ways that reverse the tendencies toward absentee ownership, concentration of economic control and the export of environmental costs.

The decade of the 1980s was in the end the decade of awakening. We must approach the 1990s as the decade of opportunity to create a new human society based on justice, peace, human dignity and accommodation to life on a wondrous living spaceship. It could also, however, prove to be a decade of disaster—a prelude to the ultimate self-destruction of human civilization. A choice is at hand between focusing on transformation or focusing on a continued path of undifferentiated growth. The outcome of a transformational choice is by no means certain. The outcome of the growth choice, however, is increasingly self-evident.

Even five years ago thoughts of achieving a transformation in values and institutions of the magnitude outlined here would have seemed little more than a naive idealist's dream. It is now a necessity, and each day brings new evidence that it is also a possibility.

NOTES

1. Tom Houston, "The Greatest Need in the World Today," *Together,* July–September 1988, p. 2.

2. Michael Renner, "Enhancing Global Security," in Lester R. Brown, *et al, State of the World 1989* (New York: Norton, 1989), pp. 135–36.

3. We still have a long way to go. The Philippine press announced in late 1989 that Malaysia, with assistance from Great Britain, is developing a submarine fleet. The Philippine air force responded with an appeal for additional funds to purchase more powerful and sophisticated aircraft. Such initiatives may enrich Northern arms merchants and enhance the stature and power of military personnel, but they do not increase global security and certainly do nothing to improve the lives of the average Malaysian or Filipino. The citizens of these and other countries should make clear that they want no part of such expensive, useless and ultimately destabilizing military projects. The major military agenda for Southeast Asia should be one of demilitarization, beginning with the removal of foreign military bases from both the Philippines and Vietnam.

4. The U.S. Congress has been insisting that open democratic elections be a condition for receiving U.S. military assistance. In fiscal year 1989, the United States provided $680 million in military aid to countries other than Israel, Egypt, and European countries. Of this money, less than 1 percent went to countries classified as full democracies. Eighty-five percent was allocated to twenty-six countries classified as partial democracies, defined specifically as democracies with strong militaries that are largely outside the control of elected civilians and the judicial system. Nearly 15 percent was earmarked for forty-eight countries with dictatorial governments or one-party states. *United States Security and the Developing World: Defining the Crisis and Forging Solutions*, A report commissioned by Mark O. Hatfield, Matthew F. McHugh and Mickey Leland (Washington, DC: Arms Control and Foreign Policy Caucus of the U.S. Congress, March 1989), p. 29.

   Note that these statistics were provided only in the draft version of the report. The final version of the report lumps all military assistance together and stresses that nearly half of all U.S. military assistance goes to fully functioning democracies and only 2 percent goes to dictatorships and one-party states. *The Developing World: Danger Point for U.S. Security*, A report commissioned by Mark O. Hatfield, Matthew F. McHugh and Mickey Leland (Washington, DC: Arms Control and Foreign Policy Caucus of the U.S. Congress, August 1, 1989), pp. 45–56. The difference is explained by the fact that the vast bulk of U.S. military assistance goes to Israel and Egypt.

   Both versions of the study stress that assistance to the military in partial democracies can inadvertently undercut the transition to democracy by strengthening military power and giving implicit sanction to politically active military forces. Even where U.S. military assistance has been linked to democratic elections and reduction of human rights abuses, the report concludes that U.S. training programs for military officers of assisted countries have given far too little attention to developing commitment to civilian control of the military and to human rights. It provides evidence suggesting that many of the officers trained in these programs are anti-democratic and disdainful of civilian rule. See pp. 45–52 of the August 1, 1989, final report.

5. Compiled from statistics reported in International Institute for Environment and Development and World Resources Institute, *World Resources 1987* (New York: Basic Books, 1987), Tables 16.1, 22.1 and 22.5. Energy figures are for 1984. Metals figures are for 1985. In 1985 these four countries accounted for 57 percent of the world's con-

sumption of aluminum, 52 percent of copper, 48 percent of lead, 66 percent of nickel, 59 percent of tin, 47 percent of zinc, 53 percent of iron ore and 55 percent of crude steel.

6. Lester R. Brown, Christopher Flavin, and Sandra Postel, "Outlining a Global Action Plan," in Lester Brown, *et al., State of the World 1989* (New York: W.W. Norton & Company, 1989), p. 175.

7. As reported in "U.S. is Worst Offender in Rise of Carbon Dioxide," *International Herald Tribune,* September 18, 1989, p. 3.

8. Many of the possibilities are outlined in Robert Repetto, *World Enough and Time: Successful Strategies for Resource Management* (New Haven: Yale University Press, 1986).

9. World Commission on Environment and Development, *Our Common Future* (Oxford: Oxford University Press, 1987), pp. 1–4, and 49–52.

10. IIED and WRI, *World Resources 1987,* Table 22.1.

11. Lester R. Brown, Christopher Flavin, and Sandra Postel, "A World at Risk," in Lester Brown, *et al., State of the World 1989,* p. 6.

12. From a 1989 fund raising letter of the Natural Resources Defense Council, 40 W. 20th St., New York, signed by John H. Adams, Executive Director.

13. For a comprehensive proposal for dealing with global warming see Christopher Flavin, "Slowing Global Warming: A Worldwide Strategy," *Worldwatch Paper 91* (Washington, DC: Worldwatch Institute, October 1989). The Worldwatch plan calls for reducing net carbon emissions to a maximum of 2 billion tons per year. According to Flavin, given a projected world population of 10 billion people, this means it will be necessary to stabilize per capita outputs at a level similar to India's today, or one-tenth the European level.

14. While conservation groups in the United States are pressuring Southern countries to preserve their rain forests, their own forests are being decimated by corporations that are clear cutting their timber holdings as a defense against unfriendly corporate takeovers. See Andrew Porterfield, "Railroaded: The LBO Trend on Wall Street is Playing Havoc with the Nation's Forests," *Common Cause Magazine,* September/-October 1989, pp. 21–23. Efforts to stop the destruction of irreplaceable tropical forests must continue with all the energy and commitment the United States can muster, but it must give at least equal attention to the destruction that is occurring in its own back yard in response to senseless policies that serve only the greed of a small group of parasitic investment bankers and financial manipulators and the politicians they have bought. The use of political contributions by the leveraged buy-out lobby to forestall essential reforms is documented in detail by Max Holland and Viveca Novak, "Buyouts: The LBO Lobby Makes its Move on Washington," *Common Cause Magazine,* September–October 1989, pp. 13–20.

15. Current methods of economic accounting make no distinction between a value extracted from the environment (the extraction of a mineral, the cutting of a tree, the loading of the air with a toxic substance, the depletion of soil fertility, or the drawing down of ground water); and a value that is created through the application of: 1)

labor, which employs an otherwise wasted resource and represents a good in itself; or 2) the application of information, which is nondepleting and environmentally benign.

Work to develop more appropriate systems of national accounting are underway at a number of institutions, including the World Resources Institute in Washington, DC, and the International Institute for Environment and Development in London. See Robert Repetto and William B. Magrath, *Wasting Assets: Natural Resources in the National Accounts* (Washington, DC: World Resources Institute, 1989). See also the report of an international conference held in Caracas, Venezuela, July 31–August 3, 1989, titled "Towards a New Way to Measure Development." The proceedings of this meeting are available in Spanish and English from the South Commission, Office of the Commissioner in Venezuela. Ave. Libertador, Centro Libertador, PH Oeste, Caracas, Venezuela.

16. Charles Elliot, *Comfortable Compassion? Poverty, Power and the Church* (London: Hodder and Stoughton, 1987); Maurice Sinclair, *Ripening Harvest, Gathering Storm* (London: Church Missionary Society, 1988); and Niall O'Brien, *Revolution from the Heart* (New York: Oxford Press, 1987).

17. Elliot, *Comfortable Compassion?*, pp. 100–41.

18. In the early 1970s I was living and working in Central America. One of my associates was a young member of an elite El Salvadoran family who held a senior position in the Ministry of Education and Culture. I became fascinated with the special mission he set for himself—raising the class consciousness of wealthy families. His basic premise was that though the elites of El Salvador lived in splendid luxury amidst the teeming masses of the poor, they were sufficiently isolated from their reality to lack a real consciousness of the fact that they were members of a privileged elite. They lacked class consciousness. His goal was to penetrate the veil that cloaked their consciousness in the belief that raising class consciousness among the elites might result in their more responsible use of power vis-a-vis the poor.

19. I sense a failure of my own courage even as I write these words. The task as outlined so far in this book is already so overwhelming as to seem nearly hopeless. To put it in terms of the need for a transformation of human nature puts us up against the task at which our religious institutions have failed for centuries. Isn't the posing of the challenge in such terms tantamount to insuring paralysis? Are we simply caught between necessity and reality? Between the proverbial rock and the hard place? Is it worth devoting our energies to the impossible? Or might we just as well set ourselves to enjoying our status as overconsumers for the few years that remain to us? Then I think of my children, their special promise, and the future they will inherit if we fail at this task. Yes, we must try.

20. Statistics prepared by staff of the Arms Control and Foreign Policy Caucus of the U.S. Congress. See *United States Security and The Developing World,* p. 39–42.

21. *Ibid.,* pp. 42 and 54.

22. In FY 1989, a total of $44 million in U.S. international assistance was allocated for promoting democratic institutions in developing countries, a minuscule amount compared to the $5.4 billion earmarked for military aid. This $44 million was allocated to three programs: the State Department's Administration of Justice program ($20 million) to train judges and police in Latin America; the National Endowment for Democracy ($16 million) providing technical assistance to elections, political parties and trade unions in other countries; and AID's Democratic Initiatives Program ($8

million) supporting legal aid and training, media groups, and advocates of democracy. *United States Security and the Developing World,* p.35.

23. What of the case where a government will not allow foreigners to channel assistance to NGOs? Do we simply allow the people to suffer? We have too long been held hostage to such blackmail by authoritarian leaders. It must be made clear that if the people suffer, they suffer by the hand of their own government, not by the hands of those who refuse to assist that government in its suppression and exploitation.

24. Capitalism emphasizes the protection of the rights of property ownership. At the same time its economic models in defense of competitive markets assume a market system dominated by small producers, in which this property ownership is vested. While there is no explicit presumption that each worker will own his or her means of production, the assumption is that control over economic assets will be widely distributed in the hands of owners who are also workers in the firm. The principle that the worker should own the means of production through some form of democratically governed collective association is much more explicit in socialist theory. Yet the basic goal of an empowered individual is much the same in both ideologies. The differences relate more to how this will be achieved.

25. For a discussion of the ideal, see Leamon J. Bennett, "When Employees Run the Company," *Harvard Business Review,* January–February 1979. In the United States some 7,000 companies have enrolled nearly 10 million workers in employee stock ownership plans. At current rates of enrollment it is estimated that by the year 2000 some 25 percent of all U.S. workers will own part or all of their companies. "ESOPs: Revolution or Ripoff?" *Business Week,* April 15, 1985, pp. 94–108.

26. There is a related problem even with pure grant assistance that provides foreign exchange free of obligation to repay, either in the form of direct goods and services or foreign currency. Even it the foreign currency is exchanged for local currency to buy local products and services, the foreign currency provided by the donor is in fact being placed in the hands of the country to purchase foreign goods and services or to repay loans. The former establishes patterns that can be sustained only through further grants or exports. The latter reduces dependence only as long as new debts are not immediately incurred to replace the ones retired.

27. The underlying arguments are developed in much greater detail by James Robertson, *Future Wealth: A New Economics for the 21st Century* (London: Cassell Publishers, Ltd., 1989).

28. The advocates of international financing and market dependence will dismiss this on the grounds that through the wonders of comparative advantage, the exporting country will gain much more through the ability to import products in which other producers have a comparative advantage and thus are able to offer them at more favorable prices. This is hardly the case, however, when export earnings are committed primarily to the repayment of debt.

29. One means of accomplishing this is to place a uniform international tax on all international trade and currency conversion transactions. See Robertson, *Future Wealth.* This is a radical, even illogical, proposal given the free trade logic of cowboy economics. It is, however, eminently consistent with the self-reliance logic of the newly emerging spaceship economics. The Robertson book is highly recommended reading for anyone interested in these issues.

30. See *Sustainable Development: A Guide to "Our Common Future"* (Washington, DC: Global Tomorrow Coalition, 1989), p. 7.

31. This argument is based on the reality that the country that in effect exports its minerals, soils, forests, ground water, etc., is giving up something substantive, in many instances permanently. These losses have real implications in terms of well-being and future productive potentials. Information based exports are entirely different. When you export a product that derives its value primarily from information content, you give up nothing in terms of your own life-style or your future productive potential, since information based products are infinitely replicable. On the contrary, the more you work with information based technologies, the more you master them and the greater the future benefit you may expect to derive. Thus, we may speak of the difference between the export of environmental and information values. The country that can trade its own information values for the environmental values of others, while preserving its own environmental resource values, is in a highly favored position.

32. The term information resources refers to the technical knowledge and rights to use advanced information based technologies, particularly those from materials science, genetic engineering, and electronics that essentially substitute information for physical materials in critical production processes.

33. "Save the Tropical Rainforests!" an information bulletin available from the Japan Tropical Forest Action Network, 501 Shinwa Building, 9–17 Sakuraoka, Shibuya-ku, Tokyo 150, Japan, *circa* 1989, p. 1.

34. Consumer groups in the Philippines have made the case that tobacco companies are consciously targeting youth to attract them as lifetime consumers.

35. This refers to transferring control over and the ability to use the technologies in question, not simply setting up a factory in which they will be applied under the exclusive control of the foreign investor.

36. By this standard, Japan and the United States are economically perhaps the two most irresponsible members of the international community for exactly opposite reasons. Japan is constraining the rise in its domestic living standards while turning the power of its formidable economic machine outward to the capture an enormous share of the world's economic resources in an effort to become the world's leading money lender and absentee owner of productive assets. The United States is living far beyond its means, using borrowed money and the sale of productive assets to maintain a level of irresponsible, profligate overconsumption that is the envy of overconsumers and aspiring overconsumers throughout the world. Both are acting irresponsibly in the global community and should be called to task for their irresponsible actions.

37. Those who expect to buy products or services from another community that involves a consequential depletion of the selling community's environmental resources should expect to pay prices that fully compensate the supplying community for its loss. Political democratization is particularly important here to limit the extent to which a ruler or entrepreneur may be in a position to turn the community's loss into a personal gain through the misuse of state power.

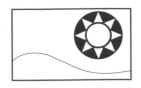

CHAPTER FOURTEEN

CITIZEN VOLUNTEERS

You see what is and ask, 'why?'
I see what could be and ask 'why not?'
— *George Bernard Shaw*

Progress toward realization of the transformation agenda will depend on the efforts of millions of citizen volunteers working toward the realization of a broadly shared vision. There is need to mobilize and focus voluntary energy on a scale without precedent in human history. It remains to be seen whether those nongovernment organizations (NGOs) that style themselves as development organizations will play a meaningful role in this process. Though many have grown out of voluntary traditions, in all too many cases the role of the volunteers has, with time, been reduced to writing checks to support paid staff who owe allegiance to the norms of bureaucratic administration. This chapter looks at four areas in which there is particular need to strengthen voluntary action, re-examine voluntary organization (VO) roles and relationships and build new VO capacities.

FOUR CRITICAL ROLES

There are at least four critical roles for voluntary action within the broader framework of a people's development movement: catalyzing the transformation of institutions, policies and values; monitoring and protesting abuses of power; facilitating reconciliation; and providing essential community services. In all of these roles, individual voluntary action is as important as the action of the formally constituted VO, each contributing to the larger synergy of the movement.

Catalyzing Systems Change
The foremost development priority of the 1990s is to transform the ways in which people perceive their world, use its resources, and relate to one another as individuals and nations.[1] There is a substantial need

for leadership and support from government. However, a lead role in catalyzing these changes—through defining issues, creating a new global consciousness, facilitating people-to-people exchange, advocating policy change, building political will and undertaking experimental initiatives—must come from people taking voluntary action.

For the VO this implies an emphasis on third and fourth generation strategies (see chapter 9) aimed at redefining policies, transforming institutions, and helping people define, internalize and actualize a people-centered development vision. At a practical level this means, for example:

- Working to achieve a more broadly distributed control of productive assets and in particular helping the disenfranchised obtain secure claims to the assets on which their livelihoods depend.
- Working for the transformation of national development agencies so that they have the capacity to support communities in the management of their own resources.
- Working with corporations to create positive demonstrations of social and environmentally responsible resource management.
- Holding seminars for military officers to educate them to their responsibilities under democratic civilian rule.
- Working for court reform to insure the rights of the weaker elements of society.
- Working to direct international assistance to positive uses in support of democratic governments and people's development action.
- Working with community organizations to create prototype resource management systems based on social and environmentally appropriate technologies and organizational relationships.
- Helping to publicize the results of such experiments.

The list could be extended indefinitely to include activities from every sector of society and every element of the transformation agenda briefly outlined in chapter 12. Sometimes the catalytic activity may involve protest actions. However, unlike the monitoring and protest role described below, the first priority of the VO in the catalyst role is *pro-action* to create positive change more than *re-action* to police negative behavior. Thus the focus is on *advocacy*—acting *for*—rather than on *protest*—acting *against*.

Education for global citizenship is another activity to which development-oriented NGOs of both North and South need to devote greater attention.[2] There has been a growing interest in development education among Northern NGOs, in part a result of admonitions from their Southern partners.[3] Yet most of what passes for development education by development-oriented NGOs in the North continues to consist mostly of fund raising appeals directed to the lowest common denominator of the public's understanding of global issues, i.e., there are starving children out there who depend on compassionate people in the North to send them food. These appeals were demonstrably effective during the 1980s from a fund-raising perspective.

Indeed, their success has created an understandable reluctance on the part of the sponsoring VOs to accept the reality that these messages carry a false image of the problem. More importantly they do nothing to build an understanding of the actions required to eliminate the conditions that give the young faces staring out from the fund raising appeals no prospect for a decent future—no matter how generous the donations of the Northern TV viewer.[4] The false image is a far cry from the type of education that the people of both North and South need in order to prepare them for active participation in a global transformation.

The international NGOs[5] typically protest that if they change their message they will bring in less money to help the needy of the South. The answer to that protest is a series of questions. Does your fund raising create complacency and inhibit essential actions in the North? Do the programs to which you apply it serve to sustain rather than change the unjust power relationships that are a crucial cause of the suffering in the South? If so, then who, other than your own paid staff and those who benefit from the status quo in the South, will really suffer from a drop in your organization's income?

System Monitoring and Protest

Many elements of the transformation agenda require actions to check abuses of power that violate both the law and accepted norms of human behavior, especially by government and business. The key to effective monitoring and protest is a system of citizen surveillance that brings abusive behavior into the open for public scrutiny and action.

Abuse feeds on silence. Often the fear of exposure is in itself enough to check the potential abuser. System monitoring and protest are not popular activities among those who are protective of what they may perceive to be their prerogative to abuse the power they hold. It requires courage to monitor and expose this abuse in the face of potential retaliation.[6]

Rarely is any organization able to effectively discipline itself through internal procedures alone. This is why democracy depends on a system of checks and balances provided by such institutions as an independent judiciary and a free press. Yet even they depend on an informed and vigilant citizenry to function effectively.

The judiciary is a passive instrument. It can act only on those cases that are brought before it—either criminal suits brought by government or civil suits brought by citizens. Public interest legal organizations from the voluntary sector are essential to the protective role of the judiciary. They give society's weaker elements access to the protection of the law and bring class-action suits to counter abuses of power by government and business.

The press can communicate only the information it has. An informed and active citizenry is its eyes and ears, calling attention to abuses that otherwise might go unseen.

Both national and international poll watching groups help to insure the integrity of election processes in countries where it has commonly been lacking.[7] Amnesty International is only one of the better known international human rights monitoring groups. Environmental organizations are becoming increasingly active in monitoring corporate performance on environmental issues. Citizen groups may also organize to monitor and draw public attention to such things as illegal logging activities and the smuggling of endangered species.[8]

In general, the successful efforts of environmental and human rights groups in bringing the international development agencies to task for their socially and environmentally destructive projects stands in sharp contrast to the comparative silence of most private international assistance agencies. Hopefully, the voices of the latter will be heard with greater frequency as they broaden the definition of their roles.

Facilitating Reconciliation with Justice

Dwight D. Eisenhower, who had commanded the Allied Forces in Europe during World War II, said in 1959, during his tenure as President of the United States:

I like to believe that people in the long run are going to do more to promote peace than are governments. Indeed, I think that people want peace so much that one of these days governments had better get out of their way and let them have it.[9]

Many VOs have worked to relieve the suffering of the victims of conflict. These VOs have often struggled with the ethical dilemmas involved in such interventions. To what extent should they remain politically neutral and risk tacitly accepting or even condoning the policies and actions of governments and others that directly create the suffering? Taking a political stance may result in their being barred from assisting the victims. The International Red Cross has consistently taken the position that one cannot at the same time be a champion of justice and a champion of charity. Groups that take this stance commonly maintain that they do not distinguish between just and unjust wars. They see only victims in need of help.[10]

Some observers argue that political neutrality in a conflict situation is impossible given the likelihood that relief efforts may affect the balance of forces in the area, or even allow the conflict to be sustained longer than otherwise possible. Relief workers have acknowledged, for example, that some food aid to the Kampucheans in Thailand has been diverted to the use of Pol Pot military forces and that humanitarian aid within Kampuchea indirectly helped to sustain the Vietnamese occupation.[11]

Given the current prevalence of communal violence and its influence on the lives of millions of people, responsible VOs must take a more proactive stance. They must turn their attention to the protagonists, as did the Sudan Council of Churches (SCC) in the 1988/89 conflict in that country. Rather than closing its eyes to the cause of the suffering, the SCC became actively involved in a peace-making effort. It established a dialogue with both the Khartoum government and the Southern People's Liberation Army (SPLA). It also sent delegations to churches and governments in Europe, North America and Africa to encourage them to become more active in peace-making efforts. This strengthened efforts by Church World Service to motivate the U.S. government to apply stronger pressure on its Khartoum ally to seek a negotiated solution.[12]

In the SCC case, the peace-making effort was the *outgrowth* of involvement in large-scale relief operations. The priorities should be reversed. Relief operations in conflict situations should be undertaken primarily and specifically to build the presence, credibility and relationships required to play an effective peace-making role. Reflection on past experience, such as in the Sudan, may provide insights into the range of opportunities that might be available to VOs to pursue peace making strategies in conflict situations.

The issues are not simple. A rejection of violence and a commitment to reconciliation must not be equated with condoning injustice. A peace that imposes or sustains injustice works its own violence on the poor and powerless. For them it is no peace at all. The goal must be reconciliation with justice.

The need for just reconciliation is one of the most fundamental development needs in our contemporary world. Religion, which commonly presumes to be society's primary arbiter of the values that govern human behavior and relationships, must surely play a central role. While religion is all too often invoked as the rallying cry of the intolerant and hateful in the cause of violence, the basic message of all of the world's great religious teachers has been one of love, brotherhood and tolerance. Those who follow in the tradition of these great teachers are among the most important development workers of our day because they are attacking a root cause of human suffering.

An inspiring example is provided by Elias Chacour's account of his efforts to bring reconciliation to a Christian community in Ibillin, a village in northern Palestine.[13] Hatred and conflict divided brother from brother and sister from sister. The community filled the church pews on Palm Sunday, but more from custom than from the desire for spiritual renewal. Indifferent to the service, they sat with sullen hatred in their eyes.

At the end of the service Father Chacour took a bold action. He went to the back of the church, pulled a heavy chain from a pocket of his robe and padlocked the doors shut. Turning to the congregation, he said,

> You are a people divided. You argue and hate each other, gossip and spread malicious lies. What do the Moslems and the unbelievers think when they see you? Surely that your religion is false. If you can't love your brother that you see, how can you

say you love God who is invisible?

Shock turned to anger. The congregation's lay leader trembled and seemed about to choke. The village policeman tapped his foot angrily and turned red around the collar. Father Chacour continued,

For many months, I've tried to unite you. I've failed, because I'm only a man. But there is someone else who can bring you together in true unity. His name is Jesus Christ. He is the one who gives you power to forgive. So now I will be quiet and allow Him to give you that power. If you will not forgive, we will stay locked in here. You can kill each other and I'll provide your funerals gratis.

There was silence. Tight-lipped, fists clenched, the congregation glared at Father Chacour as if carved from stone. More than ten minutes passed. Then suddenly, Abu Mouhib, the hard-bitten village policeman was on his feet.

I'm sorry. I am the worst one of all. I've hated my own brothers. Hated them so much I wanted to kill them. More than any of you I need forgiveness.

Suddenly there was a chaos of embracing and repentance in the church as each member sought out those whom he or she had scorned and slandered to seek and receive forgiveness. The festival continued into the streets and far into the evening, groups of believers going door-to-door asking and receiving forgiveness.

Father Chacour spoke to his congregation in the language of their faith. His message, however, is universal to all the world's great religions. This story illustrates the power of spiritual renewal in allowing society to release itself from the bondage of fear and hatred—the spiritual poverty that may well be the cause of more human suffering than economic poverty.

What happened in Father Chacour's church must be recreated innumerable times on a global-scale. Reconciliation must start within the family and the community. From there it must be extended across the boundaries of ethnic, religious, race, ideological, class and national differences.

The reconciliation agenda presents a particular challenge to religiously affiliated VOs. These organizations have often developed agendas that are indistinguishable from those of their secular counterparts, even while attempting to work through local churches as the instruments of implementation. Seldom have they asked whether local churches are the most appropriate organizations to implement well digging, food storage and road building projects. Nor have they asked what might be a distinctive role of the church in addressing the realities of underdevelopment.[14]

If the church as an institution is not being effective in this role, then a priority concern of religiously oriented-development VOs should be to help it rediscover its mission. If the institutional church is incapable of this role, then the religiously-oriented development

VOs should themselves accept a responsibility to play the role of teacher in carrying forward the universal messages of love, brotherhood and reconciliation as central to their own missions.

This is not a call for proselytizing to win religious converts. Conversion from one religious tradition to another is not the objective. Indeed, the focus of organized religion on gaining converts to a particular faith is a major contributor to the problem of religious intolerance and conflict. The objective is to help each individual discover the power of the fundamental integrative teachings of his or her own religious faith—whatever that faith may be. This role demands an advanced level of religious tolerance and ecumenism.

Implementing Large-scale Service Programs

A sustainable equity-led growth strategy must be supported by appropriate service delivery systems able to function on a national scale. It has long been assumed in development circles that government has a natural responsibility and ability to deliver essential services. That belief has contributed to a great deal of waste and all too little service.

New and more innovative approaches to large-scale service delivery and program implementation are essential, especially in such vital services family planning services, reforestation (particularly social forestry programs), basic education and small-scale credit. Most efforts to broaden the base of control over productive assets and to organize farmer's unions and cooperatives also require effective large-scale outreach capability. Many of these services and programs are best carried out on a decentralized basis.[15] Yet it is also true that large-scale program implementation requires more focused and coordinated action than characterizes the episodic, scattered and ad hoc service delivery activities of many NGOs.

There are important examples of successful large-scale program implementation by NGOs. In Bangladesh, CARE, through its food for work program, supports the construction of nearly 10,000 miles of road a year. Some 90 percent of the households have received oral rehydration training from the Bangladesh Rural Advancement Committee. The Grameen Bank has become established as a permanent banking institution that extends credit to 580,734 members, mostly women.[16]

Elsewhere, there are other examples of large-scale NGO outreach. The programs of the Sarvodaya Shramadana Movement reach over 5,000 villages in Sri Lanka. PROFAMILIA, the national family planning association of Colombia, operates one of the most effective and comprehensive national-scale programs of family planning service delivery in the world, insuring the availability of reliable contraceptive supplies and services to nearly every family in the country.

Examples such as these have contributed substantially to a growth of interest among donors and governments in funding nongovernmental organizations (NGOs) to implement large-scale service delivery programs.[17] There has been a considerable tendency to assume that any organization that calls itself an NGO will readily replicate the success achieved by other NGOs.[18] This is dangerously naive. It results in wasteful actions that risk undermining and discrediting the effective NGOs.

At the same time there has been too little attention to an important weakness of many NGO service delivery success stories, particularly those from the South. Often they depend entirely or substantially on foreign funding and therefore must be presumed to be unsustainable. Though there are exceptions, many do not lead in any systematic way toward self-reliance. Furthermore, the NGOs involved are likely to find that the demands of large-scale service delivery interfere with their ability to serve as catalysts, advocates and monitors.

From the standpoint of our concern with voluntary action, the most interesting cases of large-scale service delivery by NGOs are those that are built on true volunteer action. For example, according to Drucker, in the state of Florida in the United States, young people convicted of their first criminal offense—about 25,000 a year—are paroled into the custody of the Salvation Army. Through a strict work program, run largely by volunteers backed by a small professional staff, the Salvation Army has been able to rehabilitate 80 percent of them. Another example is the American Red Cross, which depends almost entirely on volunteer labor to run worldwide disaster relief programs, maintain thousands of blood banks, conduct training in cardiac and respiratory rescue nationwide, and give first-aid courses in thousands of schools.[19]

There is much to be learned from such examples about the effective mobilization of volunteer energy as a community resource in support of large-scale, yet decentralized, service delivery. The sharing of such experience and expertise might be an especially appropriate role for international VOs. While it remains unclear to what extent these models can be replicated in resource poor countries, greater attention is needed to exploring the possibilities.

DEVELOPING NEW COMPETENCIES

VOs that redefine their roles in line with the challenges of the 1990s will often face the need to develop new competencies. Ironically, for many development-oriented VOs learning to work through voluntary action may be their greatest capacity building challenge.[20]

As Advocates, Educators and Catalysts
The VO that attempts to catalyze system change will need a change theory that provides a basis for focusing its interventions (see chapter 9). It will need skills in social and policy analysis, political strategy, and public education, and it must be able to define and articulate policy issues clearly to lay audiences.

Compared to their counterparts in the volunteer based environmental, human rights, consumer affairs, peace and women's movements, the more professionalized development-oriented VOs and public service contractors (PSCs) have given relatively little attention to policy education and advocacy beyond lobbying to protect or increase foreign assistance levels.

By and large, the development-oriented VOs and PSCs have been content to leave the larger policy issues to the World Bank, IMF and bilateral donors. The few exceptions, such as the World Development Movement, Development Gap, International Coalition for Development Action, North-South Institute, Overseas Development Council, Results, Bread for the World, International Institute for Environment and Development, Institute for Policy Studies, Transnational Institute and World Watch Institute, are often specialists in policy analysis, education and/or advocacy and are likely to be viewed as outside the mainstream by other private international assistance organizations. Only a few, such as the Oxfams, AFSC, Lutheran World Relief and the World Council of Churches combine field operations and policy advocacy.

This is an unfortunate pattern. Those VOs that have extensive international field operations have access to a rich store of data and experience that is less available to organizations that function exclusively as Northern policy think tanks. Furthermore, greater attention to social and policy analysis might lead those international VOs that are engaged in support of field operations to insights that would greatly enhance the relevance of their field activities.

It would not be realistic, appropriate or cost effective, however, for each international VO interested in advocacy issues to develop a formal policy analysis capability of its own. In many instances development of linkages with organizations in both North and South that do specialize in such analysis may be a more realistic way to meet this need. At a minimum the operational VO that is also interested in advocacy should have some means to capture and process relevant data inputs from its own experience as a means of refining its understanding of and position on important issues. Participation in networks of VOs that share information and analysis on particular policy interests may also be valuable.

Such networks should normally involve both Southern and Northern VOs, each dealing with its own side of the selected issues. For example, suppose the issue is one of convincing a major multinational corporation engaged in conversion of local forest resources into pulp and paper to undertake a more socially and environmentally sound approach to its operations. Southern VOs may lobby their own government to make such practices a part of the licensing agreement with the company and seek to negotiate directly with local officers of the corporation to develop a planning process by which VOs might work with the company to implement the plan. The Northern VO partners might simultaneously mobilize pressure on the company's international headquarters, through threat of a consumer boycott, to work with the local VOs in good faith. More technically oriented Northern VOs might prepare the outlines of an alternative land use and business plan. The Southern VOs might provide a continuing flow of feedback on negotiations.[21]

In some instances the Southern VO may operate in a setting where open dissent might be dangerous, particularly if the interests of high level government officials are involved. In such cases the Southern VO may quietly provide the data, giving leadership to a Northern partner in disseminating the information and mobilizing public opinion.

In efforts to deal with interlinked North-South policy interventions the on-the-ground perspectives of Southern VOs are vital to appropriate action. This is demonstrated in the action taken by the U.S. Congress to increase the Philippine sugar quota. The Hunger Project's World Development Forum carried an announcement of the quota increase, lauding it as a step to relieve the suffering of the poor in the economically depressed sugar growing Philippine province of Negros Occidental. It seemed a logical and self-evident conclusion. Unfortunately it was wrong.

What is not widely known outside the Philippines is that even when the sugar industry of Negros Occidental Province is thriving, the landless sugar workers there live in destitution under some of the most oppressive labor relationships found anywhere in the world. They share in the prosperity only in the most limited ways. While the depression of the sugar industry did make it even harder than usual for landless laborers to find work, it also severely depressed the value of the landholdings of the large sugar barons. They thus became more amenable to land sharing arrangements under which the landless were able to grow their own crops on otherwise idle land. Resistance to land reform weakened as land values fell.

As soon as sugar prices recovered, following the increase in the U.S. quota, land barons began kicking the landless off their small plots and converting them back to sugar, all the while rejoicing at the return of the "good old days." Only by drawing on the perspective of the Philippine VOs that work with the landless of Negros would U.S. VOs likely be aware that rather than providing a boon to the poor, the increase in the sugar quota had helped to deprive the poor of their hope for access to land of their own.[22]

In addition to strong South-North linkages, an active and committed grass roots constituency can add greatly to the effectiveness of a VO as policy advocate and educator—irrespective of whether in the South or the North.[23] A long list of contributors may help, but an engaged constituency that is prepared to lobby parliamentarians, elicit editorials in local newspapers, give talks to civic groups, organize local seminars and participate in public demonstrations is more likely to capture the attention of decision makers. Highly qualified professional backstopping may be essential to produce the supporting analyses and polished publications. However, in the end it is voluntary action that is most likely to influence the policy process.

An important starting point for the VO seeking to play a more effective and responsible role in development education may be to apply the techniques of market analysis to identify the demographic characteristics of its natural constituencies, both contributors and non-contributors, and to assess their current levels of global knowledge in general and development knowledge in particular. Efforts might then be made to find out what issues most concern them. These issues can serve as entry points for engaging them in relevant self- and group-study programs. Such efforts might ease the VO's risk of suffering a serious revenue loss as it moves away from conventional fund-raising appeals.

As Monitors and Whistle Blowers
Often the roles of advocacy and protest are combined within the same VO. Protest action may in some instances be an essential element of advocacy. On the other hand, there are important differences in orientation and competence involved.

The heart of the monitoring function is an extensive network of volunteers, linked together by an effective information system, who serve as the eyes and ears of the monitoring network. It is equally essential, however, that the organization have the capacity to use the gathered information in ways that lead to specific political, judicial or administrative action. This is likely to require capabilities in political lobbying, litigation and mobilization of public protests through the media, demonstrations and letter-writing campaigns.

As Mediators, Conciliators and Bridge Builders
To play an effective role in the reconciliation of violent conflicts, the VO is likely to require a combination of the skills of the political organizer, diplomat, mediator and marriage counselor. Sometimes it may be necessary to bring strong international pressure to bear through broadly based public appeals. At other times working quietly behind the scenes to win the trust of the protagonists may be required. Sometimes it may be necessary to do both at once.

The groundwork for reconciliation may be prepared by facilitating direct communications and exchanges between constituent citizen groups of the contesting factions. This has been a major tactic of volunteer citizen peace groups. Even when leaders of opposing factions may not be willing to sit together to dialogue, lay members of these same factions may be more receptive.

In the United States, a quarterly journal, the *Bulletin of Municipal Foreign Policy,* has been created solely to promote and publicize efforts at citizen diplomacy. Its special focus is on initiatives by individual American cities to establish their own foreign policies. These include sister cities programs that encourage direct links between the citizens of a U.S. city and those of a city abroad, commonly in the South. More than twenty U.S. cities that have sister city relationships in Nicaragua sent delegations to participate in the monitoring of Nicaragua's election to insure that the U.S. government could not arbitrarily to dismiss these elections as fraudulent.[24]

As Large-scale Program Implementers

Large-scale service delivery by nonprofits, whether as public service contractors, large cooperatives federations, or independent agencies organized to mobilize community level volunteer resources, is an important and legitimate role for NGOs. Those that chose to assume long-term or permanent roles in such systems must be clear in their own minds, however, that this is what they are doing and approach the task accordingly. It is very different from that of short-term delivery of relief supplies and services, the implementation of conventional development projects, or catalyzing institutional and policy change—all of which assume that the NGO's participation is temporary.

When an NGO—whether VO, PSC, people's organization (PO), or a governmental nongovernmental organization—is positioning itself for a long-term implementing role, it must think not in terms of a temporary intervention, but rather in terms of institutionalizing itself and its functions. When assuming this role the NGO must deal with the issue of sustained financing. Dependence on short-term foreign grants is inconsistent with the need to sustain permanent operations.[25] The permanent service delivery NGO should also address the need to organize its own governance structures so that it can be held accountable for performance by the people who depend on its services.

In some instances a catalyst VO may create a new organization intended to serve as a permanent institutionalized service provider. For example, the Bangladesh Rural Advancement Committee (BRAC) is creating a bank that will function as an independent entity, to perform BRAC's credit delivery functions on a permanent basis.[26]

It is rarely appropriate for large, foreign-funded, professionally staffed international NGOs to become involved in large-scale program implementation in Southern countries on a permanent operational basis, except when a country is acknowledged to be a permanent, international welfare dependent. On the other hand, large VOs, such as the Red Cross, that support self-financing, self-managing local chapters staffed and managed by local volunteers may have important and appropriate roles. Here the international organization provides technical backstopping, an international constituency and credibility, and emergency resources for times of special need. A number of the larger international VOs with experience in managing volunteer based, large-scale humanitarian assistance operations might find important roles in helping mobilize and organize similar volunteer based programs in the South. International NGOs operate more as PSCs also have valuable management skills that might be passed on to local organizations that also serve as PSCs.

LEARNING TO WORK TOGETHER

Development-oriented VOs have long been known for their exclusive preoccupation with their own development projects and beneficiaries. Sometimes it almost seems as though they are competing for the right to claim accessible groups of the poor as their own. Such attitudes are an almost certain indicator that the primary orientation of the VO in question is toward relief and welfare. The more the VO becomes truly committed to a people-centered development agenda aimed at institutional and values transformation, the more it is likely to find a need to cooperate with many like-minded individuals and organizations to create a critical mass of support for change.[27]

Criticism from the South

Much of the current debate on NGO roles and relationships centers on the relationships between international NGOs based in the North and national ones in the South. This has been stimulated by often harsh criticism from Southern NGOs that many Northern based international NGOs are seriously out of step with changing times.[28]

The arguments are now familiar to most international NGOs. Their field operations are characterized as anachronisms from another era, still focused more on relief than development, negligent in the creation and strengthening of indigenous capabilities to replace themselves, and unmindful of the growth of national NGOs that have surpassed them in relevance and in size and technical and managerial skills.

In less polite company, international NGOs are accused of representing establishment interests more than those of the poor and of lacking any development theory. They are perceived to act as though the problem of poverty were entirely within the capacity of the poor themselves to solve if given sufficient food, school uniforms, education and health care—ignoring the extent to which inequitable economic and political structures at local, national and international levels make real self-help progress a false hope. There is a suspicion that their interests in sustainability center on sustaining their own jobs and a dependence on their own presence.

International NGOs are being told that if they are to have any legitimate function in development in the South, they must first transform themselves and seek new and more timely roles in developing the capabilities of indigenous NGOs and voluntary sectors. Even more important is the assumption of new functions as global partners in policy dialogue and development education.

Some of the accusations are inaccurate and unfair, and few of them apply to all international NGOs. They do not acknowledge the substantial progress that many international NGOs have made in increasing their technical and professional capabilities, becoming development-oriented, and giving more attention to the development of indigenous NGO capabilities. There are, however, few who deny the merit of the admonition that further re-examination is needed by international NGOs of their roles in the South.

North/South Partnerships

The progressive NGOs of both the North and the South are currently engaged in trying to realize a somewhat elusive concept often referred to as North/South partnership. One manifestation is an increased concern among international NGOs with the development of independent national NGOs in the South.

International NGOs based in the United States have received encouragement from the U.S. Agency for International Development (AID) to give more attention to providing such assistance. A recent study of this experience funded by AID's Office of Private Voluntary Cooperation points to the importance of the international NGO doing more than simply creating an indigenous organization that is a replica of itself and then departing. The most successful experiences have been those in which the U.S. partner maintained a long-term relationship with the local partner organization, helping it to establish and maintain linkages with both national and international networks.[29]

A dilemma is created by the growing number of instances in which national NGOs have developed capabilities equal to or greater than those of many prospective international NGO partner organizations in conventional areas of expertise such as health services, rural credit programs and community organizing. In countries such as India and the Philippines there are also a variety of local institutions able to offer high quality training on a wide range of themes. International NGOs have a difficult time justifying their presence in such settings if they can offer nothing more than what local groups are already able to provide.[30] In a growing number of countries the capacity building needs are becoming increasingly sophisticated.

For example, the more advanced Southern VOs may be looking for assistance in developing specialized technical capabilities in restoring degraded agricultural or forestry lands, policy analysis, legislative lobbying, drafting legislation to protect the coastal ecology, managing computer communications networks, designing social marketing campaigns, using television for distance education, organizing rural banks, managing press relations and policy advocacy.

They may also be looking for international partners who will be effective political allies in such matters as lobbying against the socially and environmentally unsound projects of Northern donor agencies; or bringing international pressures to bear on their own governments to guarantee the freedom of association and expression of VOs and POs.

They may seek assistance to link into international experience and data banks for such purposes as: determining whether particular pesticides or pharmaceutical products are approved for use in the United States or Europe, assessing the export market potentials of a prospective product of a sponsored cooperative, accessing new technologies, learning from the experience of women's movements in other countries, and helping access debt swap funds.

Of course organizations offering funding, especially if their procedures are not too cumbersome or obtrusive, are usually tolerated even if they bring little in the way of technical expertise or useful linkages. However, in general, the more highly developed the Southern VO community, the more advanced the capability offered by the PVO or Northern VO must be in order for it to be a relevant and useful partner. To the extent that they accept the invitation to partnership, international VOs will need to be able to establish that they are channels to relevant financial, political and technical resources. They will be expected to bring an expertise that at least equals that of the Southern partner and to share the latter's commitments to social and political change.

Another important dilemma faces Northern NGOs that respond to the call for partnership. The easiest type of capacity building assistance for one NGO to provide to another is assistance in becoming a replica of itself. Unfortunately, the need of most Southern countries is not for the replication of Northern organizations that were created to dispense Northern charity in the South.

The South needs a diverse variety of VOs skilled in mobilizing voluntary energy to catalyze system change, monitor power holders, facilitate conflict resolution through reconciliation, and establish and sustain volunteer based service delivery systems. For NGOs that have become professionalized charities to play a meaningful role in the creation of such organizations poses a challenge several orders of magnitude greater than simply replicating themselves. Yet simply to recreate themselves may well only contribute to already alarming trends toward commercialization of national NGO sectors in the South, and to institutionalizing national organizations with a strong self-interest in perpetuating what is becoming an international system of welfare dependence.[31]

Where international NGOs have devoted attention to strengthening indigenous partners, the focus has most often been on assisting individual organizations. Less common have been interventions to help strengthen an NGO community or sector. Even more rare than efforts aimed at sector development are efforts by development-oriented international NGOs aimed at strengthening voluntarism in the South. The voluntary dimension of development action needs much greater attention in future North-South partnerships among development-oriented NGOs than it has received to date.

Forming Alliances across People's Movements
A growing number of development-oriented VOs of both South and
North are discovering that many of the most critical issues to be
addressed in the 1990s are in fact more central to the agendas of
environmental, women's, peace, and human and civil rights groups
than to those of the mainstream international assistance NGOs. Furthermore, many Northern VOs involved in these movements have
already forged alliances with like-minded VOs in the South and are
making their proven capabilities in advocacy and public education
available to their Southern partners.

Southern NGOs are increasingly seeking out such alliances. For
example, Southern VOs that work closely with the rural poor see the
extent to which the burden of a deteriorating land, water and forestry
resource base is being borne by the poor. This leads them to an interest in linking into international environmental networks. Recognition
of the political dimension of poverty and the need to protect the rights
of freedom of association and expression for VOs and POs leads them
to an interest in establishing linkages with human rights groups.

Those VOs with women in development programs are coming to
appreciate the full potential of women as a development force and the
extent to which their liberation may be a key to unlocking cultural
constraints to needed economic and political change. This creates a
natural basis for alliances with organizations engaged in the women's
movement. There is also a natural, though as yet only marginally
recognized, shared interest between development VOs and peace
groups that are promoting the cause of nonviolent conflict resolution.

When the consumer movement was born in the North, the focus of
concern was on product testing and education to improve the ability of
consumers to make informed product choices. In recent years the
consumer affairs movement has developed substantial strength in the
South. Its Southern affiliates have brought important new perspectives,
asking difficult questions about who is consuming what resources and
for whose benefits. This has brought the consumer affairs movement
into the mainstream of concerns shared by human rights, environmental, peace and women's movements and makes it an important potential player within a broad social transformation coalition.[32]

Each of these movements has both its reactive and its proactive
thrusts. The reactive thrust seeks to block harmful actions: abuse of
human rights, discrimination against women, regulation of dangerous
products, increased arms expenditures and the cutting of forests. The
proactive thrust seeks the creation of new and more positive social
institutions: the strengthening of democratic institutions, introducing a
stronger feminist perspective into public policy, promoting citizen
diplomacy through sister city programs and developing markets for
sustained yield forest products. The proactive thrusts, irrespective of
the movement in question, all support elements of the transformation
agenda consistent with the people-centered development vision. It

would seem natural for these movements to build interlinking alliances with one another around shared interests in proactive transformation.

Unless the international NGOs concerned with relief and development dramatically reorient their programs and capabilities within the next few years it is likely that Southern VOs will come to view them purely as funding sources—if they bother to relate to them at all. The real energy of the Southern groups will go into forming alliances with Northern organizations engaged in environment, women, human rights and peace—for the simple reason that the commitments and capabilities of these organizations will be perceived to be more relevant.

A Voice in International Fora

Marc Nerfin has documented the increasing involvement of NGOs in UN fora. Strengthening this involvement should be an important goal of international NGO partnerships. Nerfin marks the 1972 Stockholm Conference on the environment as a turning point, noting that many of the more interesting and far-reaching discussions occurred not in the official government-to-government sessions, but rather in the adjacent NGO Forum.

Since then it has become increasingly common for NGOs to have their own fora as an adjunct to official international gatherings, and even to participate as equals with government representatives in the main meetings. In 1986, NGOs were invited to address a special session of the UN General Assembly session on Sub-Saharan Africa.[33] Nerfin makes special note of NGO contributions to a landmark WHO/UNICEF meeting in October 1979 in which NGOs participated on an equal footing with official delegates and had a major role in the important advances achieved in setting international standards for marketing infant formula.[34]

There are obvious difficulties in such efforts. Who is to say which NGOs are better representatives of the people's view than the official government representatives? The more that NGOs establish an entry to global policy fora, the more attractive they will become as avenues for the politically ambitious to advance their own careers and interests. Perhaps it is better that such involvement should be kept informal and not be institutionalized, regularized, certified and proceduralized. At the same time, NGOs, especially VOs and POs need to recognize the opportunities provided by such fora for introducing an articulate people's voice into the processes by which governments shape their global agendas. Those NGOs that seek a role for themselves in such fora must take care to assure that they do indeed represent a distinctive people's perspective derived from broadly based grass roots dialogue.[35]

There has been a parallel growth of interest among official international assistance agencies in dialoguing with NGOs. Sometimes the motivation is primarily to mobilize NGOs as lobbyist in support of official agency programs and budgets. The trend, however, is toward inviting substantive inputs to agency policy. The World Bank formed a joint World Bank/NGO Committee in 1982 to facilitate cooperation with NGOs. The members of this Committee have taken an increasingly activist position in challenging World Bank policies and programming. The 1987–88 African aid legislation passed by the U.S. Congress called for AID to hold local consultations with NGOs as they prepare their country program plans.

To date, other than in cases of specific instances of NGO efforts to block or seek the restructuring of a project perceived by NGOs to pose unacceptable social or environmental risks, NGOs have engaged in dialogue with official agencies primarily at the request of the latter and on agency defined agendas. During the 1990s, NGOs, especially VOs and POs, should seek to reverse this pattern, taking greater initiative in inviting donors, and even national planning agencies, to discuss NGO defined policy agendas relating to the directions of national and global development.[36]

NORTHERN NGOS: BECOMING RELEVANT

As suggested above, NGOs, particularly those from the North, face important challenges in the 1990s. As development priorities are redefined, the relevance of their existing programs to the needs of the South come into increasing question. This is especially true for NGOs that trace their roots to the humanitarian traditions of an earlier era.

Difficult Choices

While it is likely that international assistance NGOs with conventional missions will have access to a growing pool of public assistance resources during the 1990s, the available funding is likely to continue to be primarily for activities that focus more on the symptoms than on the causes of development failure.

Will they continue to act primarily as humanitarian assistance agencies, or will they become agents of transformation—even at the risk of alienating funders? Will they function primarily as professionally staffed bureaucracies engaged in the funding and implementation of projects, or will they build their capacities to strengthen global citizenship among their domestic constituencies and to serve as a support system for a voluntary people's development movement? If they opt for voluntarism in support transformation, how will they deal with the consequences, and what will they call on their prospective volunteer constituencies to do? For example:

- A VO is assisting people in a war zone under a government that is intent on using the starvation of civilian populations as a weapon. Is the VO prepared to expose the callous irresponsibility of the government in an effort to bring international public opinion to bear? Such action would almost certainly result in it being expelled from government-controlled areas. What sorts of citizen action are likely to produce useful results?

■ A VO is engaged in relief operations assisting people living in an environmentally devastated drought-prone area with infertile soils and a depleted water table. Is it prepared to educate contributors and the general public regarding the policies and conditions that created this situation, including the links to Northern lifestyles? If it does, will donors be offended and withdraw their support?

■ A VO is making an appeal for funds to feed the starving child whose face appears on morning TV. Is that VO prepared to explain that the child's parents are unable to provide it with a nourishing meal because a wealthy family that has gained control of the available fertile land to grow the sugar the viewers are now putting on their breakfast cereal refuses to pay the parents a living wage for their labor? The viewer may decide to eat an egg instead, but will he or she send a contribution?

The dilemmas are real. There are no easy answers. However, given the current global context, there is no escaping the need to confront these questions and their implications.

Domestic Constituencies

International NGOs often speak with pride of their grass roots constituencies as the mark of their privateness and volunteerism. A few international NGOs like Bread for the World, AFSC, Oxfam UK, Oxfam America and Results, have true grass roots volunteers engaged in public education and advocacy. For these few organizations the claims of a grass roots constituency, voluntarism and privateness have a substantive validity. They are accurately described as VOs. They have engaged constituencies that relate to the organization in many ways that go beyond merely making financial contributions.[37]

In the more typical case, however, the constituency claimed by the international NGO consists of nothing more than the people that a media blitz has succeeded in separating from their money. These constituencies are potentially the heart and soul of a true VO. To treat them only as faceless contributors is to deprive the organization of what is potentially its most valuable resource.

Few international NGOs know anything more about the broad demographic profile of their contributors, their presumed constituents, than that they have sent money in response to a particular media appeal. They are unlikely to have any idea of how their contributors think about global issues, what they expect to happen as a result of their contribution, or even what motivates their giving. These are clearly passive constituencies with respect to the organization that accepts their funds, having no more engagement in the work of the organization than the person who buys a box of soap flakes has in the company that makes it. This is the nature of a business, not a VO.

International NGOs that presume to be values driven VOs have an obligation to come to terms with their own contradictions and to expand the vision of their roles in the relief of human suffering. A serious commitment to global education to increase Northern understanding of the causes of human suffering must be an important part of that commitment. In many instances such educational efforts will appropriately begin with the organization's own staff and board of directors. Ultimately that commitment should extend to broader constituencies, seeking to turn passive constituents into active ones.

Efforts to engage the public in development concerns should extend beyond actual or prospective contributors. Many church-sponsored VOs have large natural constituencies within their affiliated churches.[38] The challenge is to reach out through human networks, study groups and forums where people can engage and dialogue on critical development issues. There is need to seek more opportunities for true people-to-people linkages, bringing together community level environmental activists, cooperatives leaders, women's rights activists and organizers of farm laborers from North and South for mutual exchange to build a shared vision and put their efforts in global perspective.[39] It is appropriate that VOs of both North and South give more attention to strengthening and engaging their natural citizen constituencies in ways appropriate to their nature. These would all be positive steps toward transforming private international assistance into a people's international development cooperation movement.

In the effort to develop engaged constituencies, lessons might be found in the experience of the international issues network campaigns that have been organized over the past few years, the best known of which was the campaign against the promotion of infant formula as a substitute for breast milk. There have been others in seeds, pesticides and pharmaceutical drugs that have brought together global education and citizen action in the fullest sense.[40]

On the whole, European VOs have taken a more activist stance in development education than have U.S. PVOs, particularly in efforts to address the causes of hunger and poverty and in the search for alternatives to more conventional development policies. These activities are often carried out by volunteers working with minimal budgets through local groups. It has been suggested that combining the type of intensive person-to-person engagement in development activism that is possible through such grass roots study and action groups with the popular appeal of mass media events like Live Aid might prove particularly powerful.[41]

Earth Day and Earth Train have emerged as examples of such sophisticated linkage of grass roots action, sustained educational efforts, and powerful media events involving massive global participation. Grass roots organizations carry out local discussion groups and mass participation events. Events such as rock concerts and the Earth Train's televised excursions across the United States with schoolchildren, entertainment personalities, and leaders of important voluntary organizations from both North and South focus attention. University students conduct environmental assessments of their immediate areas. Documentaries on the mass media provide public education, while special curriculum modules engage schoolchildren in debates on global issues. International corporations that can demonstrate a commitment to socially and environmentally sound products and practices are invited to serve as sponsors, and in so doing to publicize their efforts and affirm their commitment to responsible global citizenship.[42]

Unlike Live Aid and other such promotions, the central goal of Earth Day and Earth Train is personal change and action, not fund raising for new charities. This is an important advance that helps to set these initiatives apart.

Linkage Facilitation

To the extent that VOs are successful in advancing the people-centered development vision as a global movement, there will be a growing need for international VOs that specialize in facilitating direct people-to-people linkages.

For example, World Vision New Zealand went well beyond extracting child sponsorships from faceless contributors when it introduced the concept of *village* sponsorship. A group of church organizations in a New Zealand community undertakes the sponsorship of a village or district in India or another assisted country. In addition to contributing material assistance, the World Vision sponsors undertake a systematic study of the causes of poverty in the village or district they are sponsoring. Representatives of the sponsor group may visit the assisted village and district to meet with the people and gather further data for analysis in discussion groups back home. A member of World Vision's international staff who had visited such sponsorship groups in New Zealand reported being startled by the sophistication of their questions and observations compared to those of similar groups in the United States.

A model of a somewhat different type is provided by the Rainforest Action Network (RAN), an environmental VO based in San Francisco with some twenty-five thousand volunteer members supported by a paid central staff of only ten persons. RAN serves as an information nerve center for a decentralized network that runs entirely on local volunteer initiative. RAN's primary concern is to insure the international responsibility of U.S. companies and U.S. headquartered multilateral assistance agencies in protecting tropical forests and the rights of indigenous people who live in forest areas. However, it also provides support for local environmental groups throughout the world. Some four to five thousand members are located outside of the United States, and it is linked to affiliated networks throughout the world.

Within the United States, RAN works through Rainforest Action Groups (RAGs). RAN staff members travel around the country giving talks to colleges and community groups. When they pick out a person who looks like an organizer they give him or her a kit on how to organize a RAG. The organizer then receives regular newsletters that identify issues and campaigns in which local RAGs may wish to participate. For example, RAN has organized a campaign against a World Bank dam project in Brazil, a boycott against Burger King to protest its import of beef from Costa Rican producers who were converting rainforests to grazing lands, a program to find alternative economic uses of rainforests in Malaysia, and a campaign to strengthen a Guatemalan government commitment to protecting selected forest areas.

Local RAGs decide which campaigns they want to join and how. The central staff provides backstopping. For the Burger King campaign special packets were sent out describing how to organize a boycott of local outlets, including how to make a papier-mâche cow that appears to eat tropical foliage and poop hamburgers; and reminding the RAGs to call their local TV station to catch this photo opportunity. According to Randall Hayes, RAN's executive director, in the end it was hundreds of school children writing to the president of the company saying they would no longer eat Burger King hamburgers that made the difference. Threatened with a children's consumer boycott, Burger King ended its contract with the Costa Rican beef suppliers.

Another packet sent out by RAN to its RAGs offers guidance on how to twin directly with environmental groups in the South. Lists of Southern environmental VOs are included, along with brief descriptions of their interests and activities. RAGs are encouraged to make direct contact with any group that looks interesting to them. A U.S. RAG may offer assistance to the Southern VO in obtaining support on the latter's issues from U.S. environmental groups, fund-raising for them, organizing exchange visits, or whatever. If a RAG wants to do fund-raising for a Southern organization it is encouraged to send the funds raised directly to the assisted group, not through the RAN central office.[43] This strengthens the direct people-to-people bond and minimizes needs for expensive central administration and accounting.

NGOs have been under strong pressures to professionalize. Voluntarism has been equated with amateurism. Professionalism has become equated with salaries and formal administrative procedures. Consequently, the tendency has been to treat development, even the efforts of the "voluntary" sector, as a lifeless, monetized, technocratic activity administered by professional bureaucrats. Any role for the citizen volunteer—except as financial contributor—has been excluded from our consciousness, as has any consideration of the potential to tap the dynamic energy of people's movements as a development resource.

These tendencies cannot be allowed to survive into the 1990s. We must restore the human dimension of development. We must recognize and support the essential and central role of the global citizen volunteer. We must act on a recognition that the distinctive role of the voluntary sector is not to serve as a cheap contractor to implement government defined programs. Rather it is to mobilize and focus the social energies of a people's development movement driven by a commitment to self-help action and guided by a critical consciousness of the responsibilities of global citizenship.

Those NGOs that chose to embrace the distinctive challenges and opportunities of the 1990s are nearly certain to enter the 21st century as fundamentally transformed organizations. The alternative is likely, at best, to be irrelevance.

NOTES

1. Willis Harman, in *Global Mind Change: The Promise of the Last Years of the Twentieth Century* (Indianapolis: Knowledge Systems, Inc., 1988), notes the need for a transformation from a dominant mode of competition to one of cooperation.

2. There is a trend toward speaking of global education, rather than development education in the interest of stressing the global nature of development. I would argue for stressing the citizenship dimension of this education.

3. See Thomas B. Keehn, "After Five Years of Growth, Development Education in the U.S. Comes of Age: Or Does It?" *Ideas & Information about Development Education,* a newsletter of Interaction, New York, Fall 1989.

4. See Larry Minear, "The Other Missions of NGOs: Education and Advocacy," *World Development,* Vol. 15, Supplement, 1987, pp. 205–06. One American NGO executive has condemned the treatment of human suffering by NGOs as "one of life's most tragic and intimate experiences,...as a product to be packaged and sold." He maintains that these NGOs highlight the symptoms of hunger while ignoring its causes, peddling "a view of the world that is out of date, out of touch with reality, arrogantly conceived and potentially dangerous." Larry Hollon, "Selling Human Misery," Global Education Reprint Series (New York: Church World Service, 1983), p. 7, as quoted by Minear. This exploitation of the starving child for fund-raising purposes is perhaps development's equivalent of child pornography. This is not to argue for avoiding the reality of poverty. However, the viewer should be enlightened as to the real causes of the suffering. NGOs should not simply use the poor as promotional models to enhance their own fund raising.

5. The term international NGO is used here to refer to an NGO that has major involvement in more than one country. Most of the development NGOs based in Northern countries are of this nature. By contrast most Southern development NGOs concern themselves primarily with issues and activities specific to their country of nationality. These are referred to here as national NGOs. Of course there are thousands of national NGOs in the North as well.

6. There is a critical distinction here between the citizen monitoring the powerful and their abuses of power, and the systems of informants commonly established by totalitarian regimes to maintain their power monopoly. One maintains a check on power. The other maintains a check on citizen dissent. The former is the act of the citizen. The latter is the act of the tattle-tale seeking special favors. The two should not be confused.

7. NAMFREL, a domestic voluntary poll watching group in the Philippines, played a critical role in exposing the election frauds that brought down the Marcos regime and placed Cory Aquino in power.

8. The Haribon Foundation organizes volunteer citizen groups throughout the Philippines to monitor and report illegal logging activities and the smuggling of rare bird species.

9. As quoted in Don Carlson and Craig Comstock (eds.), *Citizen Summitry: Keeping the Peace When it Matters too Much to be Left to Politicians* (New York: St. Martin's Press, 1986), p. 59. This book describes a wide variety of citizen peace initiatives aimed at reconciliation between the United States and the Soviet Union. These include direct citizen exchanges and the use of electronic media, particularly closed circuit TV to promote dialogue and understanding.

10. Larry Minear, "Terms of Engagement," *The Ecumenical Review,* in press for January 1990 publication.

11. Larry Minear, *Helping People in an Age of Conflict: Toward a New Professionalism in U.S. Voluntary Humanitarian Assistance* (Washington, DC: Interaction, 1988), p. 25.

12. Minear, "Terms of Engagement."

13. This story is from Elias Chacour, "Can You Forgive Me, Abuna?" *Together,* July-September 1988, pp. 4–5, excerpted from Elias Chacour with David Hazard, *Blood Brothers* (Old Tappan, N.J.: Chosen Books, 1984).

14. These questions are examined within the historical context of church involvement in development work by Charles Elliot, *Comfortable Compassion? Poverty, Power and the Church* (London: Hodder and Stoughton, 1987). See especially chapter 4, pp. 39–50.

15. In a classic study John D. Montgomery, "Allocation of Authority in Land Reform Programs: A Comparative Study of Administrative Processes and Outputs," *Administrative Science Quarterly,* March 1972, concluded that the implementation of land reform programs in twenty-five countries that devolved administrative functions to local non-career officials produced significantly better results for peasant welfare than arrangements using professional administrators in either a centralized or decentralized bureaucratic system.

16. Statistics for July 31, 1989, reported in *Grameen Dialogue,* a newsletter published by the Grameen Trust, Bangladesh, Vol. 1, No. 1, September 1989, p. 8. What is distinctive about the Grameen Bank is not its particular approach to credit. Many NGOs have quite similar programs. Rather it is the scale of operations and their institutionalization in a formal bank. From this perspective it is ironic and disappointing that so many NGOs throughout the world that have formed one or more five person credit groups claim to be "replicating" the Grameen Bank. Such claims reflect a serious misunderstanding of the substance of the Grameen Bank experience. It should be noted here that though the bank began as an NGO initiative, it has been integrated into government and now quite self-consciously identifies itself as a governmental, not a nongovernmental, organization.

17. In the Philippines the Asian Development Bank (ADB) and AID are both planning programs with the Philippine government to engage NGOs in the implementation

of social forestry projects on a very large scale. AID is pursuing forestry programs in Africa based on NGO implementation. The ADB is planning a project in the Philippines for large-scale financing of NGO rural credit programs. The World Bank is talking with NGOs in Bangladesh about implementing large-scale programs of primary education.

18. The case can be made that to the extent such donor initiatives attract the participation of true VOs, there is substantial risk that enticing them into contractor roles for which they are ill-suited will distort their fundamental nature and ultimately discredit them as a development force when they fail to perform to donor expectations. An important issue here is that most donors do not recognize and understand the difference between an NGO that is a VO and one that is a PSC. For that matter, few NGOs clearly recognize the difference. See L. David Brown and David C. Korten, "Understanding Voluntary Organizations: Guidelines for Donors," Working Papers, WPS 258, Country Economics Department, The World Bank, Washington, DC, September 1989. Whether or not such donor initiatives are ill-advised is, however, a moot issue. The driving force behind them is too strong to stop. Energy is better directed to reducing the risks of distortion and failure.

19. The Salvation Army and American Red Cross cases are described by Peter E. Drucker, "What Business Can Learn from Nonprofits," *Harvard Business Review,* Vol. 67, No. 4, July-August 1989, pp. 88–93.

20. NGOs that are prepared to give this issue serious attention may be interested in the decision of LSP (the Institute of Indonesian Studies), an innovative Indonesian NGO, to commit itself to recapturing its voluntary roots. LSP began as a policy analysis and human rights organization staffed by volunteers and supported by financial contributions from sympathetic professionals. With time, LSP developed a paid professional staff that became increasingly dependent on foreign donor funding. It gave less and less time to policy advocacy and human rights activities, becoming increasingly occupied in implementing the types of community development activities that donors preferred to fund.

   In the course of carrying out a comprehensive review of the organization's history and objectives, LSP's leadership decided to take a bold step to restore its voluntary roots, eliminate anti-developmental foreign dependence, and recapture its social agenda. It would no longer provide a salary to staff, nor would it accept foreign donor funding. These decisions were taken within the context of an effort to craft a new development philosophy focused on working to increase the social and economic productivity of under-utilized domestic resources. The more innovative LSP projects that resulted involved working with local governments, private investors and Indonesian banks on development of market schemes and housing projects that produced attractive returns to the private developers. Simultaneously, these projects provided the poor with improved housing and business opportunities that substantially increased their earning potentials. LSP financed its involvement by charging consultant fees to the developers and brokerage fees on loans it helped arrange with local banks for assisted cooperatives. Staff members were expected to support themselves, either by taking outside work for remuneration and working for LSP as volunteers, or collecting fees for contract services.

21. These are difficult and complex processes. In broad outline the hypothetical situation described here is essentially what was happening in response to a project being planned by Scott Paper in the province of Irian Jaya, Indonesia. Scott had given indications to both government and to the NGOs involved that it would cooperate in such an effort. Unfortunately, Scott ended up canceling the project, presumably out of

concern that its best efforts might not satisfy the more activist environmental groups and consequently lead to a public boycott. Since it appears likely that Scott's role in the concession will now be taken over by other investors with less commitment to environmental and social issues, some of the NGOs involved are speaking of having won the battle and lost the war.

22. In his book *Comfortable Compassion?* Charles Elliot cites three lightly disguised cases to demonstrate the workings of unjust economic and social structures (pp. 105–10). One of them is clearly based on the plight of the landless sugar workers in Negros Occidental. He documents the miserable conditions under which they work and the injustice of their working relationships. He then describes the reactions of two foreign development assistance agencies that wanted to do something to help these wretched people. A German agency proposed building a school so that the children could be educated and be able to compete for better jobs. In a country with rampant unemployment, the landless leaders wanted to know where these jobs were that the Germans had in mind. Another small agency thought it might be able to help the local Catholic priests with their work by providing them a typewriter, stationery and some visual aids. Then they asked the people what they wanted. After long discussion one of the leaders arose and said:

> We know your country is the headquarters of a large and important company that buys sugar and coconut oil on this island. We want you to go to that company and say to it: "We will ask our people not to buy your products unless you, as a company, tell the landowners on this island to treat their workers better."

The villagers applauded and others rose to endorse the idea. The visitors, knowing their agency would never back such an idea, admitted they could be of no help and were told by the villagers to go home and not bother them again.

The message is clear. Most of what the international NGOs have to offer the oppressed is irrelevant or worse, unless these NGOs are prepared to take concrete action such as mobilizing economic sanctions. If the U.S. PVO that is running a U.S. government funded feeding program in Negros is really concerned with the well-being of the poor children of that province, it should be educating the American people to the reality of Negros and urging them to demand that the U.S. Congress eliminate the Philippine sugar quota until such time as the sugar lands of the Philippines have been subjected to a radical land reform and are in the hands of the poor whom Americans really want to help. If this PVO is not prepared to do that, then perhaps it should do what Elliot reported the villagers in his case requested of the European NGO—go home.

23. This is the conclusion of Michael Bratton, based on an assessment of African experience. "Non-governmental Organizations in Africa: Can They Influence Public Policy?" *Development and Change,* Vol. 21, 1989, pp. 87–118.

24. Sheldon Rampton, "Sister Cities Gear Up for Nicaraguan Elections," *Bulletin of Municipal Foreign Policy,* Vol. 3, No. 4, Autumn 1989, pp. 34–36.

25. If foreign money is to be used to finance operations, it should be with a clear understanding that the foreign donor expects to provide a long-term subsidy.

26. David C. Korten, *Bangladesh Rural Advancement Committee: Strategy for the 1990s* (New York, NY: PACT, forthcoming).

27. In many instances NGOs serve as bridging institutions that bring together a variety of organizations in synergistic combinations to address complex problems that are

beyond their individual capabilities. See L. David Brown, "Bridging Organizations and Sustainable Development," paper prepared for the Conference on Social Innovations in Global Management at Case Western Reserve University, November 13–15, 1989.

28. These criticisms have often been particularly focused on international, private voluntary organizations based in the United States. This may simply reflect the fact that they control approximately 50 percent of all financial resources channeled to the South through private assistance agencies and thus have a dominant presence. Based on data reported in OECD, *Voluntary Aid for Development: The Role of Non-Governmental Organizations* (Paris: OECD, 1988). There is a general consensus that European NGOs tend to be relatively more progressive and politically aware, perhaps because their activities more often center on channeling funds to Southern NGOs in preference to running their own field operations.

29. See *Accelerating Institutional Development*, PVO Institutional Development Evaluation Series, Bureau for Food for Peace and Voluntary Assistance, Office of Private and Voluntary Cooperation, U.S. AID, Washington, DC, May 1989.

30. International NGOs interested in local institutional development need to base their assistance strategies on a well-developed understanding of local conditions. For example, NGO communities are well established in Asia and Latin America, less so in Africa. Initiatives by international NGOs to support the formation of new NGOs in Africa might make important contributions. Similar action in the Philippines or Bangladesh, with their dense populations of NGOs and a continuing rapid spontaneous creation of new organizations, would seem redundant. In the latter countries it may be more appropriate to offer specialized capacity building services.

31. I refer here to the emergence in many countries of NGOs formed purely as a response to the availability of funding. These trends are especially strong in Bangladesh and India. Though legally nonprofits, many of these organizations are purely a response to funding opportunities and are driven more by the profit motive than by any social commitment.

32. See Wayne Ellwood, *Generating Power: A Guide to Consumer Organizing* (Penang: International Organization of Consumers Unions, 1984), especially pp. 6–10.

33. Robert Berg, personal fax communication, December 20, 1989.

34. Marc Nerfin, "Neither Prince nor Merchant: Citizen — An Introduction to the Third System," *IFDA Dossier 56*, November/December 1986," p. 17.

35. In 1992 a second international conference on environment and development will be held in Brazil, marking the twentieth anniversary of the 1972 Stockholm Conference. NGOs throughout the world are preparing to participate in this potentially landmark meeting. They are carrying out their own country analyses and organizing grass roots fora to gain broadly-based people's perspectives on priority issues linking environmental and development concerns. Results of these consultations are being shared in regional meetings to feed shared perspectives back into further local consultations. It is a diffuse process involving many centers of initiative and leadership. To the extent that it is successful it may provide a prototype for true citizen input to the formal fora in which the representatives of governmental bodies too commonly give precedence to the interests of princes and merchants over those of the citizen.

36. This suggestion was offered by Robert Berg, president of the International Devel-

opment Conference and one of the drafters of the 1987–88 U.S. legislation requiring that U.S. AID missions in Africa consult with NGOs on country programming strategy.

37. Berg, *Non-Governmental Organizations,* p. 33, has argued that U.S. PVOs should redefine themselves as mass movements, using Bread for the World, which he indicates has mobilized over 40,000 Americans to lobby for development, as a positive example.

38. The Episcopal Church in the United States makes an effort to develop direct linkages between its U.S. parishes and partner parishes in the South.

39. The New York-based Asia Society is developing a plan for such an undertaking, bringing activist Asian NGO leaders to the United States to conduct public fora and to meet with counterparts engaged in parallel undertakings in communities throughout the United States.

40. Thierry Lemaresquier, "Prospects for Development Education: Some Strategic Issues Facing European NGOs," *World Development,* Vol. 15, Supplement, 1987, p. 195. See also Wayne Ellwood, *Generating Power.*

41. Lemaresquier, "Prospects for Development Education," pp. 189–200.

42. Information on Earth Day is available from P.O. Box AA, Stanford University, Stanford, California 94309, U.S.A. Information on Earth Train is available from Gateway Pacific Foundation, 465 California Street, Suite 830, San Francisco, California 94104, U.S.A.

43. This description is based on an interview on August 17, 1989, with Randall Hayes. Further information may be obtained from Rainforest Action Network, 301 Broadway, Suite A, San Francisco, California 94133, U.S.A.

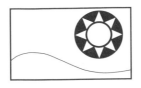

END OF INNOCENCE

The late 1980s marked an historic change in human consciousness perhaps best described as a loss of innocence. For millennia, from the time humans first appeared as a new species, we, the people of earth, were little more than small, inconsequential parasites hosted by a living planet unmindful of our physical presence. The idea of human stewardship of nature might well have seemed a pretension. Nature obviously was more than capable of caring for herself. With the innocence of childhood we focused on our own needs and pleasure. Does the young child presume to protect the parent?

Gradually at first, and then with a growing momentum, we increased our numbers and our dominion over nature. Somewhere during the middle of the 20th century we began to leave a visible mark. Nature did become mindful of our physical presence. Species were disappearing because of our acts. Lakes and rivers were dying. In some localities the air became difficult to breath. The momentum continued to build. Across the surface of the planet a mass of human flesh was consuming and displacing other forms of life with growing speed and upsetting what in reality were delicate ecological balances.

Yet we held tenaciously to our innocence. Allowing for her occasional fits of temper, Mother Nature had always provided for our needs. We advanced through our ability to take what she offered and reshape it to these needs. We accepted on faith the admonition of princes and merchants that we could not allow idealists' concern for the environment to interfere with economic growth and the sanctity of the market that represented the hope of the poor for a better life.

Then in the last two years of the past decade the veil of innocence was penetrated. We became conscious of our reality, of our responsibility for our planet and ultimately for our own destiny. In our childish innocence we had become a parasitic population grown out of control, and we were progressively killing our own host. For the first time as a collective body we are able to see this reality. We have yet to come to terms with it.

FROM PRODIGAL CHILD TO STEWARD

One implication is self-evident. We must adjust our collective thought and behavior from that of the prodigal child to that of the parent in whose hands rests responsibility for the stewardship of earth's treasure. From accepting the prodigal child's view that society is well served by the pursuit of unrestrained consumption, we must accept that with the power we have attained comes a responsibility to exercise stewardship over the resources we command—especially for future generations and for the powerless of our own generation.

The most fundamental issues of development are, at their core, issues of power. Yet most power issues may also be viewed as value issues that, in our conflict ridden world, we must learn to resolve through the application of integrative values. We must recognize and come to terms with the essential values dimension of development. The great religious teachers provide useful guidance through their insights into the values of humility, moderation, and love—the integrative values by which we now must learn to live.

We have no more than an instant of historical time to accomplish a transformation in our values and institutions if we are to save ourselves and our host from the violence to one another and to nature caused by our short-sightedness. This transformation depends on overcoming the conditioning of our history, culture, and institutions—acting on a new awareness to break the pattern of profligate and individualistic lifestyles, and applying our accumulated intellectual and technological resources to the conscious creation of a viable future consistent with the potentials within our reach.

APPLYING OUR GLOBAL INTELLIGENCE

Fortunately, we enter this period with important resources that we have only begun to learn to use. Communication technology links the world's people into a single instantaneous communication system. This gives us a powerful new collective intelligence that is at once reassuring and frightening. We find it difficult to grasp the full potentials of this power as the possibilities lie too far beyond our experience. They also raise deeply troubling questions.

What are the implications for freedom and individuality, for the deviant whose non-conformity provides the gene pool for social innovation? What ethics will guide the actions of this global intelligence? Will we live by fleeting global fads. Will we bind ourselves into a collective social and intellectual tyranny? Or will we succeed in maintaining diversity within our unity, individuality within an ethic of collective responsibility? The latter is essential. No period in human history has faced comparable needs for the rapid social innovation that only a free and pluralistic society can produce.

We have become masters of *technical* discovery and innovation. We must now set ourselves to becoming masters of *social/institutional* discovery and innovation. The latter do not come from tightly-controlled experiments in hidden sterile laboratories for later dissemination through technical journals and application by corporate engineers. They are created by people engaged in social action aimed at solving immediate problems, who continuously monitor their own progress, reflect on emerging experience and adapt approaches to changing circumstances and the lessons of their errors. Dissemination comes through person-to-person exchange using a host of media.

INTERNATIONAL NGOS AS RESOURCES FOR CHANGE

International nongovernmental organizations (NGOs) are an important existing resource that may be brought to bear in support of a global, social learning process. Many of them already have international networks and communications systems that link influential constituencies throughout the world. They have established sources of financing. Most were formed originally as voluntary organizations (VOs) around strong value commitments. Most, however, need to change in significant ways if they are to contribute to realizing their potentials to serve the needs of the 1990s. For many NGOs:

■ The first step toward realizing this potential may be simply to accept and acknowledge the existing limitations of their programs and modes of operations when set against the priorities of the transformation agenda;

■ The second step may be to regain their vision, to tap into the core values that inspired their creation and bonded the commitment of their pioneers;

■ The third step may be to articulate and re-examine their assumptions about the underlying causes of major problems they are committed to resolving and then to re-align their strategies accordingly; and

■ The fourth step may be to activate their natural constituencies, challenge them to become the life force of the organization as engaged citizen-volunteers, and support them in that undertaking.

NGO leaders concerned with the relevance of their organizations to the 1990s might begin this process by posing to their directors and senior staff the questions presented in Appendix C.   Hopefully this might lead to a reaffirmation of their organization's nature as a VO and a renewal of its vision within the context of a changing world in need. In many instances it will be necessary to move beyond a view of development as a time and space bounded project energized by money, to a more dynamic vision of development as a people's movement that gains energy from the voluntary commitment of its participants. Having accomplished this, the organization should be ready to assume a role of leadership within a people-centered development movement, helping to prepare us for entry into the 21st century as responsible stewards of the collective future of humankind.

In the end, our future depends on millions of citizen volunteers, each serving as a center of voluntary energy, adding strength to a dynamic, evolving people's movement. Each individual can and does make a difference. Each helps to shape the global consciousness and the collective pattern of behavior by which we define our relationship with our host planet. Each contributes to the emerging global intelligence.

If you have read this book, you are in all likelihood a power holder, though you may not feel like it. It is almost certain that you are among the world's overconsumers, though you may not intend to be. The powerless underconsumers seldom have the means to read such books.

Being among the world's privileged you and I have a special obligation to think and act as a global citizen, to be a steward of whatever power we hold, to contribute to the transforming forces that are reshaping our world. The future of human society, of our children, depends on each of us.

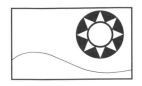

THE MANILA DECLARATION ON PEOPLE'S PARTICIPATION AND SUSTAINABLE DEVELOPMENT[1]

> "If you have come to help me you can go home again. But if you see my struggle as part of your own survival then perhaps we can work together."
> — *Australian Aborigine Woman*

We, the participants of the Inter-Regional Consultation on People's Participation in Environmentally Sustainable Development, held in Manila, Philippines from 6-10 June 1989 share a concern that the results of current development practice are not just, sustainable, or inclusive. Current development practice is based on a model that demeans the human spirit, divests people of their sense of community and control over their own lives, exacerbates social and economic inequity, and contributes to destruction of the ecosystem on which all life depends. Our work with grassroots communities brings us into daily contact with the results of this development.

Furthermore, we are concerned that foreign assistance, particularly debt financing, too often has contributed more to the problem than to its solution. It places the initiative and responsibility in the hands of foreigners rather than in the hands of the people. It weakens the accountability of governments to their own citizens. It promotes and sustains an inappropriate development model driven by the export market. It primarily finances resource-based projects that destroy the natural environment and deprive the poor of access to the productive

---

1. A statement of the participants in the Inter-Regional Consultation on People's Participation in Environmentally Sustainable Development, Hotel Nikko Manila Garden, Philippines sponsored by the Asian NGO Coalition (ANGOC) (Manila, Philippines), and the Environmental Liaison Center International (ELCI) (Nairobi, Kenya). Thirty-one NGO leaders from Africa, Southeast Asia, South Asia, the South Pacific, Latin America, the Caribbean, North America and Europe participated. The proceedings are available from the ANGOC Secretariat, 47 Matrinco Building, 2178 Pasong Tamo, Makati, Metro Manila, Philippines. Telex: 23136 VMI-PH.

assets upon which they depend for their livelihoods. National economies remain burdened with debt. And finally it results in the imposition of policies intended to facilitate debt repayment, orienting the
national economy and its resources to the needs of foreign consumers,
at the expense of the poor and the environment.

Our Vision: A People-Centered Development

There is current need for a fundamentally different development
model based on an alternative development. Authentic development
enhances the sustainability of the community. It must be understood
as a process of economic, political and social change that need not
necessarily involve growth. Sustainable human communities can be
achieved only through a people-centered development.

A people-centered development seeks to return control over resources to the people and their communities to be used in meeting
their own needs. This creates incentives for the responsible stewardship of resources that is essential to sustainability.

A people-centered development seeks to broaden political participation, building from a base of strong people's organizations and
participatory local government. It seeks the opportunity for people to
obtain a secure livelihood based on the intensive, yet sustainable, use
of renewable resources. It builds from the values and culture of the
people. Political and economic democracy are its cornerstone.

It seeks to build within people a sense of their own humanity and
their links to the earth, its resources, and the natural processes
through which it sustains all life. The relationship of the people to the
land is of particular importance. Alienation from the land creates a
symbolic alienation from community and from nature.

A people-centered development model calls for active mutual self-
help among people, working together in their common struggle to deal
with their common problems. Recognizing the importance of the self-
respect of the individual and the self-reliance of the community, it
does not look to international charity as the answer to poverty. It
seeks the productive use of local resources to meet local needs. There
is only a limited role for international debt financing or for the institutions that provide that finance.

Three principles are basic to a people-centered development.

1. Sovereignty resides with the people, the real social actors of positive change. Freedom and democracy are universal human aspirations. The sovereignty of the people is the foundation of democracy. The legitimate role of government is to enable the people to set
   and pursue their own agenda.
2. To exercise their sovereignty and assume responsibility for the
   development of themselves and their communities, the people must
   control their own resources, have access to relevant information,
   and have the means to hold the officials of government accountable. Freedom of association and expression, and open access to

information are fundamental to the responsible exercise of this sovereignty. Governments must protect these rights. People from all countries must work together in solidarity to insure that governments accept and act on this responsibility.

3. Those who would assist the people with their development must recognize that it is they who are participating in support of the people's agenda, not the reverse. The value of the outsider's contribution will be measured in terms of the enhanced capacity of the people to determine their own future.

TRANSFORMING NATIONAL AND INTERNATIONAL SYSTEMS: AN AGENDA FOR TRANSITION

The international system of state dominated development institutions built on international financial transfers has been a major contributor to the current situation, in part because it has not acknowledged the above principles. Transformation of this system represents an important priority. Thus, we will work with allies in governments and donors to transform the existing system into a system of people-to-people international development cooperation in solving the problems that all people share in common. Though the need is urgent, we recognize that there must be a transitional period. This transition period must feature a dual strategy. Simultaneous steps must be taken to: 1) stop the damage; and 2) create alternatives. The balance of attention will depend on local circumstances.

Redefining Participation

There must be a basic redefinition of participation as applied by most official development assistance agencies, and many voluntary development organizations. Conventional practice too often has called for the participation of the community in donor or voluntary development organization defined agendas and projects. Donors seek the assistance of voluntary development organizations in the implementation of donor agendas.

Since sovereignty resides with the people, not with the state, development assistance must be responsive to the people. In authentic development an assisting agency is a participant in a development process that is community driven, community led and community owned—basic conditions for sustainability. When voluntary development organizations are involved, their commitment must be to serve the people, not the donor.

Opening Access to Information

Not only is full consultation with the community essential at all stages of project identification, including pre-project identification, there must also be full disclosure of information on the part of donors, lenders and governments to the people concerned. Donors and lenders commonly withhold information on the grounds that it is privileged information that they can release only to government.

Governments, public donors including voluntary development organizations, and the multilateral banks are public agencies dealing with other public agencies. As public agencies they are agencies of the people engaged in the expenditure of people's money on activities that have considerable impact on people's lives. The sovereign people have the right to be fully informed, and donors must learn to respect this right. Where this right is not respected, development too often becomes a conspiracy between the donor or the lender and government against the people. It is a charade to talk of people's participation under such circumstances.

Building Inclusive Alliances

Alliances must be built across classes and sectors. It is important to recognize and work with natural allies within existing institutions, including government and the international donors and financial institutions, who share the vision or can be enlisted to its cause. Those who are working for internal reform can benefit from the pressures of citizen action. Care must be taken, however, to avoid co-optation, recognizing that the objective requires the transformation, not simply the fine tuning, of inappropriate institutions.

Reducing Debt Dependence

Another concern is to raise awareness that while international loan assistance may contribute to short-term prosperity, in the long-term the burden of the resulting debt falls on the poor and the environment. Long-term international debt financing is basically inconsistent with a sustainable development. Voluntary development organizations should encourage governments to reduce their international borrowing that does not specifically enhance sustainability. The incentive for successful policy changes, toward a sustainable development, including action to reduce population growth rates, should be provided through debt relief rather than through new loans that ultimately add to debt burdens.

Reducing Resource Exports

Sustainability depends on the conservation of natural resources and their judicious use by the people to preserve and enhance their quality of life. Too often the exploitation of natural resources for export deprives local people of their land and livelihoods—in order to repay loans that benefitted only the rich by catering to the overconsumption of wealthy foreign consumers. Resources must be conserved for the use of the people, particularly those who have had the least opportunity to share in development benefits.

Strengthening People's Capacity for Participation

People's capacity for participation in the creation of sustainable communities must be strengthened through efforts to rapidly expand people's organization and awareness. Voluntary development organizations will need to reappraise their roles and methods in this process. It is important to recognize and build from existing organizations and make resources available. There must be use of mass media. Communities must be encouraged to strengthen self-organizing processes and to support one another's initiatives. Governments must be encouraged and assisted in creating a policy environment for citizen action.

Creating Demonstrations of Self-Reliant Community

Simply organizing the people is not sufficient. The goal is the re-creation of society from the bottom up on a foundation of productive, sustainable communities. There is need for large-scale experimentation to demonstrate the creation of communities that exemplify sustainability, justice and inclusiveness. These must also demonstrate the potentials of small-scale community action on a replicable scale.

Creation of National and International Monitoring Systems

Voluntary development organizations and people's organizations must act directly to increase access to information and enhance people's ability to make rational choices toward a sustainable future. Voluntary development organizations working at international levels should collaborate in developing a system to monitor the plans and actions of development donors, financial institutions, and multi-national corporations. National voluntary development organizations must create similar systems to monitor and make known the plans and actions of national governments and corporations. The purpose is to insure that the people have access to the relevant information to assess social and environmental impacts and to take necessary actions to protect their interests.

There should also be a broadly based historical assessment at national and regional levels of the social and environmental impact of foreign assistance, and trade and corporate investment policies. These studies will create greater understanding of the dynamics of the international system and of the issues at stake.

Many of the changes called for by a people-centered development present a fundamental challenge to well established interests. A call for such changes would be unrealistic, were it not for the depth of the crisis of deepening poverty and environmental destruction that now confronts human society. The future of all people depends on a basic transformation in thought and action, leading people to rediscover their essential humanity and to recreate their relationships with one another and among themselves and their environment. It is pragmatism more than idealism that makes the change possible.

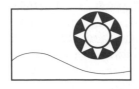

STUDY GROUP DISCUSSION TOPICS

Eleven topics are presented here for consideration by study group participants. Each topic is introduced with a brief assertion. This is followed by one or more related questions intended to relate the assertion to specific concerns of Northlandian [substitute the name of your country] nongovernmental organizations (NGOs) and public. Discussants may be urged to challenge, confirm, revise, or elaborate on these assertions and then proceed to examine the related questions.

1. **Global Trends.** Several global trends experienced during the 1980s—including those relating to ecology, incidence of poverty, communal violence, drugs, population growth, refugees, trade, and debt—suggest a breakdown in the systems by which human societies manage their relationships with one another and with their environment. At the same time the easing of East-West tensions, advances in basic technologies, and trends toward democratization are creating important new opportunities. It is argued that these developments present both a need and an opportunity to rethink basic assumptions about development and society.

   What are the implications of current global trends for Northlandian society in the 1990s? Do these trends suggest a need to question basic assumptions underlying previous thinking, behavior and policies? What role does and should Northlandia have within the global community in shaping or redirecting current trends?

2. **Universal Issues.** Past thought and practice have divided the world between the developed and the underdeveloped, the North and the South. The developed have considered it their responsibility to develop the underdeveloped in their own image. However, a growing number of social, environmental, political, economic and spiritual problems are shared in common by North and South, East and West. The traditional concept of international assistance as the one way transfer of money and technology may need to be replaced by a concept of mutual problem solving.

> *What day to day social, environmental, political, economic and spiritual problems requiring effective community level action do the Northlandian people face in common with people of the South? To what extent would exchange of experience in dealing with such problems between the Northlandian people and the people of Southern countries be useful?*

3. **Role of Religion.** Development has long been treated as primarily a financial and technical problem. The importance of values has been generally neglected. This neglect contributes to many of the current global crises, in particular a high incidence of communal violence, the destructive use of natural resources, drug abuse, and social injustice. Religiously oriented NGOs have commonly defined their roles as instruments of charity engaged in transferring material resources to those in need. Few have asked basic questions about the larger role of religion in dealing with issues of social justice and conflict that are substantial contributors to the conditions of human suffering that most NGOs seek to relieve.

> *What distinctive roles can and should religious organizations and religiously affiliated NGOs play toward the creation of a just, sustainable, and inclusive global society? Are religiously oriented Northlandian NGOs currently encouraging and supporting their affiliated religious organization in their most relevant and potentially powerful roles in this undertaking?*

4. **People's Movements.** The term movement is often used loosely to refer to any large membership organization. It is more accurately applied to decentralized collective action by large numbers of active and committed people in support of a basic idea or value. Commonly, in a true movement, these people will be joined only through loosely defined networks rather than through formal organizational structures and memberships. Examples include the environmental, peace, consumer rights, women's and human rights movements. There is a tendency over time for movements to become formalized into bureaucratic-type organizations with a resulting loss of the creative energy that made them important and effective forces for social reform.

> *What initiatives in Northlandia are accurately classified as people's movements? To what extent do these national movements address critical global issues and have active international links? How do and should Northlandian international assistance NGOs relate to these movements and what might they contribute to strengthening them? Are any*

of the Northlandian international assistance NGOs engaged in facilitating people's movements as defined above?

5. **Voluntarism.** NGOs commonly refer to themselves as voluntary organizations. Yet pressures to "professionalize" generally lead toward assigning more and more of the control and responsibility to full-time paid staff who function much as the paid staff of a business or a government agency. The role of "volunteers" may become limited to making financial contributions to support the work of paid staff, resulting in a loss of the ability to mobilize voluntary energy that is one of the distinctive qualities of true voluntary organizations.

    Do Northlandian international assistance NGOs mobilize the voluntary energy of Northlandian citizens to participate actively in revolving global issues, or do they look to their constituents only as a source of financial contributions? How might they mobilize and apply voluntary energy in more productive ways?

6. **Redefining Affluence.** There is growing evidence that affluent lifestyles in the North are important contributors to social injustice and environmental destruction in the South. Northern demands for timber, beef, and the repayment of loans are direct contributors to the destruction of tropical forests in the South. The demands of Northern consumers generate the toxic wastes that are dumped in Southern countries. High per capita energy consumption from fossil fuels in the North is the major contributor to carbon dioxide buildup that is raising global temperatures in both North and South. Policies of the Northern dominated International Monetary Fund put the interests of Northern banks and their affluent shareholders far ahead of the interests of the Southern poor. Demands for cheap consumer goods in the North create incentives for the exploitation of child labor in the South. Arms sales by Northern countries to generate the foreign exchange that allows them to purchase cheap consumer goods from the South fuel local conflicts mainly in the South. These examples suggest that improving the quality of life in the South may depend more on changing how the people of the North define and pursue the good life than it does on their token contributions to well-intentioned charities.

    Is there validity to the charge that affluent lifestyles in the North create a barrier to achieving a just, sustainable and inclusive development in the South? Are the examples offered valid? Are there other examples? What is Northlandia's responsibility? What should Northlandian NGOs do?

7. **Multilateral Development Agencies.** It is commonly suggested that the lead role in resolving current global development crises, particularly the debt and environmental crises, must be borne by the multilateral development agencies. The most important of these organizations, the World Bank and the regional development banks, exist to mobilize loan financing to Southern countries to purchase more products and services from the North in support of their development. They act primarily through lending. Thus their actions almost inevitably add to the debt of the assisted country and increase pressures to gear domestic policies toward the generation of foreign exchange to finance debt repayment to maintain credit worthiness to finance further imports. The reduction of social services and the short-term exploitation of resources for export are two important consequences.

> *To what extent are existing multilateral development agencies able to provide needed leadership in achieving a just, sustainable and inclusive global society. What should be Northlandia's role in the reform or retirement of existing multilateral agencies and/or in the creation of new agencies more appropriate to the tasks at hand?*

8. **An Alternative Development Vision.** The conventional vision that has driven development policy and action equates progress with short-term increases in economic activity. It gives little regard to considerations of justice, sustainability or inclusiveness. It encourages extravagant and wasteful consumption supported by debt financing and the mining of environmental resources. It gives preference in investment and trade policies to the wants of affluent foreign consumers over the needs of the domestic poor. It legitimates authoritarianism and the concentration of economic and political power.

Many NGOs, especially in the South, argue the need for an alternative development vision that views progress in terms of just, sustainable and inclusive improvements in human well-being. This vision encourages moderation in physical consumption, financial self-reliance, and the conservation and recycling of resources. It focuses on the local ownership and use of local resources to meet local needs. It calls for economic and political democratization as the cornerstone of economic and political justice.

> *Do you agree with the argument that there is need for an alternative development vision and theory? If so, what distinctive contributions might Northlandia, including Northlandian NGOs, make to its definition and acceptance?*

9. **Consequences versus Causes.** There is a strong tendency to respond to human suffering with direct action intended to obtain an immediate relief of that suffering. The starving child needs food. There is neither time nor inclination to ask: Why is the child hungry? Furthermore, to ask that question is to confront difficult and seemingly unresolvable political, social, economic and spiritual issues that it is more comfortable to avoid. Thus assistance agencies go into conflict zones with a single-minded purpose—to feed and care for the hungry and the sick—not to question the politics that led to the human misery they seek to relieve. They sponsor the child of a landless family without asking why his father has neither land nor employment. We have consistently avoided asking the difficult questions. Perhaps this explains why human misery appears to be on the increase around the world, even after decades of international assistance directed to relief, welfare and conventional development. There is every reason to believe that the number of people needing relief assistance will increase at a growing rate during the coming decade, while the availability of surplus food stocks to relieve it is almost certain to decline.

> *Can we continue to avoid the difficult questions? Given current global realities, how should Northlandia divide its contribution to international assistance between relief activities intended to relieve the consequences of violence, injustice, and mismanagement of resources; and activities directed to eliminating the causes of these conditions? How does this compare to the current allocation of Northlandian NGO resources and attention?*

10. **Reconciliation.** Public and private agencies engaged in relief operations for the victims of political violence observe that the numbers of victims of such violence are increasing. Furthermore, the nature of the violence is changing. No longer is it primarily a result of wars between states. Increasingly it is a result of wars between peoples, in particular between political, ethnic and religious factions. This is the reality of Lebanon, Sri Lanka, Cambodia, El Salvador, Ireland, the Philippines, Sudan, many areas of India, and urban slums throughout the world. It results from an unraveling in the social fabric of society. Deepening poverty, injustice and environmental degradation are destroying the hope of the poor for a better future. The resulting anger is being turned inward against one's neighbor and ultimately against oneself. The resulting violence cannot be resolved through the ultimate victory of one state over another as in conventional warfare. It is an enduring violence in which there are only growing numbers of victims.

*In what ways might Northlandian NGOs use relief activities
as a means to promote reconciliation in conflict situations?
To what extent should they do so? Should this be a particular priority of church affiliated NGOs? Are there useful
examples or case studies that demonstrate potentials, pitfalls
and possible approaches?*

11. **North/South and North/North NGO Relations.** Conventional
practice in international assistance has defined relations between
Northern and Southern NGOs in terms of the transfer of financial
resources from the former to the latter. While the need for such
resource transfers will likely continue for the immediate future,
the idea that the relationships are built primarily around such
transfers is increasingly questioned. Such transfers do not by
themselves address the more compelling issues facing either Northern or Southern NGOs. Similarly, in a world defined by financial
relationships, the relations among Northern NGOs have been
those of competitors vying for the same limited sources of financing. As the relationships between Northern and Southern NGOs
are redefined, a corresponding redefinition of relationships among
the international NGOs based in Northern countries may also be
in order.

*Are relationships between Northlandian NGOs and South-
ern partner NGOs appropriate to current global priorities
and realities? In what ways, if any, should they be modi-
fied? What are the implications for relationships among
Northlandian NGOs and other international NGOs based
in Northern countries?*

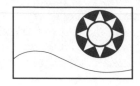

NGO SELF-ASSESSMENT QUESTIONS

While there will be need for a wide variety of NGO initiative in the 1990s, individual NGOs will face increasing demands to define their roles with a greater clarity than is commonly the case and to develop specialized capabilities appropriate to those roles. To be relevant to the 1990s, most NGOs will need to undertake serious strategic assessments that include questioning fundamental assumptions regarding who they are and what they do. Such assessments must be tailored to the particular needs and situation of each organization. The following questions may, however, help interested NGO leaders decide whether their organizations are candidates for such a process.

The Basic Questions: Identity and Role
Two sets of questions are fundamental for most NGOs that want to determine who they are and what they want to be.

- **Identity:** Are we predominantly a voluntary organization (VO) driven by a distinctive social mission? Or are we a public service contractor offering reliable, high quality contract services to public and private donors? Which do we want to be? If both, have we been able to differentiate between the two adequately to serve as well as we would like in each of these roles?

- **Role:** Are we primarily a humanitarian assistance agency engaged in or supporting the delivery of a range of humanitarian services to alleviate the consequences of human suffering? Or are we a development catalyst engaged in temporary interventions aimed at bringing about permanent systemic changes that remove the causes of suffering? Which do we want to be? If both, have we been able to differentiate between them in ways that allow us to do both jobs well? Have we achieved a balance that is appropriate to the need and to our own commitment?

Questions for the Voluntary Development Catalyst

Those NGOs that decide they either are, or aspire to be, VOs working as development catalysts might also consider the following questions:

- What do we see as the major challenges of the 1990s that coincide with our distinctive ability and commitment? Do we have an adequate theory for identifying the underlying causes of the problems with which we are most concerned? Which underlying causes are we in the best position to address? Are we now focusing our resources effectively on those causes?

- Have we developed effective alliances with other organizations that may be able to bring complementary resources to bear on other important dimensions of the selected problem? Are we actively seeking to broaden the alliance?

- Do we have a natural grass roots constituency? Do we actively engage this constituency as a voluntary people-to-people development force? Or do we look to our constituents only as a source of financial contributions?

- Is our contribution to an improved world really a function of the amount of money we raise and spend? Or might there be opportunities to substantially increase our effective contribution to resolving critical global problems by focusing more on catalytic actions that depend less on financing and more on voluntary energy?

- Do we honor both professionalism and voluntarism? What provision do we have for continually affirming and renewing our value commitment? How do our professionals contribute to strengthening the voluntary spirit and commitment of the organization?

A serious effort to answer these questions should lead the directors and senior staff of an NGO to a well considered judgement as to whether the organization is adequately on track with regard to what it seeks to be and do in the 1990s, or needs to engage in a basic re-examination of roles and strategy.

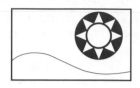

APPENDIX D

INTERNATIONAL PUBLIC FINANCIAL TRANSFERS

There is substantial need and opportunity to restructure existing flows of official international assistance and the agencies that administer that assistance in line with the analyses of this book. A number of principles are proposed below for consideration. Some of these might be considered fairly radical. I am among those who believe it is time to consider radical restructuring on the grounds that on balance the existing system of official international assistance may be doing more harm than good, at least in so far as the interests of the poor of the South are concerned.

Humanitarian Assistance: *Humanitarian assistance should be accurately labelled. If used to finance services that meet basic needs of a chronic or predictably recurring nature, the funds should be appropriated with a clear understanding that a commitment to long-term assistance is involved.* There should be a clear distinction between humanitarian and development assistance depending on whether the assistance is addressed to the consequences or the causes of poverty.[1] If the wealthier countries of the world want to finance a global welfare system, that is a noble—if currently misguided—objective. Under no circumstances, however, should commitment to an international welfare system be confused with efforts to eliminate the conditions that have created the need for such a system.

The provision of humanitarian assistance directly to or through governments represents basic budget support and should be limited to democratically elected governments that have demonstrated budgetary discipline, including an ability to hold military spending to a minimum.

---

1. It is true that part of the task of building an institutional base for equity-led growth involves strengthening human resources through improved education. It is also true that people cannot be fully productive if they lack basic health and nutrition. This is not, however, a justification for funding free standing social services programs in the name of development in the absence of basic reforms, such as land reform, aimed at insuring the beneficiaries served will have the opportunity to apply their education and good health in productive remunerative activities.

Provision of such assistance to countries with non-democratic governments should be only through NGOs.

Public Borrowing: *The use of debt as the means of transferring international assistance resources should be sharply reduced.* Selective and disciplined use of international credit for economically viable projects with good prospects to generate foreign exchange resources in excess of debt repayment can be a sound policy. Unfortunately few internationally funded development projects meet these stringent criteria. As a consequence, loan-funded international assistance tends to contribute to a bias toward bimodal enclave development oriented to the generation of foreign exchange to repay debt rather than to meet the needs of the presumed loan beneficiaries. This runs directly contrary to the requirements of an equity-led sustainable growth strategy and is developmentally counterproductive. Such types of international financial transfers should be sharply reduced. The focus should be on helping poor countries eliminate their current debt burdens as part of a program to drastically and permanently reduce or eliminate the use of international debt financing from either official or commercial sources.

The provision of credits to compensate for temporary fluctuations in foreign exchange earnings is a legitimate use of public debt, when the problem is truly temporary. The International Monetary Fund should continue to serve this need in accordance with its original mandate.

Structural adjustment policies have stressed the need to eliminate subsidies, apply free-market principles, and privatize investments. In line with these generally sound principles, international borrowing should be limited to economically viable projects that meet the standards for commercial borrowing and should be obtained from private commercial banks, not from government subsidized multilateral agencies. To the extent that multilateral agencies have a role it should be limited to assisting governments to plan sound projects and negotiate favorable loan terms from commercial banks.

Guarantees for such loans should be limited assigning the loan funded assets, or to the assets of the specific agency responsible for the project being financed as collateral. International loans should not be guaranteed by the general credit of the borrowing government as this is an open invitation to fiscal irresponsibility.

Soft Loans: *Loans should bear market interest rates and be limited to financing economically sound bankable investment projects.* The use of soft loans for international development assistance should be eliminated. While soft loans generally go to poor countries, they do not necessarily assist poor people. The case for subsidizing the projects of the rich people of poor countries is not particularly strong.

The reason for eliminating soft loans is exactly the same as that used by the multilateral banks when they require borrowing countries to eliminate subsidies and charge market rates of interest on their own credit programs. Subsidized credit undermines economic discipline and encourages the diversion of investment resources to unsound projects.[2] If donors want to provide a grant component in conjunction with loan financing, this should be made explicit and the grant packaged accordingly.

Grant Financing: Development assistance provided primarily in the form of grants and should be used to help recipient countries: 1) transform their institutional structures and develop their human resources in ways that create the foundation for an equity-led sustainable growth strategy; and 2) master and apply technologies that allow them to make more productive use of their own resources in environmentally sustainable ways to provide for the basic needs of their own people. Public assistance for these purposes should be channeled through independent grant making foundations that have substantial flexibility and freedom of action and are able to make their decisions entirely on the basis of development criteria without regard to the short-term foreign policy concerns of the funding government.

These foundations should have a mandate to support the programs of a wide variety of private and public agencies and should seek to engage a broad range of nongovernmental organizations beyond those traditionally involved in development work. It should be made clear to the governments of recipient countries that the funds provided by these foundations are intended primarily to support private voluntary initiatives and are not a government entitlement.

Much of their focus would be on activities neglected by current international assistance agencies, such as policy advocacy and development education work, the strengthening of independent judicial systems, development of a free press, and the training of military personnel in the nature and responsibilities of the military in a democratic society.

---

2. According to Nick Eberstadt, "The Perversion of Foreign Aid," *Commentary,* Vol. 79, No. 6, June 1985, p. 23, those who initially crafted the American foreign assistance program in 1946 ruled out any use of concessional loans on the grounds that they would create a dangerous and needless confusion between charity and commerce. Within ten years they had become a preferred vehicle for foreign assistance. Concessional loans are good politics. Taxpayers are assured they are not really giving anything away because their principle will be repaid. Foreign governments are told that they should think of the loan as having a large grant component. One of the major costs of the soft loan is usually forgotten: "their impact on beneficiary governments' conception of, and attitude toward, capital transfer from abroad."

Trade Credits: *Countries that want to offer trade credits to promote their own exports should provide them under their trade promotion programs and agencies.* These credits represent disguised export subsidies and should not be confused with development assistance. As subsidies they distort international markets, encourage inefficiency in the exporting country, and limit the development of indigenous productive capacity in the importing country. These programs should be labeled for what they are and be open to the same international scrutiny as any other trade subsidy program.

Analytic and Capacity Building Support: *A new multilateral development assistance agency should be established to assist requesting countries in developing the analytic and institutional capacities required to support development processes consistent with the people-centered vision.* This agency should equal the World Bank in the quality of its analytical and technical capability. It should, however, differ from the World Bank in two fundamental respects. First, it should not have a loan program to absorb its staff in pushing new debt on recipient countries. Second, its guiding vision should be a people-centered rather than a growth-centered vision.

The job of this agency would be to advise Southern countries on how to reduce their debt burdens and restructure their institutions and their economies for an equity-led, broadly-based, sustainable growth. It would help assisted countries develop and institutionalize their own analytical and technical capabilities, evaluate proposals from foreign investors, reshape trade patterns in line with the patterns of a people-centered vision and access various sources of technical and financial assistance from appropriate sources. It would also serve as a people-centered development think tank for the international community.

This agency should have the capability to make grants to assisted countries for use in institutional capacity building. These funds should not, however, be used to fund operating programs or infrastructure.

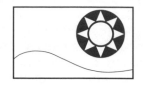

BIBLIOGRAPHY

"A Survey of the Third World: Poor Man's Burden." *The Economist,* September 23, 1989.

Accelerating Institutional Development. PVO Institutional Development Evaluation Series. Bureau for Food for Peace and Voluntary Assistance, Office of Private and Voluntary Cooperation, U.S. Agency for International Development, Washington, DC, May 1989.

Adelman, Irma. "A Poverty-Focused Approach to Development Policy." In *Development Strategies Reconsidered,* edited by John P. Lewis and Valeriana Kallab, 49–66. Washington, DC: The Overseas Development Council, 1986.

——. "Development Economics—A Reassessment of Goals." *Development Economics* 65 (May 1975): 302–309.

Adelman, Irma, and Cynthia Taft Morris. *Economic Growth and Social Equity in Developing Countries.* Stanford, CA: Stanford University Press, 1973.

Annis, Sheldon. "Costa Rica's Dual Debt: A Story About a Little Country that Did Things Right." Study prepared for the World Resources Institute by the Overseas Development Council, Washington, DC, May 1987.

Ayres, Robert L. *Banking on the Poor.* Cambridge, MA: The MIT Press, 1983.

Bangladesh Rural Advancement Committee. "Unraveling Networks of Corruption." In *Community Management: Asian Experience and Perspectives,* edited by David C. Korten, 135–56. West Hartford, CT: Kumarian Press, 1986.

Bennett, Leamon J. "When Employees Run the Company." *Harvard Business Review* (January–February 1979): 75–90.

Berg, Robert J. *Non-Governmental Organizations: New Force in Third World Development and Politics.* East Lansing, MI: Center for Advanced Study of International Development, Michigan State University, May 1987.

Bhagwati, Jagdish N. "Rethinking Trade Strategy." In *Development Strategies Reconsidered,* edited by John P. Lewis and Valeriana Kallab, 91–104. Washington, DC: The Overseas Development Council, 1986.

——. *The Economics of Underdeveloped Countries.* New York, NY: McGraw-Hill, 1966.

Boulding, Kenneth E. "The Economics of the Coming Spaceship Earth." In *Environmental Quality in a Growing Economy*, edited by Henry Jarrett, 3–14. Baltimore, MD: The Johns Hopkins University Press, 1968.

————. *Three Faces of Power.* Newbury Park, CA: Sage Publications, 1989.

Bourguignon, François, William H. Branson, and Jaime de Emlo. "Adjustment and Income Distribution: A Counterfactual Analysis." WPS 215, Working Paper, Country Economics Department, The World Bank, Washington, DC, May 1989.

Bradford, Colin I., Jr. "East Asian 'Models': Myths and Lessons." In *Development Strategies Reconsidered*, edited by John P. Lewis and Valeriana Kallab, 115–28. Washington, DC: The Overseas Development Council, 1986.

Bratton, Michael. "Non-governmental Organizations in Africa: Can They Influence Public Policy?" *Development and Change* 21 (1989): 87–118.

————. "The Politics of Government — N.G.O. Relations in Africa." *World Development* 17 (April 1988): 569-87.

Britain and the Brundtland Report: A Programme of Action for Sustainable Development. London, England: International Institute for Environment and Development, *circa* 1989.

Broad, Robin. *Unequal Alliance, 1979–1986: The World Bank, the International Monetary Fund, and the Philippines.* Quezon City, Philippines: Ateneo de Manila University Press, 1988.

Broad, Robin, and John Cavanagh. "No More NICS." *Foreign Policy* (Fall 1988): 81–103.

Brown, L. David. "Bridging Organizations and Sustainable Development." Paper presented to the Conference on Social Innovations in Global Management at Case Western Reserve University, November 13–15, 1989.

Brown, L. David, and David C. Korten. "Understanding Voluntary Organizations: Guidelines for Donors." WPS 258, Working Paper, Country Economics Department, The World Bank, Washington, DC, September 1989.

Brown, Lester R. "Analyzing the Demographic Trap." In *State of the World 1987*, edited by Lester R. Brown, *et al.*, 20–37. New York, NY: W. W. Norton and Company, 1987.

————. "Feeding Six Billion." *World Watch* 2 (September–October 1989).

————. "Redefining National Security." In *State of the World 1986*, edited by Lester R. Brown, *et al.*, 195–211. New York, NY: W.W. Norton & Company, 1986.

————. "Reexamining the World Food Prospect." In *State of the World 1989*, edited by Lester R. Brown, *et al.*, 41–76. New York, NY: W.W. Norton & Company, 1989.

————. "The Changing Food Prospects: The Nineties and Beyond." *Worldwatch Paper 85.* Washington, DC: Worldwatch Institute, October 1988.

Brown, Lester R., and Christopher Flavin. "The Earth's Vital Signs." In *State of the World 1988,* edited by Lester R. Brown, *et al.,* 1–21. New York, NY: W. W. Norton & Company, 1988.

Brown, Lester R., Christopher Flavin, and Sandra Postel. "A World at Risk." In *State of the World 1989,* edited by Lester R. Brown, *et al.,* 1–20. New York, NY: W. W. Norton & Company, 1989.

————. "Outlining a Global Action Plan." In *State of the World 1989,* edited by Lester R. Brown, *et al.,* 174–94. New York, NY: W.W. Norton & Company, 1989.

Brown, Marck Malloch, ed. *Famine: A Man-Made Disaster.* A report for the Independent Commission on International Humanitarian Issues. London: Pan Books, 1984.

Brzezinski, Zbigniew. "The Crisis of Communism: The Paradox of Political Participation." *The Washington Quarterly* 10 (Autumn 1987).

Capra, Fritjof. *The Turning Point: Science, Society and the Rising Culture.* New York, NY: Simon and Schuster, 1982.

Carlson, Don, and Craig Comstock, eds. *Citizen Summitry: Keeping the Peace When it Matters too Much to be Left to Politicians.* New York, NY: St. Martin's Press, 1986.

Carner, George. "Survival, Interdependence, and Competition among the Philippine Rural Poor." In *People-Centered Development: Contributions Toward Theory and Planning Frameworks,* edited by David C. Korten and Rudi Klauss, 133–43. West Hartford, CT: Kumarian Press, 1984.

Cassen, Robert. "The Effectiveness of Aid." *Finance & Development* (March 1986): 11–14.

Cernea, Michael M. "Farmer Organizations and Institution Building for Sustainable Development." *Regional Development Dialogue* 82 (Summer 1987): 1–19. (Published by the United Nations Centre for Regional Development, Nagoya, Japan.)

Chacour, Elias. "Can You Forgive Me, Abuna?" *Together* (July-September 1988): 4–5.

Chambers, Robert. *Managing Rural Development: Ideas and Experience from East Africa.* Upsala: Scandinavian Institute of African Studies, 1974. (Reprint edition available from Kumarian Press.)

————. *Rural Development: Putting the Last First.* London: Longman, 1983.

Chambers, Robert, Arnold Pacey, and Lori Ann Thrupp, eds. *Farmer First: Farmer Innovation and Agricultural Research.* London: Intermediate Technology Publications, 1989.

Chenery, Hollis, Montek S. Ahluwalia, C.L.G. Bell, John H. Duloy, and Richard Jolly. *Redistribution with Growth.* London: Oxford University Press, 1974.

Clark, John. "World Bank and Poverty Alleviation—An NGO View." Paper prepared for the 1988 Meeting of the World Bank-NGO Committee. Development Policies Unit, Oxfam, 174 Banbury Road, Oxford OX27DZ, England, 1988.

Conroy, Czech, and Miles Litvinoff, eds. *The Greening of Aid: Sustainable Livelihoods in Practice*. London: Earthscan Publications, Ltd., 1988.

Cook, James. "The Molting of America." *Forbes,* November 22, 1982, 161-67.

Cornia, Giovanni Andrea, Richard Jolly, and Frances Stewart, eds. *Adjustment with a Human Face: Protecting the Vulnerable and Promoting Growth.* Oxford: Clarendon Press, 1987.

Costanza, Robert. "What is Ecological Economics?" *Ecological Economics* 1 (1989): 1-7.

Daly, Herman E., and John B. Cobb, Jr. *For the Common Good: Redirecting the Economy Toward Community, the Environment, and a Sustainable Future.* Boston, MA: Beacon Press, 1989.

de Soto, Hernando. *The Other Path.* New York, NY: Harper & Row, Publishers, 1989.

"Development Alternatives." *World Development* 15 (Autumn 1987). Special issue edited by Anne Gordon Drabek.

Diamond, Larry. "Beyond Authoritarianism and Totalitarianism: Strategies for Democratization." *The Washington Quarterly* (forthcoming).

Dorner, Peter. *Land Reform & Economic Development.* Middlesex, England: Penguin Books, 1972.

Dover, Michael, and Lee M. Talbot. *To Feed the Earth: Agro-Ecology for Sustainable Agriculture.* Washington, DC: World Resources Institute, 1987.

Drucker, Peter E. "What Business Can Learn from Nonprofits." *Harvard Business Review* 67 (July-August 1989): 88–93.

Durning, Alan B. "Action at the Grassroots: Fighting Poverty and Environmental Decline." *Worldwatch Paper 88.* Washington, DC: Worldwatch Institute, January 1989.

Eberstadt, Nick. "The Perversion of Foreign Aid." *Commentary* 79 (June 1985): 19–33.

Elliot, Charles. *Comfortable Compassion? Poverty, Power and the Church.* London: Hodder and Stoughton, 1987.

Ellis, Susan J., and Katherine H. Noyes. *By the People: A History of Americans as Volunteers.* Philadelphia, PA: Energize, 1978.

Ellwood, Wayne. *Generating Power: A Guide to Consumer Organizing.* P.O. Box 1045, Penang, Malaysia: International Organization of Consumers Unions, 1984.

Ensminger, Douglas. "Agriculture, Food and Employment: Agenda for the Coming Century." *Kidma* 10 (1988).

Esman, Milton J., and Norman T. Uphoff. *Local Organizations: Intermediaries in Rural Development.* Ithaca, NY: Cornell University Press, 1984.

"ESOPs: Revolution or Ripoff?" *Business Week,* April 15, 1985, 94–108.

Firstenberg, Paul B. *Managing for Profit in the Nonprofit World.* New York, NY: The Foundation Center, 1986.

Flavin, Christopher. "Slowing Global Warming: A Worldwide Strategy. *Worldwatch Paper 91.* Washington, DC: Worldwatch Institute, October 1989.

Foley, Dolores. *Non-Governmental Organizations as Catalysts of Policy Reform and Social Change: A Case Study of the International Planned Parenthood Federation.* Ph.D. Dissertation. Los Angeles, CA: University of Southern California, May 1989.

Fujioka, Masao. "Alleviating Poverty Through Development: The Asian Experience." *Development* 2/3 (1988): 26–33.

Gawthrop, Louis C. *Public Sector Management, Systems, and Ethics.* Bloomington, IN: Indiana University Press, 1984.

George, Susan. "The Debt Crisis: Obstacle to Development or Path to Democracy?" Briefing Paper No. 14, Australian Development Studies Network, October 1989.

Global Tomorrow Coalition. *Sustainable Development: A Guide to "Our Common Future."* Washington, DC: Global Tomorrow Coalition, 1989.

"Gorbachev Reforms Facing Easy Approval." *The Manila Chronicle,* February 7, 1990, 2.

Gran, Guy. *Development by People: Citizen Construction of a Just World.* New York, NY: Praeger Publishers, 1983.

Gupta, Ranjit. "The Poverty Trap: Lessons from Dharampur." In *Bureaucracy and the Poor: Closing the Gap,* edited by David C. Korten and Felipe B. Alfonso, 114–34. West Hartford, CT: Kumarian Press, 1983.

Hale, David C. "Global Finance and the Retreat to Managed Trade." *Harvard Business Review* 90 (January-February 1990): 150–62.

Hardin, Garrett. "Lifeboat Ethics: The Case Against Helping the Poor." *Psychology Today* 8 (September 1974), 38+.

Harman, Willis. *Global Mind Change: The Promise of the Last Years of the Twentieth Century.* Indianapolis, IN: Knowledge Systems, Inc., 1988.

Hellinger, Stephen, Douglas Hellinger, and Fred M. O'Regan. *AID for Just Development: Report on the Future of Foreign Assistance.* Boulder, CO: Lynne Reinner Publishers, 1988.

Henderson, Hazel. *Creating Alternative Futures: The End of Economics.* New York: Perigee Books, 1978.

Hewlett, Sylvia Ann. *The Cruel Dilemmas of Development: Twentieth-Century Brazil.* New York, NY: Basic Books, 1980.

Holland, Max, and Viveca Novak. "Buyouts: The LBO Lobby Makes Its Move on Washington." *Common Cause Magazine,* September–October 1989, 13–20.

Houston, Tom. "The Greatest Need in the World Today." *Together,* July–September 1988.

"Hunger Profile for the 1990s." *Bostid Development* 9 (Summer 1989): 5.

Huntington, Samuel P. *Political Order in Changing Societies.* New Haven, CT: Yale University Press, 1968.

Ickis, John C., Edilberto de Jesus, and Rushikesh Maru, eds. *Beyond Bureaucracy: Strategic Management of Social Development.* West Hartford, CT: Kumarian Press, 1987.

Independent Commission on International Humanitarian Issues. *Modern Wars: The Humanitarian Challenge.* London: Zed Books, Ltd., 1986.

International Institute for Environment and Development, and the World Resources Institute. *World Resources 1987.* New York, NY: Basic Books, 1987.

Jacobson, Jodi L. "Environmental Refugees: A Yardstick of Habitability." *Worldwatch Paper 86.* Washington, DC: Worldwatch Institute, November 1988.

Johnston, Bruce F. "Agriculture and Economic Development: The Relevance of the Japanese Experience." *Food Research Institute Studies* 6 (1966): 251–312.

Johnston, Bruce F., and Peter Kilby. *Agriculture and Structural Transformation: Economic Strategies in Late-Developing Countries.* New York, NY: Oxford University Press, 1975.

Johnston, Bruce F., and William C. Clark. *Redesigning Rural Development: A Strategic Perspective.* Baltimore, MD: The Johns Hopkins University Press, 1982.

Kohli, Atul. "Democracy and Development." In *Development Strategies Reconsidered,* edited by John P. Lewis and Valeriana Kallab, 153–82. Washington, DC: The Overseas Development Council, 1986.

Korten, David C. *Bangladesh Rural Advancement Committee: Strategy for the 1990s.* New York, NY: PACT (forthcoming).

————, ed. *Community Management: Asian Experience and Perspectives.* West Hartford, CT: Kumarian Press, 1986.

————. "Community Organization and Rural Development: A Learning Process Approach." *The Public Administration Review* 40 (September–October 1980): 480–511.

————. "Micro-Policy Reform: The Role of Private Voluntary Agencies." In *Community Management: Asian Experience and Perspectives,* edited by David C. Korten, 309-18. West Hartford, CT: Kumarian Press, 1986.

————. *Planned Change in a Traditional Society: Psychological Problems of Modernization in Ethiopia.* New York, NY: Praeger, 1972.

————. "Practical Problems of Project Design and Implementation." In *Institutional Development: Improving Management in Developing Countries.* Washington, DC: American Consortium for International Public Administration, 1986.

————. "Private Aid Enters Third Phase." *Development Forum,* June 1986, 14.

————. "Third Generation NGO Strategies: A Key to People-Centered Development." *World Development* 15, Supplement (Autumn 1987): 145–59.

Korten, David C., and Felipe B. Alfonso, eds. *Bureaucracy and the Poor: Closing the Gap.* West Hartford, CT: Kumarian Press, 1983.

Korten, David C., and Rudi Klauss, eds. *People-Centered Development: Contributions Toward Theory and Planning Frameworks*. West Hartford, CT: Kumarian Press, 1984.

Korten, Frances F., and Robert Y. Siy, Jr. *Transforming a Bureaucracy: The Experience of the Philippine National Irrigation Administration*. West Hartford, CT: Kumarian Press, 1989.

Kuhn, Thomas S. *The Structure of Scientific Revolutions*. Chicago, IL: University of Chicago Press, 1970.

Landim, Leilah. "Non-Governmental Organizations in Latin America." *World Development* 15, Supplement (Autumn 1987): 29–38.

Lecomte, Bernard J. *Project Aid: Limitations and Alternatives*. Paris: OECD, 1986.

Lemaresquier, Thierry. "Prospects for Development Education: Some Strategic Issues Facing European NGOs." *World Development* 15, Supplement (Autumn 1987): 189–200.

Lewis, John P., and Valeriana Kallab, eds. *Development Strategies Reconsidered*. Washington, DC: The Overseas Development Council, 1986.

Lipnack, Jessica, and Jeffrey Stamps. *Networking: People Connecting with People, Linking Ideas and Resources*. New York, NY: Doubleday and Co., 1982.

—————. *The Networking Book: People Connecting with People*. New York, NY: Routledge and Kegan Paul, 1986.

Lutz, Mark A., and Kenneth Lux. *The Challenge of Humanistic Economics*. Menlo Park: The Benjamin/Cummin Publishing Company, 1979.

Luz, Juan Miguel, and Ernesto D. Garilao. "The NGO as Advocate: Savar Gonoshasthaya Kendra, Bangladesh." Case written for the APPROTECH V Organizational Strategy Planning Workshop, Manila, October 20–21, 1985.

Maass, Peter. "Seoul Radicals Invade Home of U.S. Envoy to Protest Trade Pressure." *International Herald Tribune*, October 14–15, 1989, 2.

McBeth, John. "The Boss System." *Far Eastern Economic Review* 14 (September 1989): 36–43.

Mackintosh, Maureen. *Gender, Class and Rural Transition: Agribusiness and the Food Crisis in Senegal*. London: Zed Books, Ltd., 1989.

Marcus, Tessa. *Commercial Agriculture in South Africa: Modernizing Super-Exploitation*. London: Zed Books, Ltd., 1989.

Mathews, Jessica Tuchman. "Redefining National Security." *Foreign Affairs* 68 (1989): 162–77.

Mayfield, James B. *Go to the People: Releasing the Rural Poor Through the People's School System*. West Hartford, CT: Kumarian Press, 1985.

Meadows, Donella H., *et al. The Limits to Growth*. New York, NY: New American Library, 1972.

Minear, Larry. "Terms of Engagement." *The Ecumenical Review,* January 1990.

—————. "The Other Missions of NGOs: Education and Advocacy." *World Development* 15, Supplement (Autumn 1987): 201–12.

—————. *Helping People in an Age of Conflict: Toward a New Professionalism in U.S. Voluntary Humanitarian Assistance.* Washington, DC: Interaction, 1988.

Montgomery, John D. "Allocation of Authority in Land Reform Programs: A Comparative Study of Administrative Processes and Outputs." *Administrative Science Quarterly* (March 1972).

Neil, Robert E. "What Makes History Happen?" In *People-Centered Development: Contributions Toward Theory and Planning Frameworks,* edited by David C. Korten and Rudi Klauss, 33–46. West Hartford, CT: Kumarian Press, 1984.

Nerfin, Marc. "Neither Prince nor Merchant: Citizen—An Introduction to the Third System." *IFDA Dossier 56,* November/December 1986, 3–29.

NGO Strategic Management in Asia: Focus on Bangladesh, Indonesia, and the Philippines. Manila: Asian NGO Coalition, 1988.

Nugent, Jeffrey B., and Pan A. Yotopoulos. "Orthodox Development Economics versus the Dynamics of Concentration and Marginalization." In *People-Centered Development: Contributions Toward Theory and Planning Frameworks,* edited by David C. Korten and Rudi Klauss, 107–20. West Hartford, CT: Kumarian Press, 1984.

O'Brien, Niall. *Revolution from the Heart.* New York, NY: Oxford University Press, 1987.

O'Neill, Michael. *The Third America: The Emergence of the Nonprofit Sector in the United States.* San Francisco, CA: Jossey-Bass Publishers, 1989.

OECD. *Voluntary Aid for Development: The Role of Non-Government Organizations.* Paris: OECD, 1988.

Ornstein, Robert, and Paul Ehrlich. *New World New Mind: Moving Toward Conscious Evolution.* New York, NY: Doubleday, 1989.

Owens, Edgar, and Robert Shaw. *Development Reconsidered: Bridging the Gap Between Government and People.* Lexington, MA: D. C. Heath and Co., 1972.

Paul, Samuel. *Managing Development Programs: The Lessons of Success.* Boulder, CO: Westview Press, 1982.

Payer, Cheryl. *The World Bank: A Critical Analysis.* New York, NY: Monthly Review Press, 1982.

Pearce, David, Anil Markandya, and Edward B. Barbier. *Blueprint for a Green Economy.* London: Earthscan Publications, Ltd., 1989.

Poerbo, Hasan, Daniel T. Sicular, and Vonny Supardj. "An Approach to Development of the Informal Sector: The Case of Garbage Collectors in Bandung." *Prisma* 32 (June 1984): 85–100.

"Population of World's Largest Cities." In *The World Almanac and Book of Facts 1989*, 738–39. New York, NY: St. Martin's Press, 1989.

Porterfield, Andrew. "Railroaded: The LBO Trend on Wall Street is Playing Havoc with the Nation's Forests." *Common Cause Magazine*, September/October 1989, 21–23.

Rajaratnam, S. "The Ethnic Fires Won't Die Out." *International Herald Tribune*, January 12, 1990, 4.

Rampton, Sheldon. "Sister Cities Gear Up for Nicaraguan Elections." *Bulletin of Municipal Foreign Policy* 3 (Autumn 1989): 34–36.

Ranis, Gustav. "The Dual Economy Framework: Its Relevance to Asian Development." *Asian Development Review* 2 (1984): 39–51.

————. "The Philippines, the Brady Plan and the PAP: Prognosis and Alternatives." Yale University, May 1989 (photocopy).

Renner, Michael. "Enhancing Global Security." In *State of the World 1989*, edited by Lester R. Brown, *et al.* New York, NY: W. W. Norton & Company, 1989.

Repetto, Robert. *World Enough and Time: Successful Strategies for Resource Management.* New Haven, CT: Yale University Press, 1986.

Repetto, Robert, and William B. Magrath. *Wasting Assets: Natural Resources in the National Accounts.* Washington, DC: World Resources Institute, 1989.

Report of the Task Force on Foreign Assistance to the Committee on Foreign Affairs, U.S. House of Representatives. Washington, DC: U.S. Government Printing Office, 1989.

Richard E. Feinberg, and Catherine Gwin. "Reforming the Fund: Overview." In *The International Monetary Fund in a Multipolar World: Pulling Together,* edited by Catherine Gwin and Richard E. Feinberg, 3-32. New Brunswick, NJ: Transaction Books, 1989.

Robertson, James. *Future Wealth: A New Economics for the 21st Century.* London: Cassell Publishers, Ltd., 1990.

Roxas, Sixto K. "Industrialization through Agricultural Development." Speech before the Philippine Agricultural Economics and Development Association, August 25, 1989.

————. "Recovery, Reconstruction and Reform in the Philippines." Presentation before the Japanese JCCI Mission, March 15, 1988.

————. "Strengthening the Capability of the Philippine Food Industry to Address the Crucial Issues of Food Supply, Demand, Technology and Marketing in the Context of Regional and Global Competition." Notes for the Food Congress of the Philippine Chamber of Food Manufacturers on Innovative Approaches to Food Sector Development (undated, circa 1989, photocopy).

Sachs, Jeffrey. "Making the Brady Plan Work." *Foreign Affairs* (Summer 1989): 87–104.

"Save the Tropical Rainforests!" Information bulletin of the Japan Tropical Forest Action Network, 501 Shinwa Building, 9–17 Sakuraoka, Shibuya-ku, Tokyo 150 Japan, *circa* 1989, 1.

Schneider, Bertrand. *The Barefoot Revolution: A Report to the Club of Rome.* London: Intermediate Technology Publications, 1988.

Serrano, Isagani R. "Developing a Fourth Generation NGO Strategy." Working paper of the Philippine Rural Reconstruction Movement, Manila, Philippines, *circa* 1989.

Sinclair, Maurice. *Ripening Harvest, Gathering Storm.* London: Church Missionary Society, 1988.

Smith, Brian H. "U.S. and Canadian PVOs as Transnational Development Institutions." In *Private Voluntary Organizations as Agents of Development,* edited by
• Robert F. Gorman, 115–64. Boulder, CO: Westview Press, 1984.

Soedjatmoko, Ambassador. *The Primacy of Freedom in Development,* edited by Anne Elizabeth Murase. Lanham, MD: University Press of America, 1985.

Sommer, John G. *Beyond Charity: U.S. Voluntary Aid for a Changing Third World.* Washington, DC: The Overseas Development Council, 1977.

Stepan, Alfred, ed. *Authoritarian Brazil.* New Haven, CT: Yale University Press, 1973.

Tandon, Rajesh. "The State and Voluntary Agencies in Asia." In *Doing Development: Government, NGOs and the Rural Poor in Asia,* edited by Richard Holloway, 12–29. London: Earthscan Publications, Ltd., 1989.

Tendler, Judith. *Inside Foreign Aid.* Baltimore, MD: The Johns Hopkins University Press, 1975.

The Developing World: Danger Point for U.S. Security. Report commissioned by Mark O. Hatfield, Matthew F. McHugh, and Mickey Leland. Washington, DC: Arms Control and Foreign Policy Caucus of the U.S. Congress, August 1, 1989.

"The Hunger Report: Update 1980." Alan Shawn Feinstein World Hunger Program, Brown University, Providence, RI.

Till, John Van. *Mapping the Third Sector: Voluntarism in a Changing Social Economy.* New York, NY: The Foundation Center, 1988.

Toffler, Alvin. *The Third Wave.* New York, NY: William Morrow and Company, Inc., 1980.

Trainer, Ted. *Developed to Death: Rethinking Third World Development.* London: The Merlin Press, Ltd., 1989.

"U.S. is Worst Offender in Rise of Carbon Dioxide." *International Herald Tribune,* September 18, 1989, 3.

United Nations Food and Agriculture Organization. *Land, Food and People.* Rome: Food and Agriculture Organization, 1984.

United States Security and the Developing World: Defining the Crisis and Forging Solutions. Report commissioned by Mark O. Hatfield, Matthew F. McHugh, and

Mickey Leland. Washington, DC: Arms Control and Foreign Policy Caucus of the U.S. Congress, March 1989 (draft).

Uphoff, Norman T. "Introduction to East Asian Cases." In *Rural Development and Local Organization in Asia: East Asia,* Vol. 2 edited by Norman T. Uphoff, 1–11. Delhi: MacMillan India, Ltd., 1982.

————, ed. *Rural Development and Local Organization in Asia: East Asia,* Vol. 2. Delhi: MacMillan India, Ltd., 1982.

Werner, David. "Empowerment and Health." The Hesperian Foundation, P.O. Box 1692, Palo Alto, CA 94302, January 1988.

Woods, Alan. *Development and the National Interest: U.S. Economic Assistance into the 21st Century, A Report.* Washington, DC: U.S. Agency for International Development, 1989.

World Bank. *Sub-Saharan Africa: From Crisis to Sustainable Growth, A Long-Term Perspective Study.* Washington, DC: World Bank, 1989.

————. *World Development Report, 1987.* Washington, DC: World Bank, 1987.

————. *World Development Report, 1988.* Washington, DC: World Bank, 1988.

————. *World Development Report, 1989.* Washington, DC: World Bank, 1989.

World Commission on Environment and Development. *Our Common Future.* Oxford: Oxford University Press, 1987.

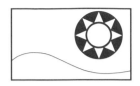

INDEX

THE AUTHOR

David C. Korten is president and founder of the People-Centered Development Forum (PCDForum), and a visiting professor at the Asian Institute of Management. A former faculty member of Harvard University's graduate schools of business and public health, staff member of the Ford Foundation and advisor to the United States Agency for International Development, Korten has more than thirty years of field experience in Asia, Africa and Latin America as a writer, teacher and consultant on development management, alternative development theory and the strategic roles of nongovernmental organizations. The holder of Ph.D. and M.B.A. degrees from the Stanford University Graduate School of Business, he is the author of *Getting to the 21st Century: Voluntary Action and the Global Agenda,* editor of *Community Management* and co-editor of *Bureaucracy and the Poor* and *People-Centered Development,* and has contributed to numerous books and professional journals. Known for their challenge to conventional development wisdom and management practice, his publications are assigned reading in universities throughout the world.

The PCDForum is an international voluntary organization dedicated to advancing voluntary action toward the realization of a people-centered development vision through a global people's development movement. This movement envisions a just, sustainable, and inclusive society that celebrates the richness and diversity of life, enhances personal freedom, lives by non-violence, and enables the growth of community and the human spirit. The forum carries out its work in close association with the Asian NGO Coalition, and cooperating individuals and organizations throughout the world.

A few words about the book...

*"... **explodes popular myths** about the true engines of progress that really shape global change."*

— **Denis Hayes**
Chair
Earth Day 1990

*"Bravo to David Korten. **Getting to the 21st Century** is a must for anyone concerned about the future of development and of our planet. I urge our 160 citizen groups in seven countries not only to read the book, but to study it and to take its challenge seriously."*

— **Sam Harris**
Results
Washington, DC

[David Korten] establishes even higher ground for us all by showing the global power of the people's movement. Those who hold or wish power in the 1990s and beyond will want to read this book!"

— **Robert J. Berg**
International Development Conference
Washington, DC

David Korten's understanding of the international development scene and voluntary development organizations reaches a new level of perception in this provocative and insightful work... imperative reading for students and teachers as well as for PVO leaders."

— **Tom Keehn**
InterAction
New York

Other important books from the
Kumarian Press Library of Management for Development

A Winner!
Best Book, World Hunger Media Awards

Change in an African Village: Kefa Speaks
by Else Skjønsberg

❖   ❖   ❖

Keepers of the Forest:
Land Management Alternatives in Southeast Asia
edited by Mark Poffenberger

Reports that get Results:
Guidelines for Executives
by Ian Mayo-Smith

Training for Development
Second Edition
by Rolf P. Lynton and Udai Pareek

Working Together:
Gender Analysis in Agriculture, Vol. 1, Vol. 2
edited by Hilary Sims Feldstein and Susan V. Poats

❖   ❖   ❖

Gender Roles in Development Projects: A Case Book
edited by Catherine Overholt, Mary B. Anderson,
Kathleen Cloud, and James E. Austin

Managing Organizations in Developing Countries:
A Strategic and Operational Approach
by Moses N. Kiggundu

Reforming Public Administration for Development:
Experiences from Eastern Africa
by Gelase Mutahaba

Transforming a Bureaucracy: The Experience of the
Philippine National Irrigation Administration
edited by Frances F. Korten and Robert Y. Siy, Jr.

Women's Ventures: Assistance to the
Informal Sector in Latin America
edited by Marguerite Berger and Mayra Buvinić

❖   ❖   ❖

For a complete catalog of Kumarian Press titles, please write or call:

Kumarian Press, Inc.
630 Oakwood Avenue, Suite 119
West Hartford, CT 06110-1529 USA

Tel: (203) 953-0214   ❖   **Fax:** (203) 953-8579